An Artist's World,
Tricks of Illusion

Author: Dan Wetta

Published by Daniel Wetta Publishing

Copyright 2015

Please visit Author Page:

http://danielwetta.com/master-artistauthor-dan-wetta/

Table of Contents

Prologue

This is my third paper-back book.

All three of my printed paper-back books are an inventory of my paintings and cartoons, a diary of my life, and contain stories behind my works and stories about my ancestors.

Chapter 1 of this book is a little bit of everything, and it includes poetry and paintings by my great-grandchildren and even poetry by a great- grand-niece, who wrote about one of my paintings!

In Chapter 2, I challenge the reader to look at the sketches I did of fellow passengers while I was riding the bus. What were they thinking? This is your chance to be a mind reader.

In Chapter 3, I take the reader to some fast food restaurants with my sketches on Richmond Road.

Chapter 4 – Several years ago, I took a beginner's course in stained glass, but I couldn't get the hang of cutting glass, so I began painting designs for stained glass windows instead.

Chapter 5 explains how I conquered my fear of flying by concentrating on my sketches as the plane took off.

Chapter 6 – A tick-tock clock at the art gallery relentlessly reminds you not to waste time.

Chapter 7 contains miscellaneous paintings and cartoons.

Chapter 8 looks at the bible through the eyes of a cartoonist.

Chapter 9 examines stories of the Old Testament in various works of media.

Chapter 1: A Little Bit of Everything

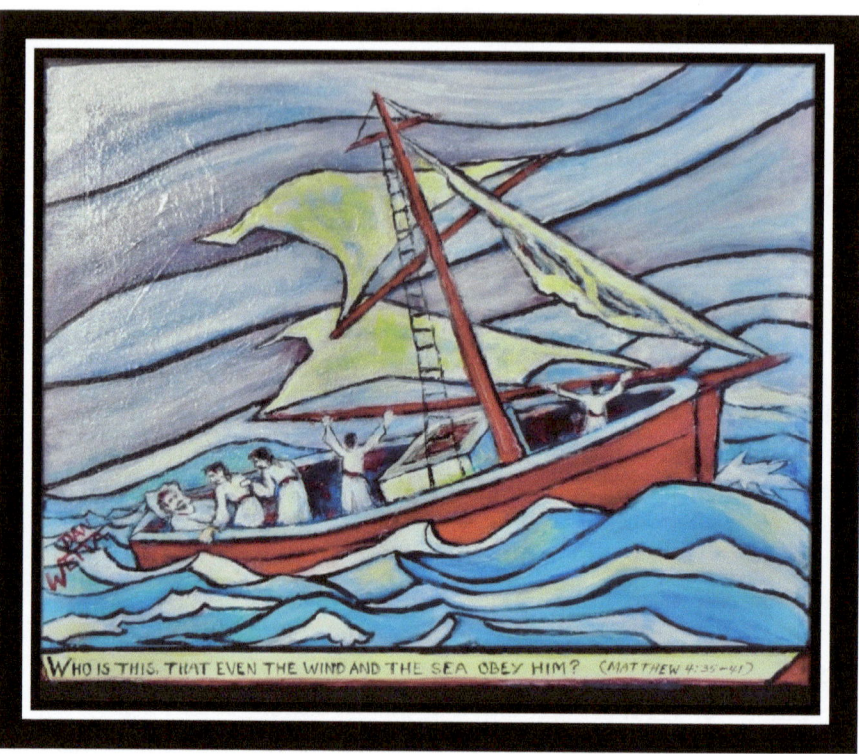

Title: Storm on Sea of Galilee
Size: 16 x 20 inches
Medium: Acrylic on canvas
Copyright 2015 by Dan Wetta

This is my most recent painting done just in time for the third printed book of my series. "Storm on the Sea of Galilee" is the finished painting I did from the original pencil sketch. That sketch follows, so you can see the evolution.

When I audited the bible years ago, I discovered that it was a warehouse full of ideas for paintings, and this story about Jesus ordering the wind and sea to calm down is one of those stories.

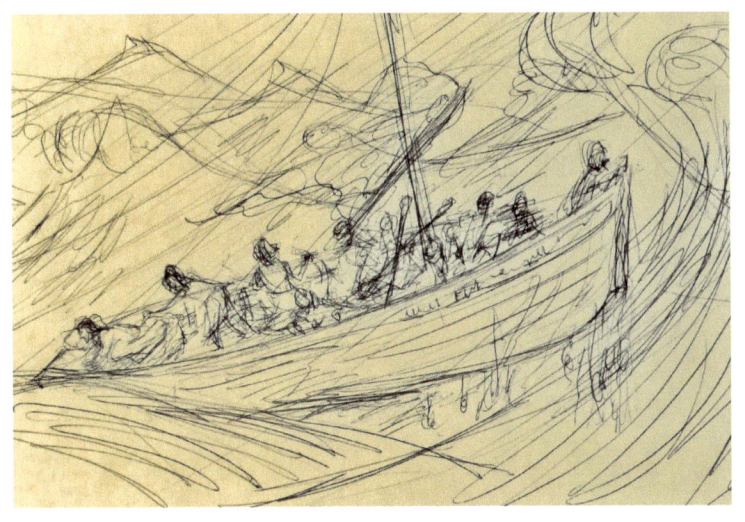

Title: Storm in Sea of Galilee
Medium: Pen on paper

This is the preliminary sketch in which I tried to capture the fury of the storm which frightened the apostles on the Sea of Galilee. They could not believe that Jesus was sound asleep and unconcerned about the wind and waves.

See Matthew 8:23 forward for the full story: When Jesus got into the boat, His disciples followed Him, and a great storm arose on the lake, so that the boat was covered with the waves.

Note that the Sea of Galilee is also called a lake, so this storm reminded me of the summer- time afternoon squalls on Lake Pontchartrain in Louisiana. Lake Pontchartrain is oval- shaped and measures about 40 by 24 miles, whereas the Sea of Galilee is pear-shaped and smaller, about 13 by 7 miles.

I hope I don't sound like a bible thumper, but whenever my mind is blank, and I can't come up with an idea for a painting, I peruse the bible, looking for ideas. Most of them are in the Old Testament.

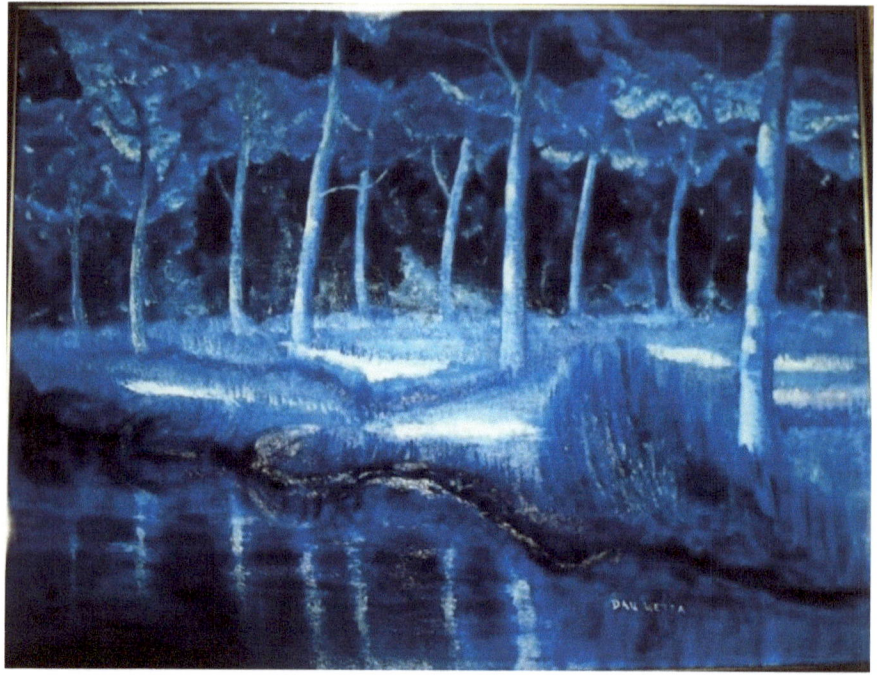

Title: The Blue Forest
Media: Acrylic on canvas

There is a lot of artistic talent in the Wetta family, especially in art and writing. I have the pleasure of living long enough to see my great-grandchildren and the family children three generations back who like to draw, paint, tell stories and write poetry.

I gave this painting to my sister, Joan, and then Joan gave it to my great-grand-niece, Megan Wetta, who wrote the following poem about this painting:

The Blue Forest
by Megan Wetta

Blue Forest
When the night falls
And the moon rises
Shades of blue
Icy, dark, and deep
Descends on the Forest

Running along the river
As my ears fill
With sounds of moving water
I search for the end of this place
Hoping for escape

Unable to find any
I stop-sweat drips down
Hitting the ground in blue silence
As I sit down to wait
For the colorful sunrise
Without blue

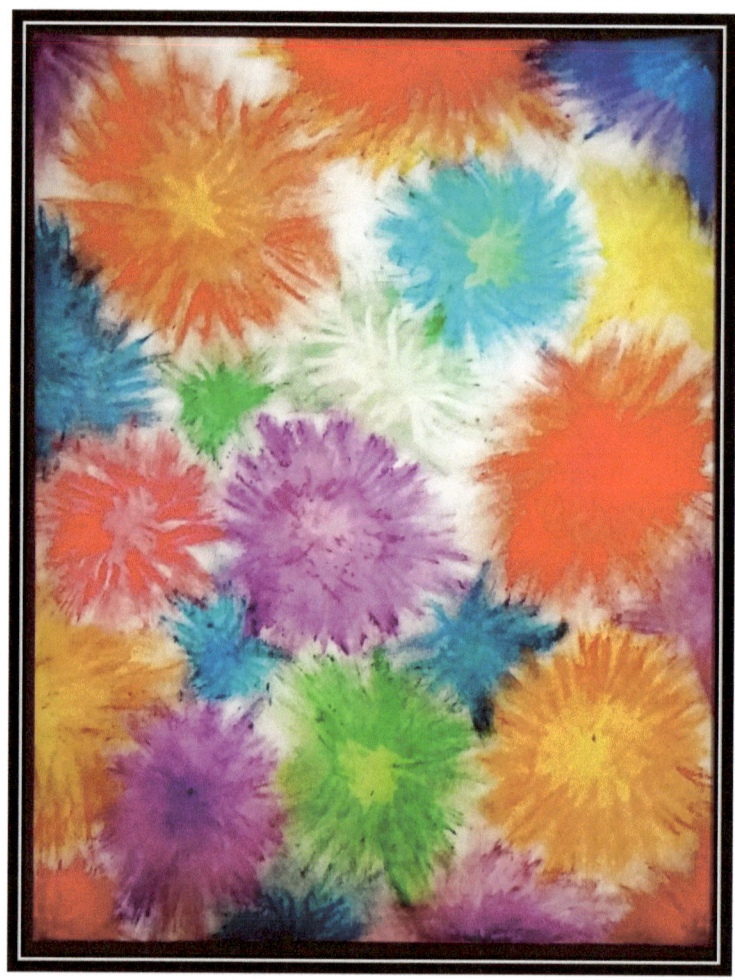

Title: Maya's Flowers
Artist: Maya Reese
Medium: Oil crayons on oil cloth.
Copyright 2015

My twelve-year-old great- granddaughter, Maya, painted this
flower design.

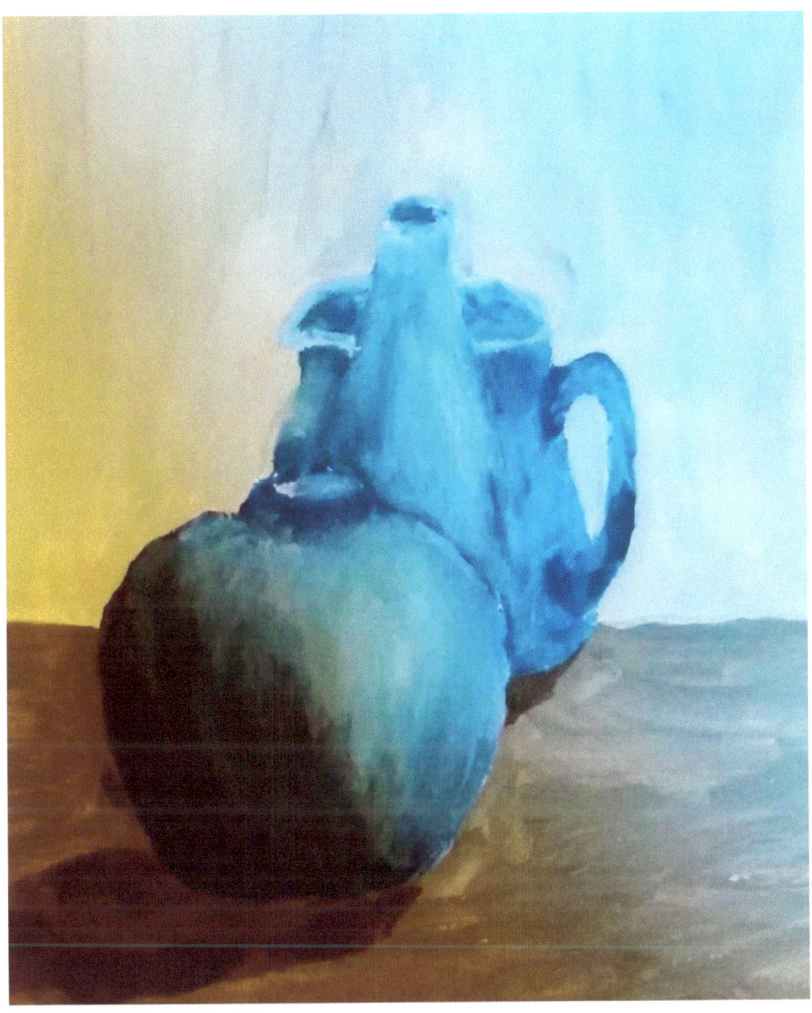

Title: Anna's Still Life
Artist: Anna Stinger
Medium: Acrylic on canvas Paper
Copyright 2015

This still life was an art-class assignment that my thirteen-year-old great-granddaughter Anna painted in 2015.

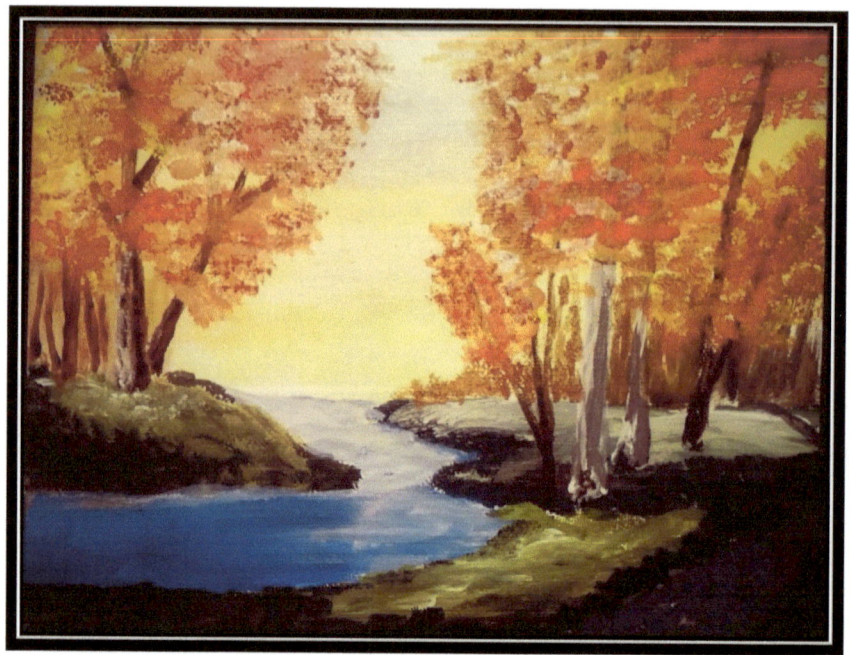

Title: Anna's Landscape
Artist: Anna Stinger
Medium: Acrylic on canvas board
Copyright 2015

My thirteen year old great granddaughter, Anna, painted this landscape for her mom as a mother's day gift.
Pretty good for a thirteen year old.

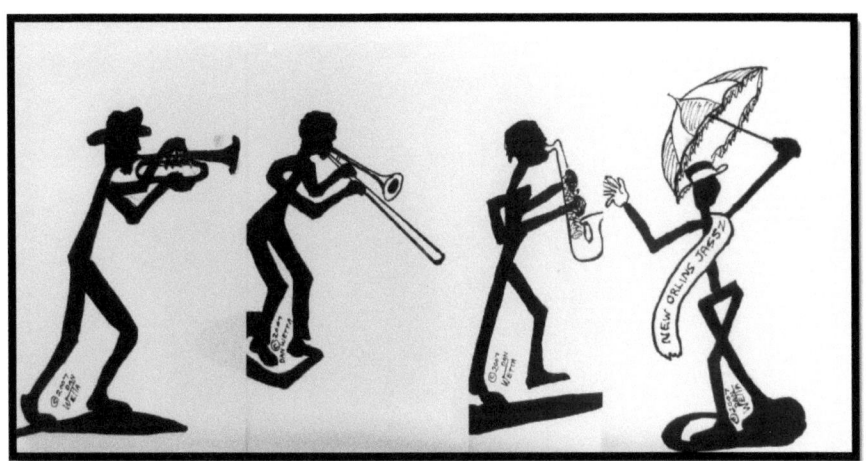

Title: New Orleans Street Parade
Copyright by Dan Wetta 2007

Silhouettes remind me of shadows.

Years ago I read a story about a quick-frozen man who was brought back to life.

However, you could tell that his soul had left his body because he did not have a shadow, and a man without a soul has no conscience, and a man without a conscience has no qualms about doing evil things.

So if you ever see anybody without a shadow, run away as fast as you can.

P.S. Don't worry about the silhouettes in this cartoon. They're just having fun.

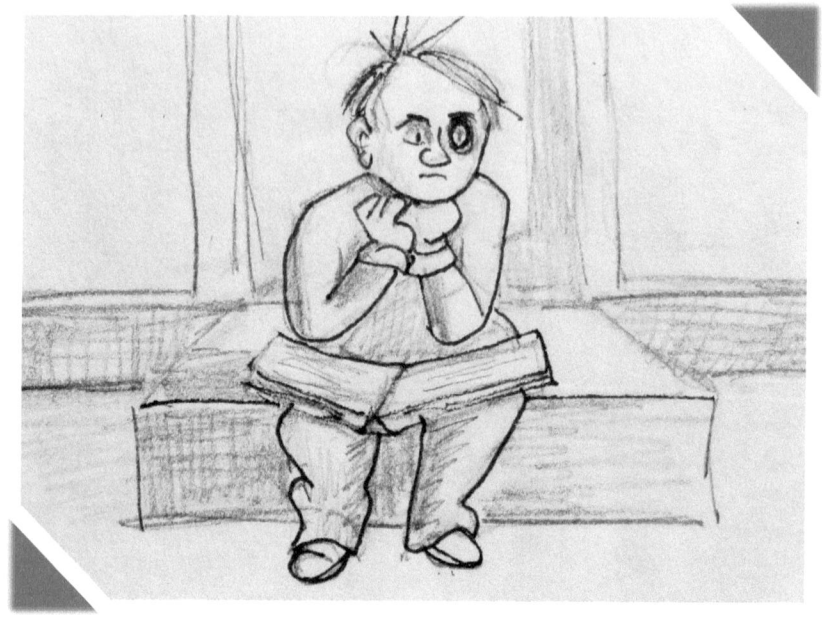

Title: Black Eye Kid

Did you ever get a black eye when you were a kid? Yeah, one time I walked into a door knob.

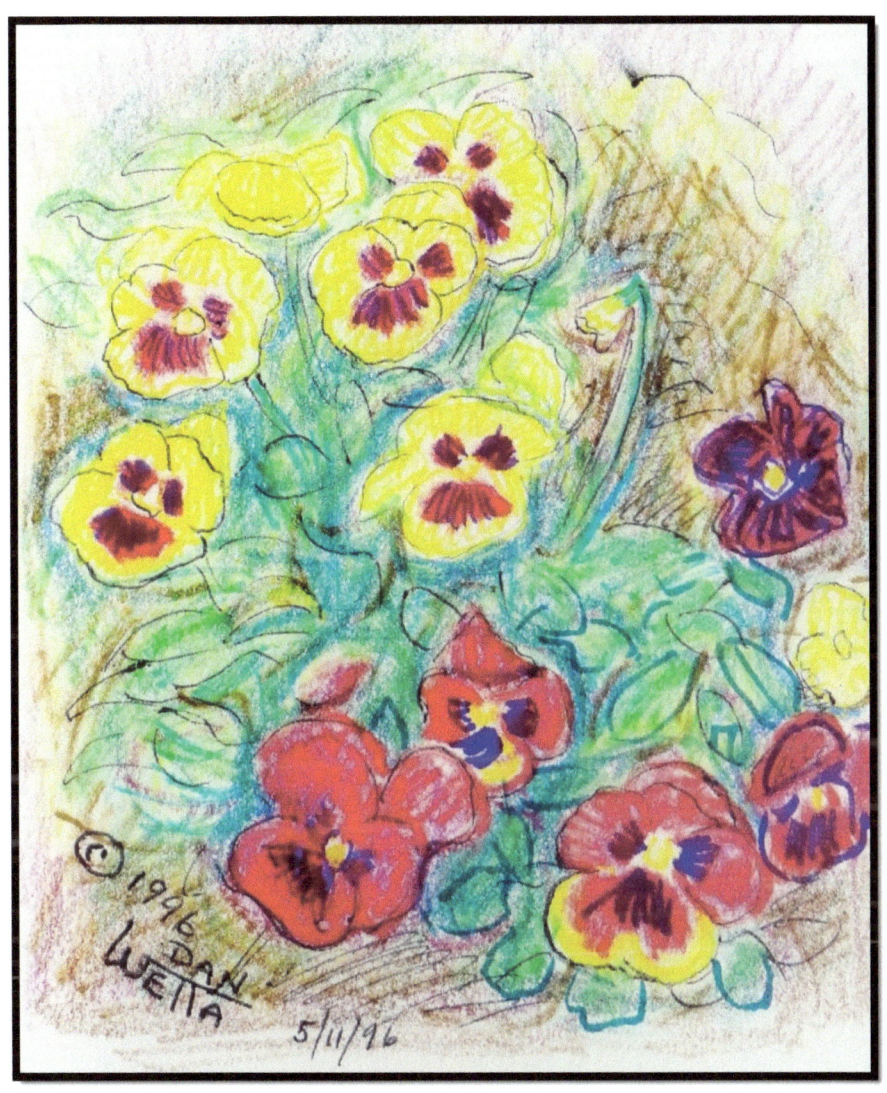

Title: Pansies and Violas Next Door
Medium: Mixed media on paper
Copyright 1996

I like flowers but I don't know their names. It took me two weeks fishing around on the internet before I located the names of these flowers.

Although flowers in a garden are pretty, borer bees are attracted to them, and borer bees will make a mess of your house. They will buzz all around your head and face when you sit on your porch to admire the flowers.

However, even though they have been aggravating me for twenty years, I have never been stung or bitten by them.

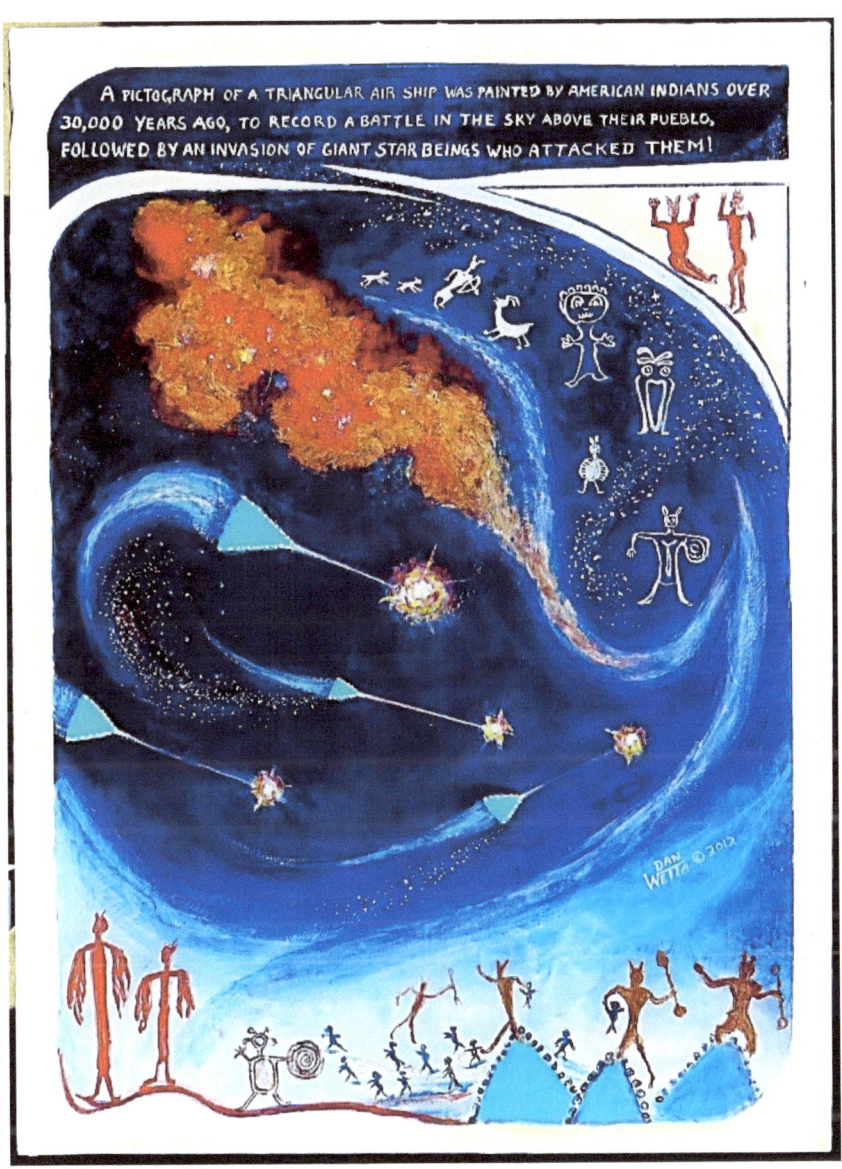

Title: Ancient Sky Battle
Size: 30 inches x 40 inches
Medium: Acrylic on canvas

In the 1960's, people began reporting that they had seen UFO's in the night sky in Goochland County, Virginia, not far from where I was living. My friend, George Bailey, said: "Let's go riding around Goochland County and take a look." We took my two sons, Steve and Dan Jr with us. We did this for three nights, but never saw anything in the sky except for the moon and a lot of stars.

However, some Indians who lived along the Snake River in Central Idaho 30,000 years ago did not have to go driving all around to look for UFO's in the night sky. The UFO's came to them, and put on a show that the Indians have never forgotten. They carved petroglyphs and painted pictographs on huge rocks of a battle in the sky above their pueblo. After the battle, the victors came down to their pueblo and attacked the Indians. The invaders were giants who probably came from a far-away planet in triangular-shaped spaceships.

This painting is my interpretation of that legend, and I do have a vivid imagination.

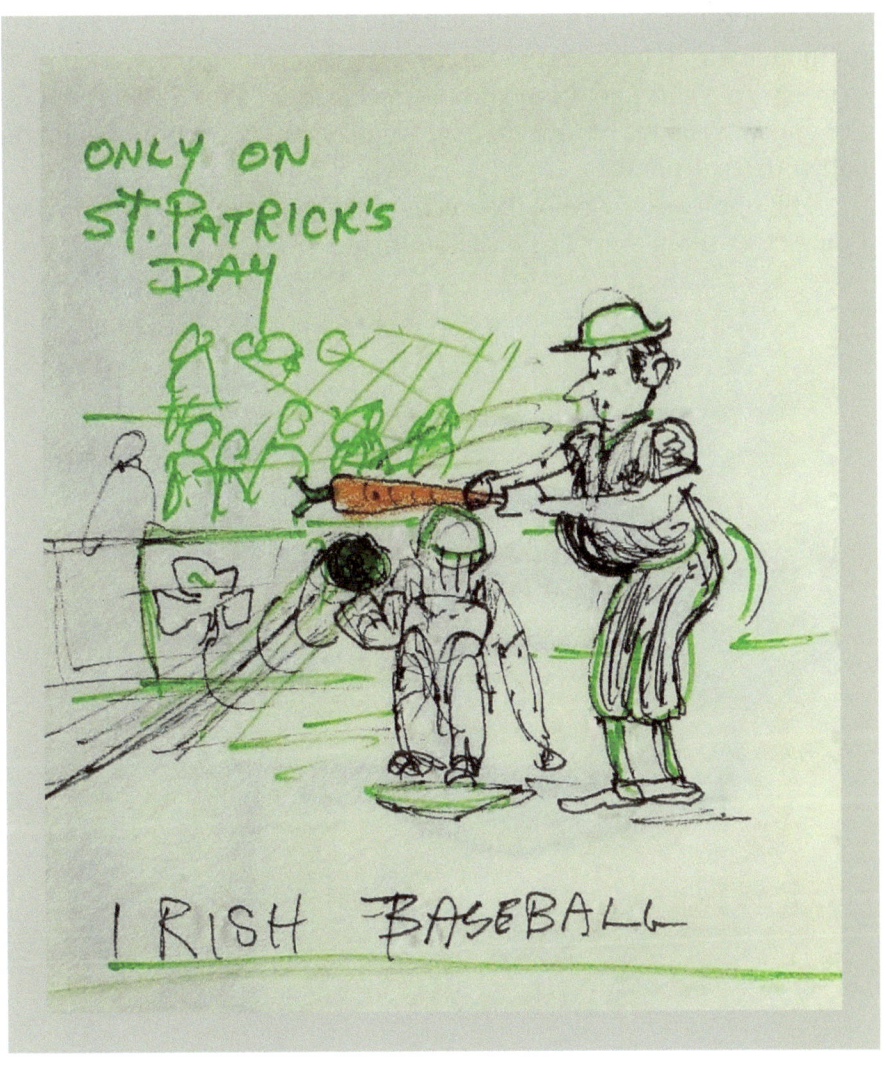

Title: Irish Baseball
Medium: Mixed media on paper

"Irish Baseball" is a good example of a cartoon "ruff." A ruff is a preliminary sketch to get an idea for a finished cartoon.

Several years ago, I tried doing some cartoons for St. Patrick's Day, and this is one of them, where the player at bat is trying to hit the ball with a carrot.

But don't ask me what the carrot has to do with St. Patrick's Day. I guess that's why I never finished this ruff.

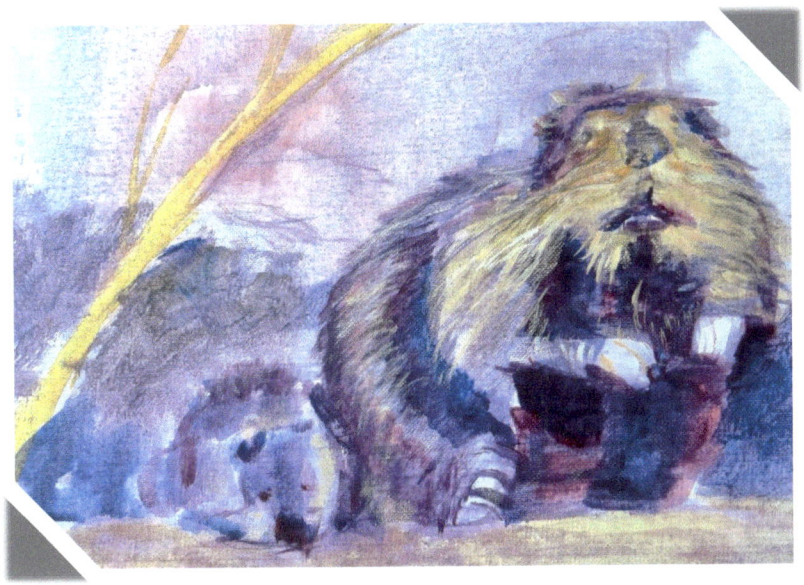

Title: Mama Beaver and Baby
Medium: Acrylic on canvas board

A few months ago, I was surfing the internet and came across a video of what looked like several tourists on a rural road, watching and photographing a beaver walking on the road. When one man began following close behind the beaver with his camera, the beaver turned around and began to run at the man. The man ran back to his car, but the beaver bit him, and went back about his business.

The video did not show the wounded man, but a text message said that the man bled to death!

If a beaver can chew a tree down, think what he could do to your leg. As the park rangers warn tourists, you never know what a wild animal will do.

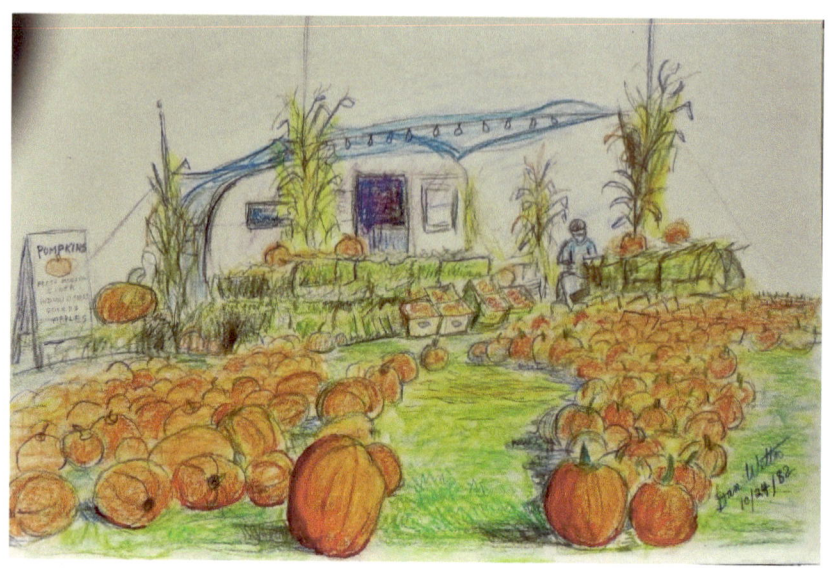

Title: Pumpkins for Sale
Medium: Mixed media on paper
Copyright by Dan Wetta 1982

Pumpkin carving has become very sophisticated over the years.

Chapter 2: Bus People

HOW GOOD ARE YOU AT MIND READING?

I used to sketch the bus passengers when I was on my way to work in downtown Richmond, Virginia. I have selected a few of these more interesting sketches to let you guess what are they thinking, what are they daydreaming about, what are they fantasizing?

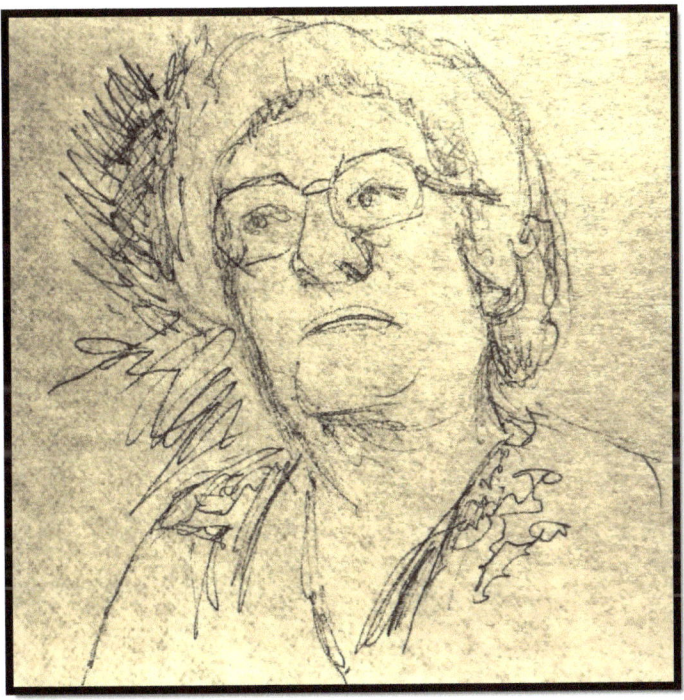

Title: Bus People – Lost in Thought
Medium: Pen on paper

Let's start off with this lady. Is she experiencing nostalgia? one way to travel back in time is through memory.
But maybe she is wondering about the future?

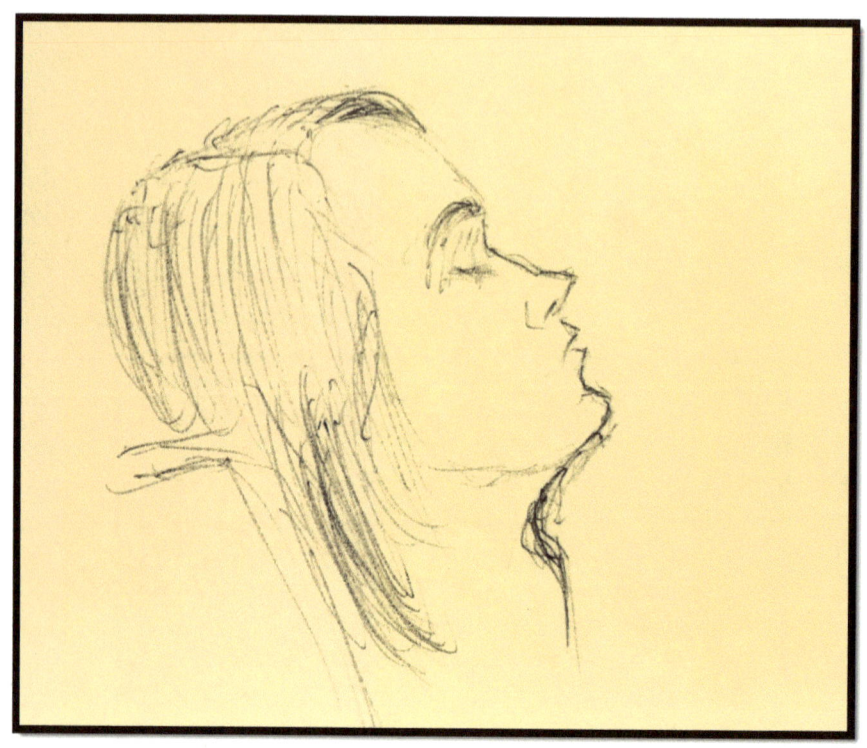

Title: Bus People – Dozing Off
Medium: Pencil on paper

What is this girl dreaming about, but, more importantly, will she wake up to get off at her stop and get to work on time?

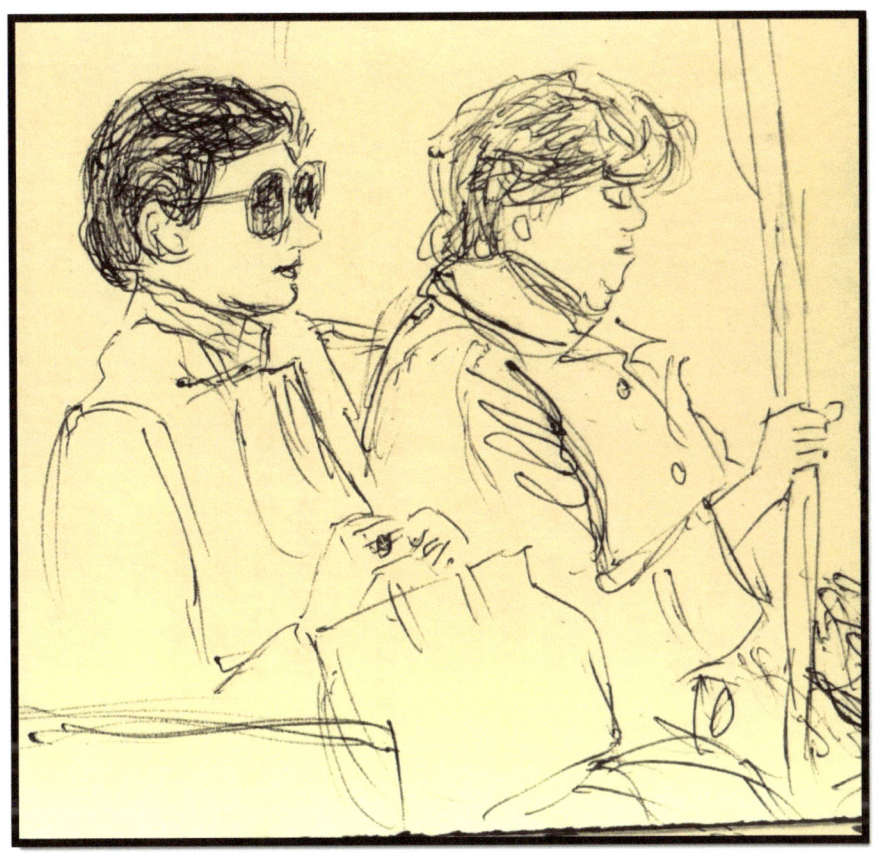

Title: Bus People – Two Women
Medium: Pen on paper

The lady in sunglasses seems to be pleased about something –
what?

The other lady is clutching a bus pole to keep her balance while
dozing off. She is probably dreaming also. How can she do these two
things at the same time?

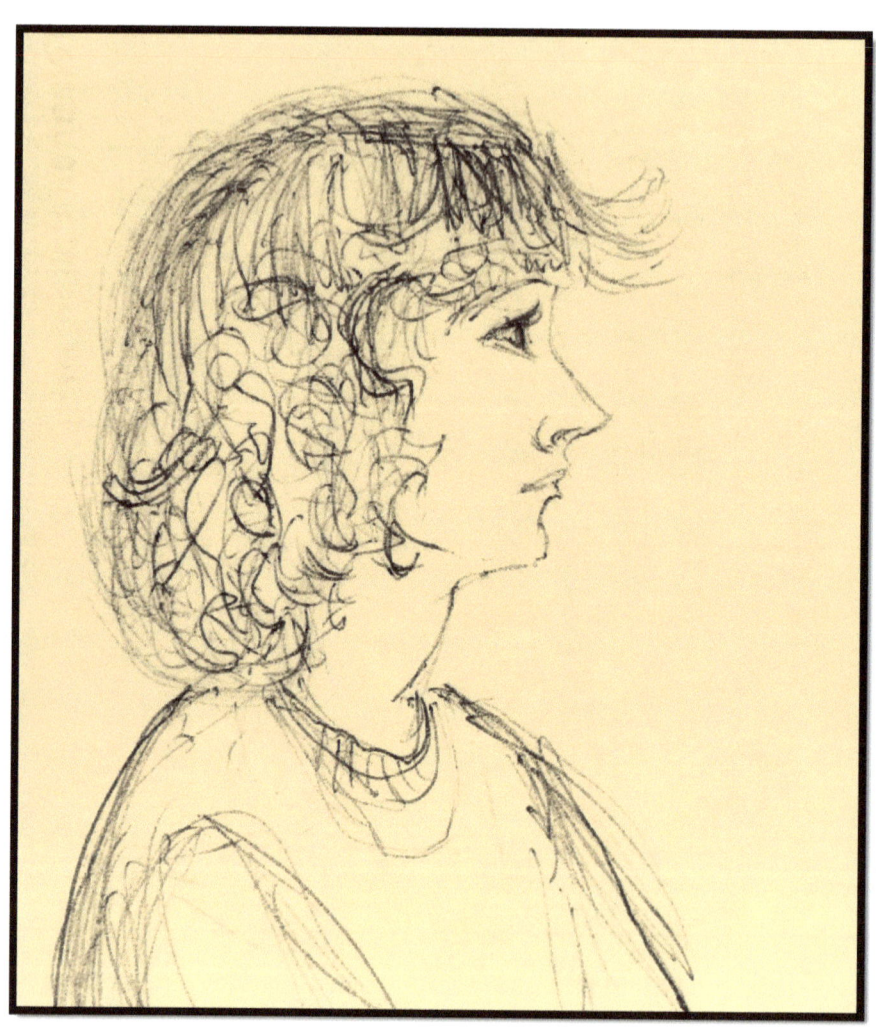

Title: Bus People – Daydreaming
Medium; Pen and pencil on paper

Is this lady daydreaming, or is her mind just blank?
I don't think your mind can ever be blank, because that would mean you are brain dead.

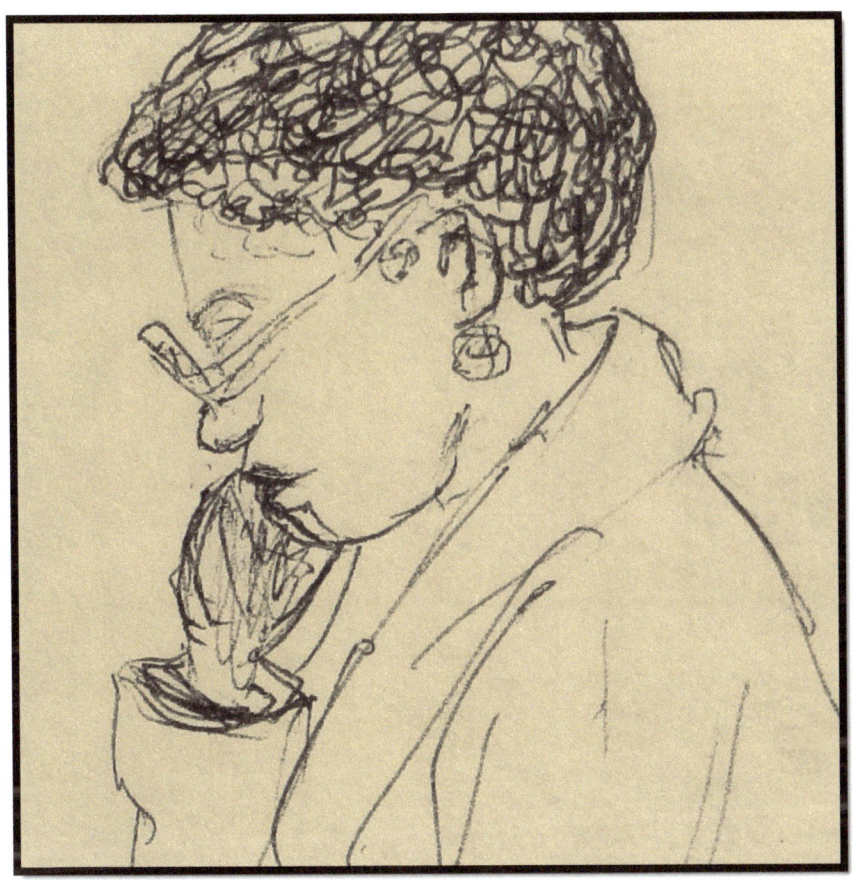

Title: Bus People – Wish I Were Somewhere Else
Medium: Pen on paper

Don't be influenced by the title of this sketch – it is only my guess what the lady is thinking, and I am an artist, not a mind reader.

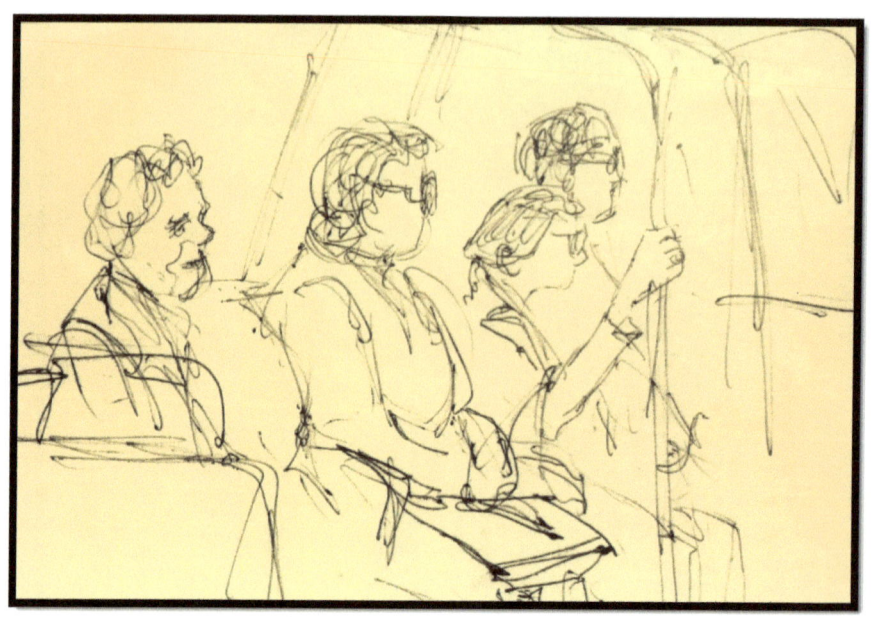

Title: Bus People – Three Unhappy People
Medium: Pen on paper

Again, do not be influenced by the title. These are three women passengers sitting behind the male bus driver.

I hope the bus driver is alert and watching out for pedestrians and traffic in general, but the women look unhappy to me.

Chapter 3: Richmond Road
(Route 60, Williamsburg, Virginia)

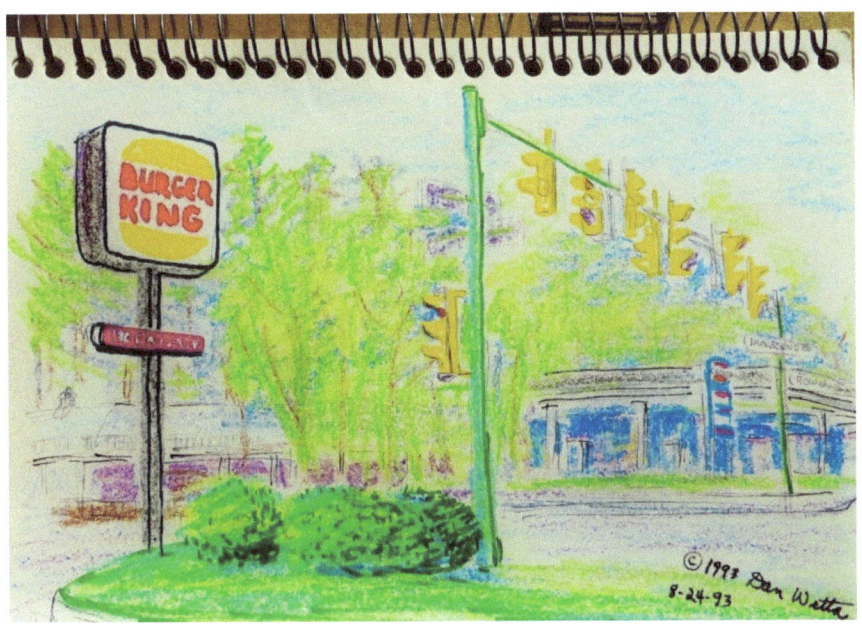

Title: Traffic Lights on Richmond Road
Medium: Mixed media on paper
Copyright Dan Wetta 1993

What would we do without traffic lights? Every once in a while, we lose electricity during a storm, and then driving on a busy road like Richmond Road is unsafe, not to mention that you can't buy gasoline, because the gas pumps operate on electricity.

PS - I left the note book binding rings on this sketch to show that this is a page out of my note book.

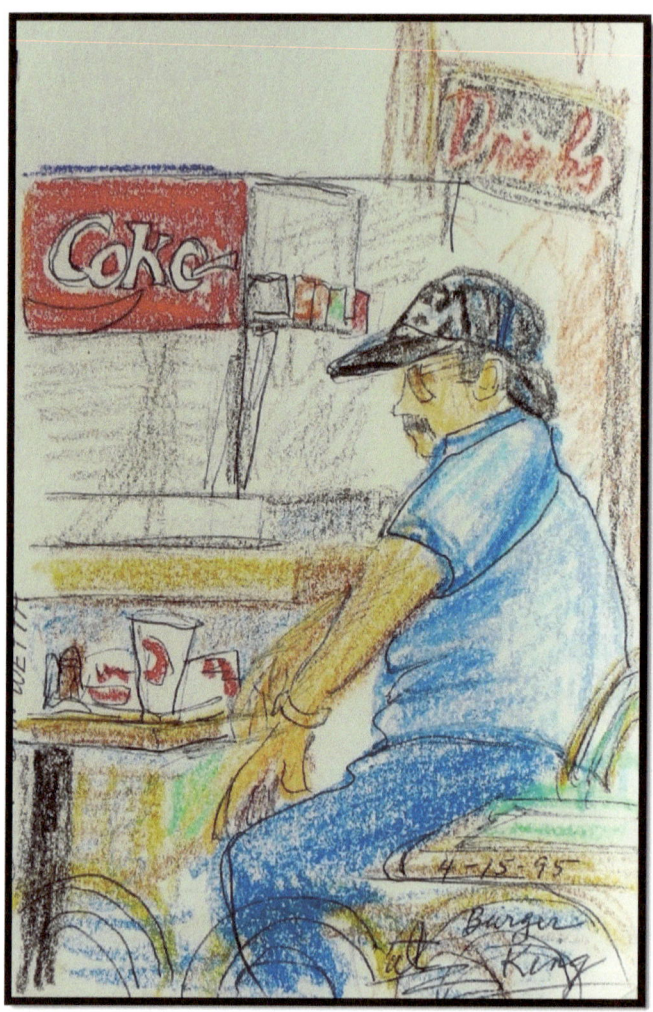

Title: Burger Customer
Medium: Mixed media on paper

I used to do a lot of sketching for practice and for fun and to keep the blues away.

If you keep busy doing something you like, you will never get bored.

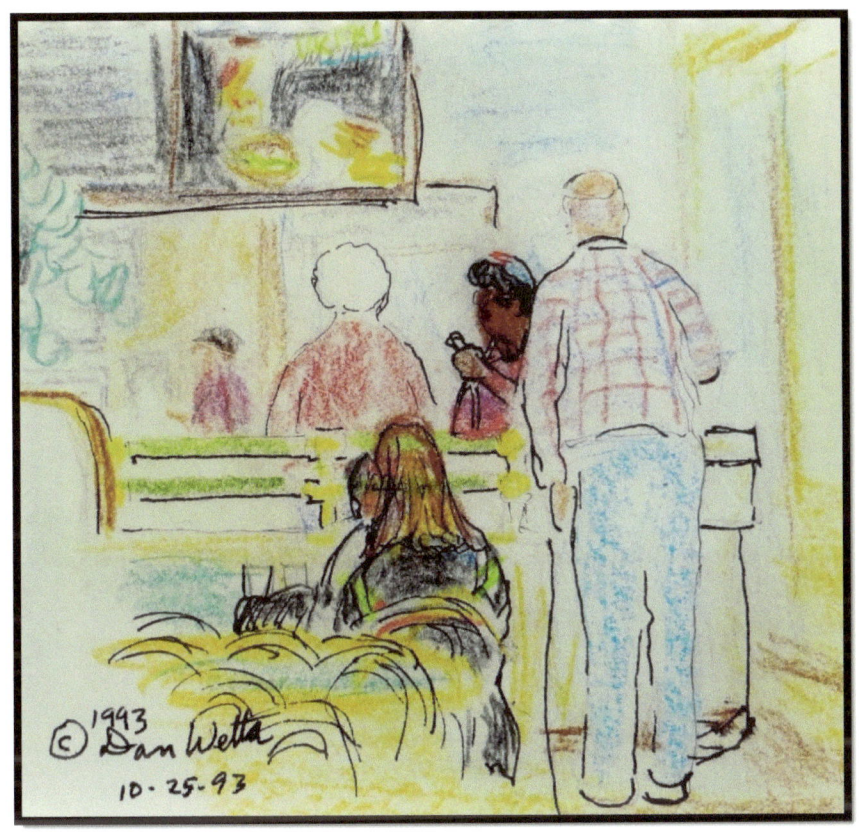

Ordering a Burger
Medium: Mixed media on paper

I used to get a couple hamburgers two or three times a week.
However, in my old age I find that all prepared foods have too much
salt. I tried eating fresh fruits and salads for three days, and the
swelling in my ankles and feet decreased about 50%. My blood
pressure also dropped several points.

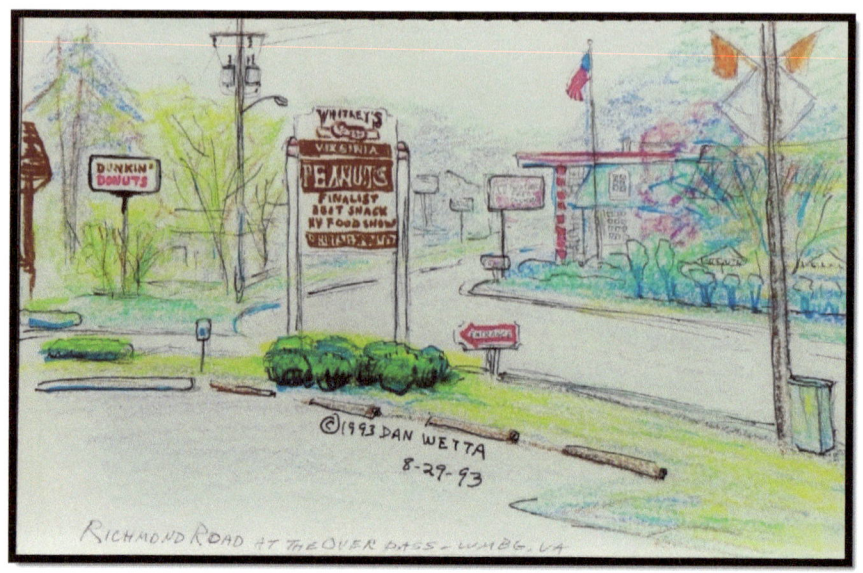

Title: Richmond Road at the Overpass
Medium: Mixed media on paper

This is another sketch of Richmond Road that I did in the early 1990's. Although Richmond Road is commercialized, it is colorful, and the only change is that it has grown. It probably has three times more restaurants than it did twenty years ago.

Since this is a tourist town, many new motels have been built on Richmond Road. There was an old mom-and-pop motel only a few yards from the above location that had a small swimming pool. Not long after I did this sketch, the parents of two teenage boys left them alone in the pool. Both boys drowned. The rumor was that the brothers did not get along too well, and that they may have gotten into a dunking contest in the pool, which caused the drowning.

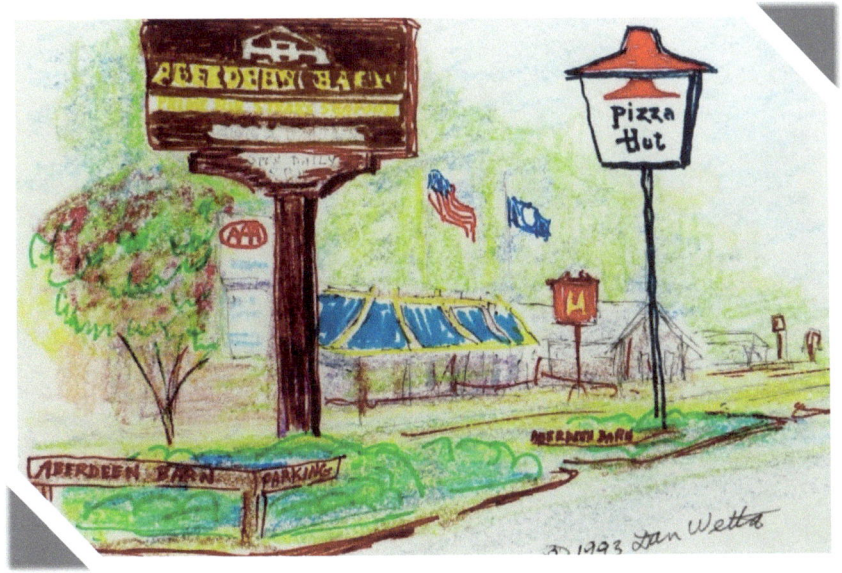

Title: Richmond Road, - Williamsburg VA
Medium: Mixed media on paper

Since the tourists outnumber residents of the Williamsburg area, there are numerous restaurants and fast food restaurants on Richmond Road. I sketched a few of them.

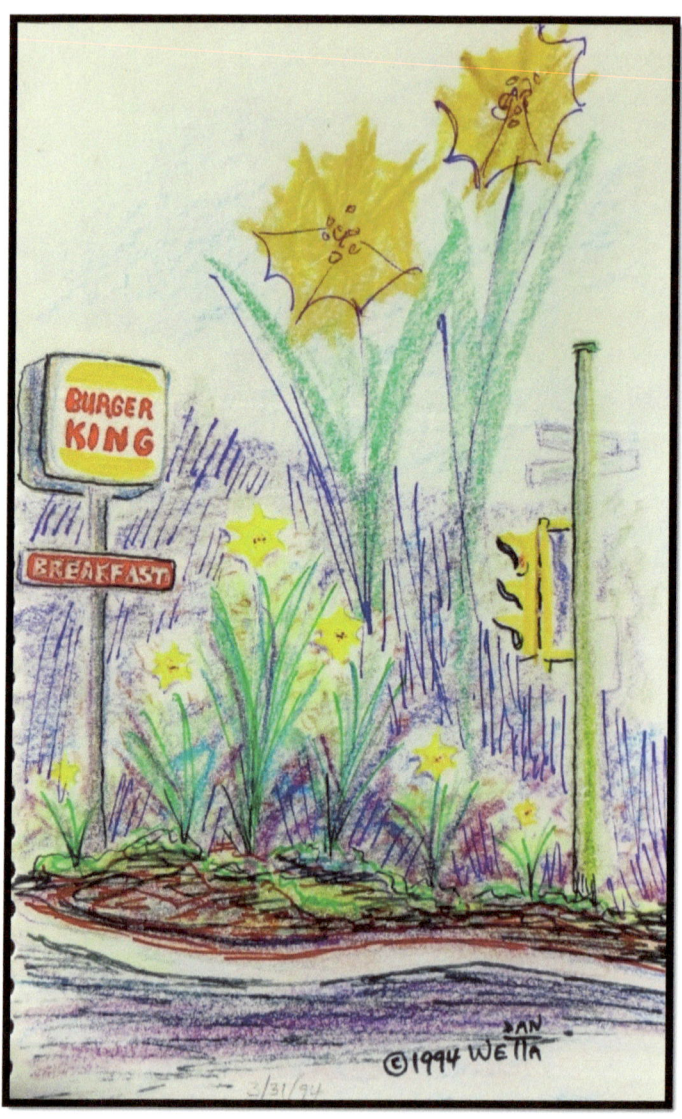

Title: Burgers and Flowers for Breakfast
Medium: Mixed media on paper

Look at the lower left side of this sketch and you will see that it is a page from my sketch book.

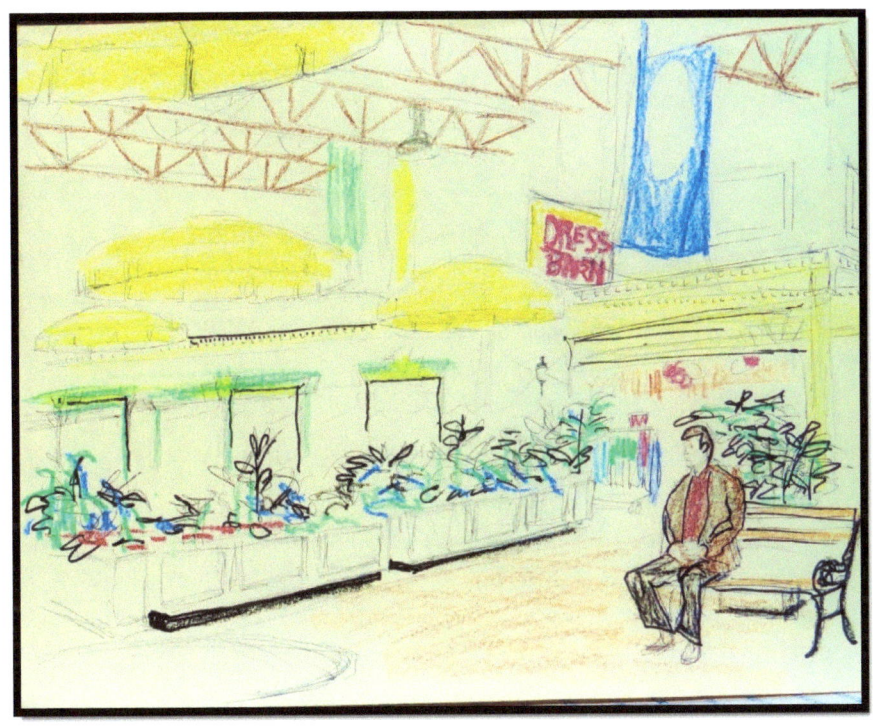

Bored Husband at Outlets Mall
Medium: Mixed media on paper

It looks like the man on the bench was bored waiting for his wife
to finish shopping.

I did this sketch over twenty years ago, shortly after the Outlets
Mall opened on Richmond Road in Lightfoot, Virginia. However,
when a strip mall opened a few miles away on Richmond Road, this
Outlets Mall lost most of their customers. This mall has been torn
down to make way for a supermarket.

Williamsburg was once a sleepy little town, but it has grown about
twenty times larger in the last twenty five years.

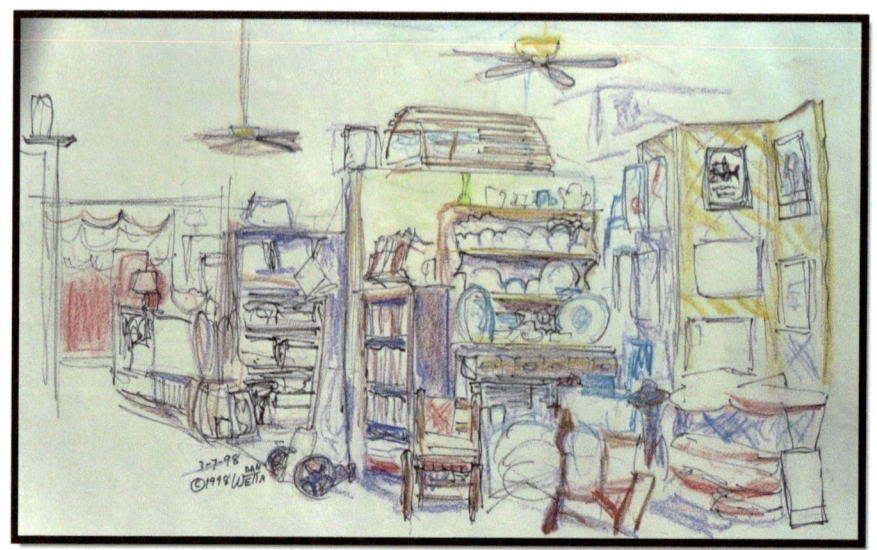

Title: Inside a Store
Medium: Mixed media on paper

I have done so many sketches that I cannot remember doing some of them. I have no idea what store this is, but my guess is that it is on Richmond Road.

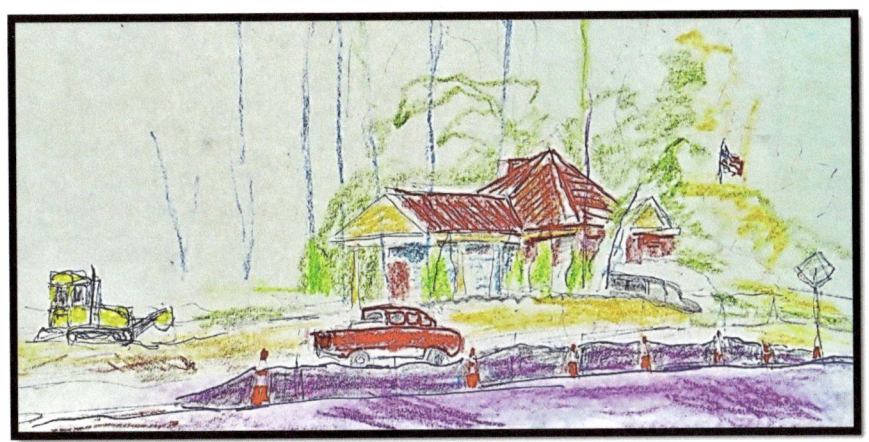

Title: Construction Site
Medium: Mixed media on paper

This is a quick sketch I did of a Federal Credit Union which is about a quarter mile from my condo. I now have an account there.

As I mentioned in one of my Richmond Road sketches, this area has increased in size from a sleepy little town into a bedroom community. People now live here and commute to work in Richmond to the west or to Newport News to the east.

Chapter 4: Designs For Stained Glass Windows

I took a beginner's course in stained glass media several years ago, but I just couldn't get the hang of cutting glass, so I decided to design stained glass scenes instead. My first illustration in this book, "Birds in Spider Web," is one such example of my art that simulates stained glass. After I finished this design for a window, I realized that the birds seem to be caught up in a spider web.

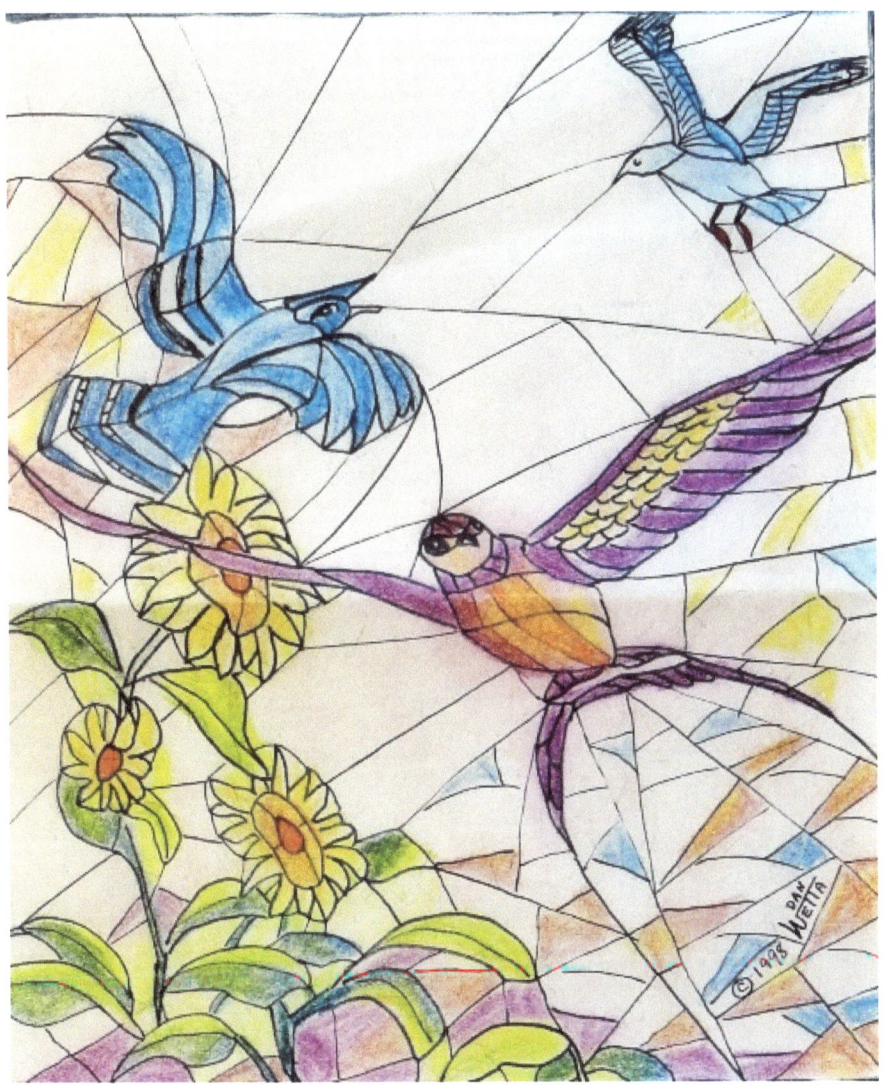

Title: Birds in Spider Web
Size: 12 x 15 inches
Medium: Mixed media on paper
Copyright by Dan Wetta

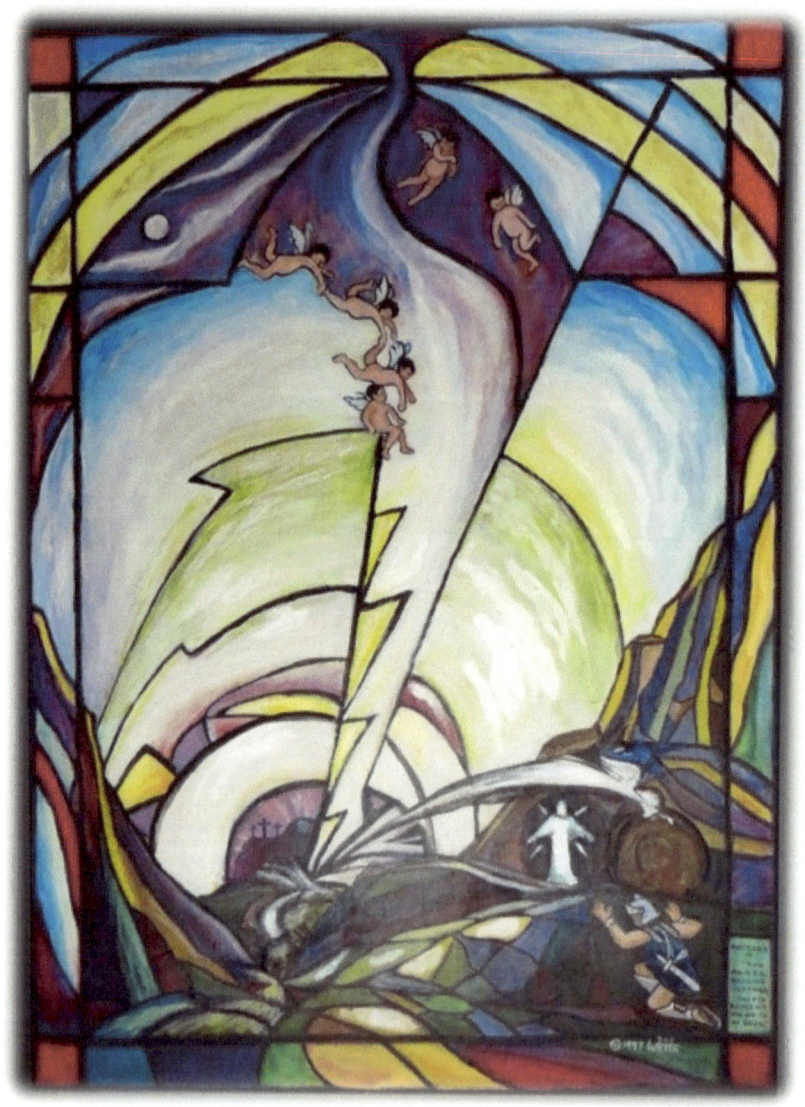

Title: Resurrection Lightning Bolt
Size: 22x30 inches
Medium: Acrylic on canvas
Copyright by Dan Wetta 1997

In the second illustration, "Resurrection Lightning Bolt," I tried to capture the image burned into the memory of the frightened Roman soldier who witnessed the miraculous event described in Matthew 28:3: "In appearance, the angel of the Lord resembled a flash of lightning."

The third stained glass illustration, "Purgatory," deals with a very Catholic concept: Catholic saints go straight to heaven when they die, but the ordinary lay Catholic has to stop off at Purgatory on the way to the Golden Gates.

Purgatory is a place where Catholics have to do penance for their sins. That lightning in Purgatory's head (see the following painting) is designed to literally scare the hell out of them.

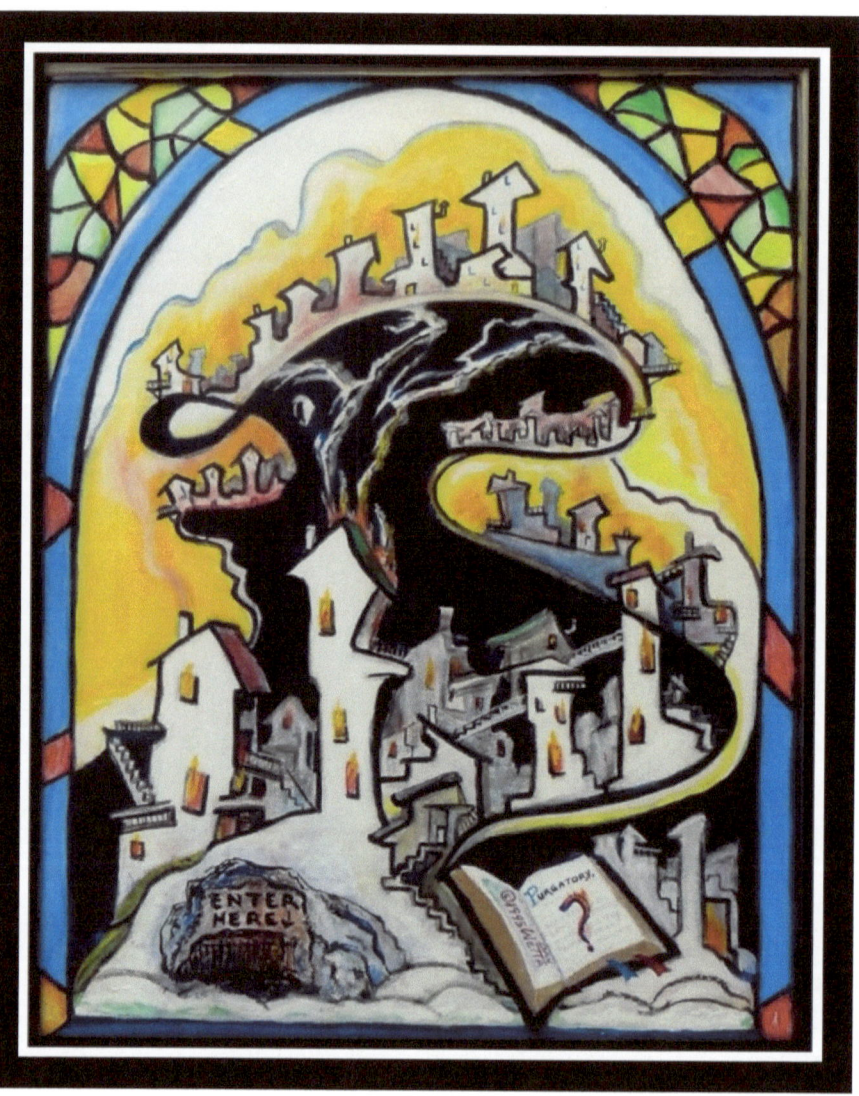

Title: Purgatory
Size: 16x20 inches
Medium: Acrylic on canvas
Copyright by Dan Wetta 1995

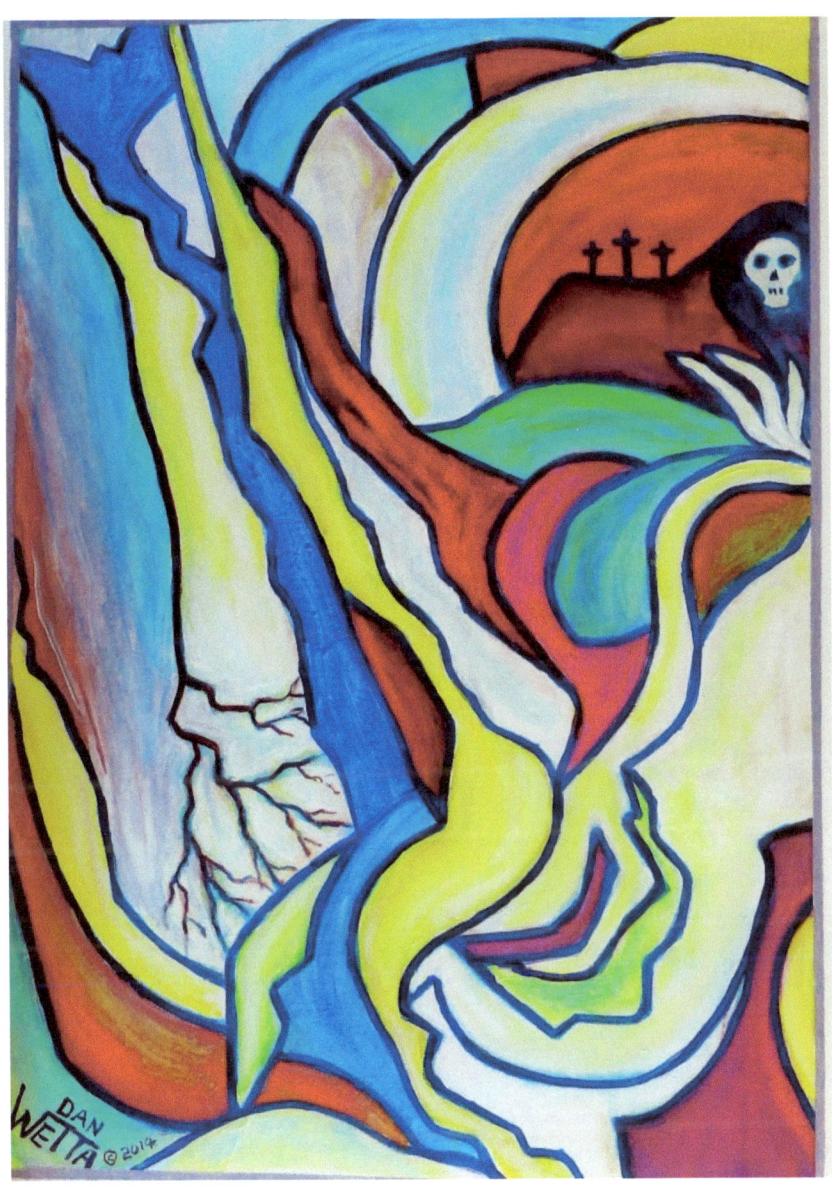

Title: Mount Golgotha
Size: 30x40 inches
Medium: Acrylic on canvas
Copyright by Dan Wetta 2014

Regarding this abstract entitled, "Mount Golgotha": I think that color stimulates the brain and abstracts stimulate the imagination. Each viewer's conception of the abstract work will differ from the other. Also, I think that the title of an abstract affects what the viewer sees.

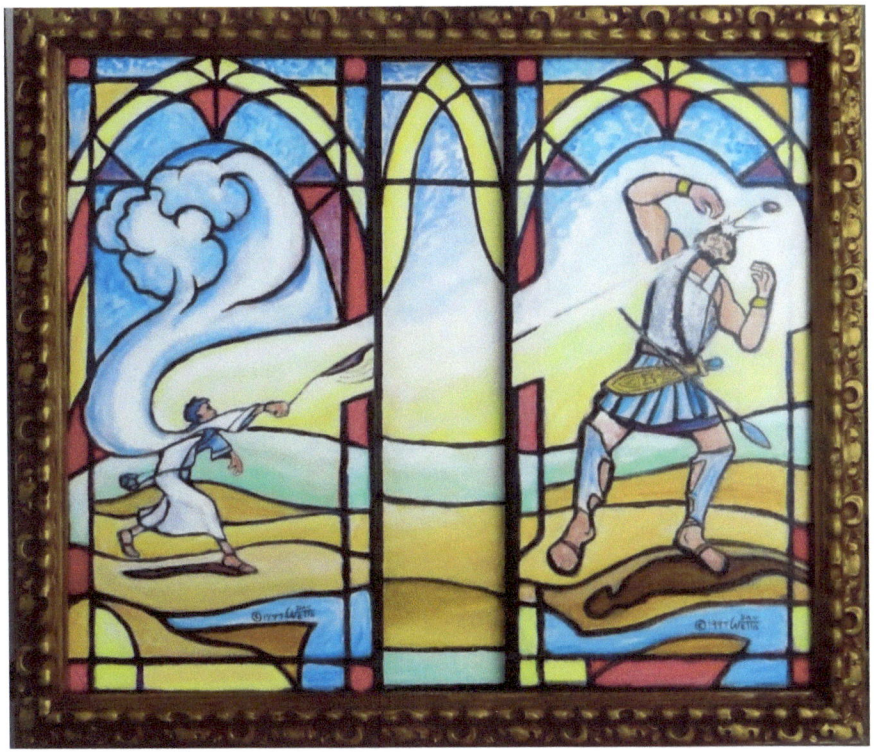

Title: David and Goliath
Size:24x20 inches
Medium: Acrylic on canvas
Copyright by Dan Wetta 1997

After the encounter between David and the Giant, people started saying: "Don't bring a sword to a rock fight."

My brain wasn't functioning properly when I did this scene. First, I painted David slinging a rock on a 10x20 inch canvas, and then I painted Goliath on a second 10x20 inch canvas.

I wanted to leave some space between them, so I framed them in a 24"x20" frame, which left a four inch space in the middle!

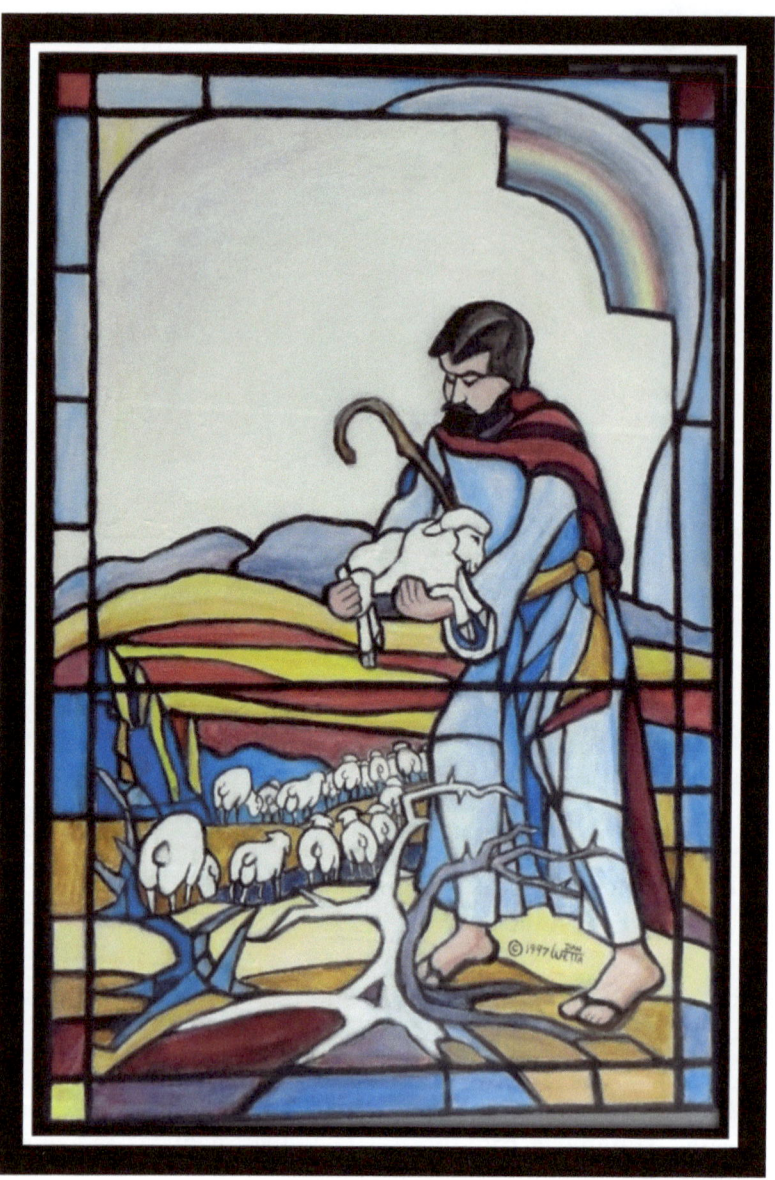

Title: Lost Lamb
Size: 20x30 inches
Medium: Acrylic on canvas
Copyright by Dan Wetta 1997

Most paintings about the parable of the lost sheep depict Jesus as the finder of the lost sheep, and I did the same thing; however, Jesus was telling a parable about a shepherd who went looking for a lost lamb. So the man holding a lamb in this painting should be a shepherd, not Jesus.

See Matthew 18:10-14 if you want to read the full story about the lost lamb.

By the way, if you search all the New Testament, you will realize that nobody knows what Jesus looked like.

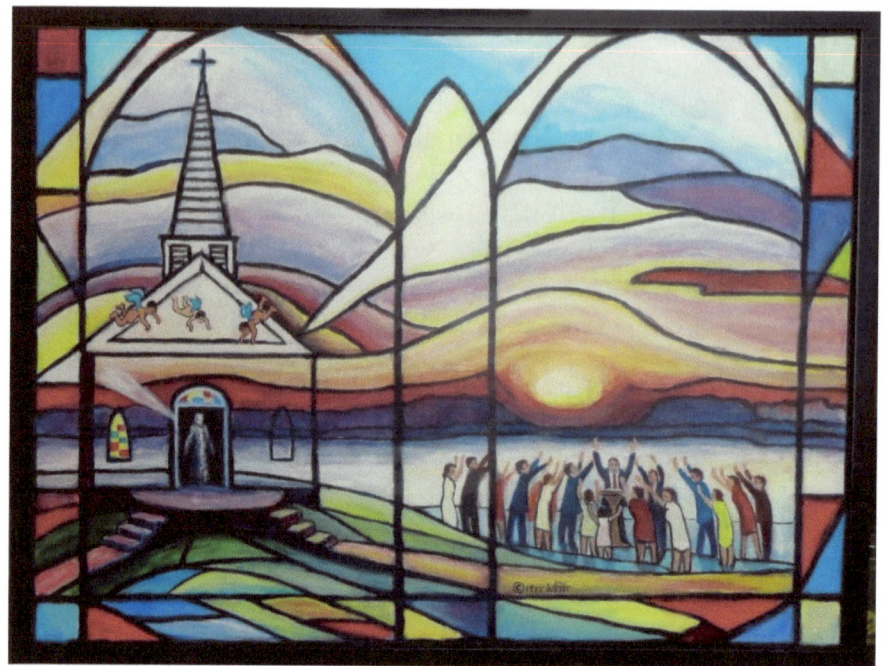

Title: Sunrise Service
Size: 20x30 inches
Medium: Acrylic on canvas
Copyright by Dan Wetta 1997

While the preacher is holding an Easter Morning Sunrise Service, the Risen Lord is watching them from their church.

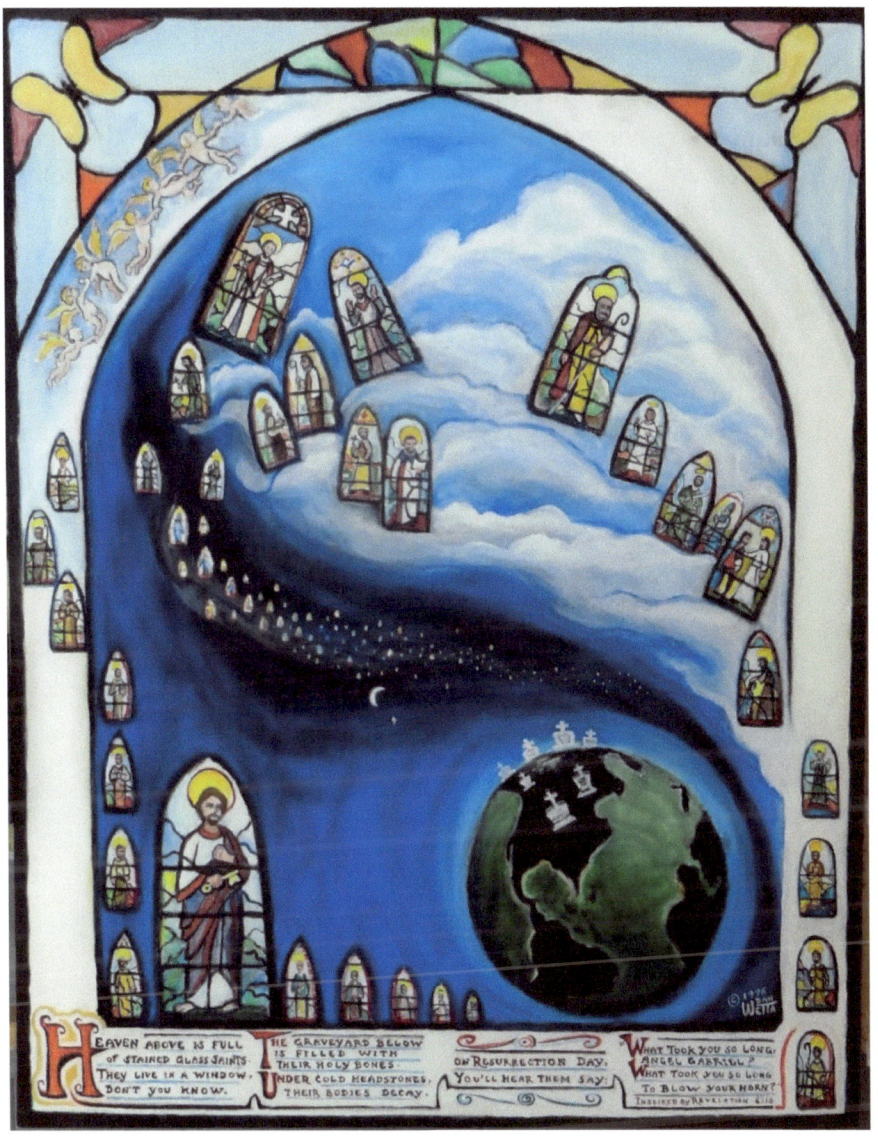

Title: Stained Glass Saints
Size: 24x30 inches
Medium: Acrylic on canvas
Copyright by Dan Wetta 1996

The bottom panel of this acrylic painting reads thus:

"Heaven above is full of stained glass saints. They live in a window, don't you know. The graveyard below is filled with their holy bones. Under cold headstones, their bodies decay. On Resurrection Day, you'll hear them say, 'What took you so long, Angel Gabriel? What took you so long to blow your horn?' Inspired by Revelation 6:10."

Sometimes it doesn't pay to be a saint. Thousands of them are imprisoned in the stained glass windows of Cathedrals all over the world, waiting for the Angel Gabriel to blow his horn on Judgment Day.

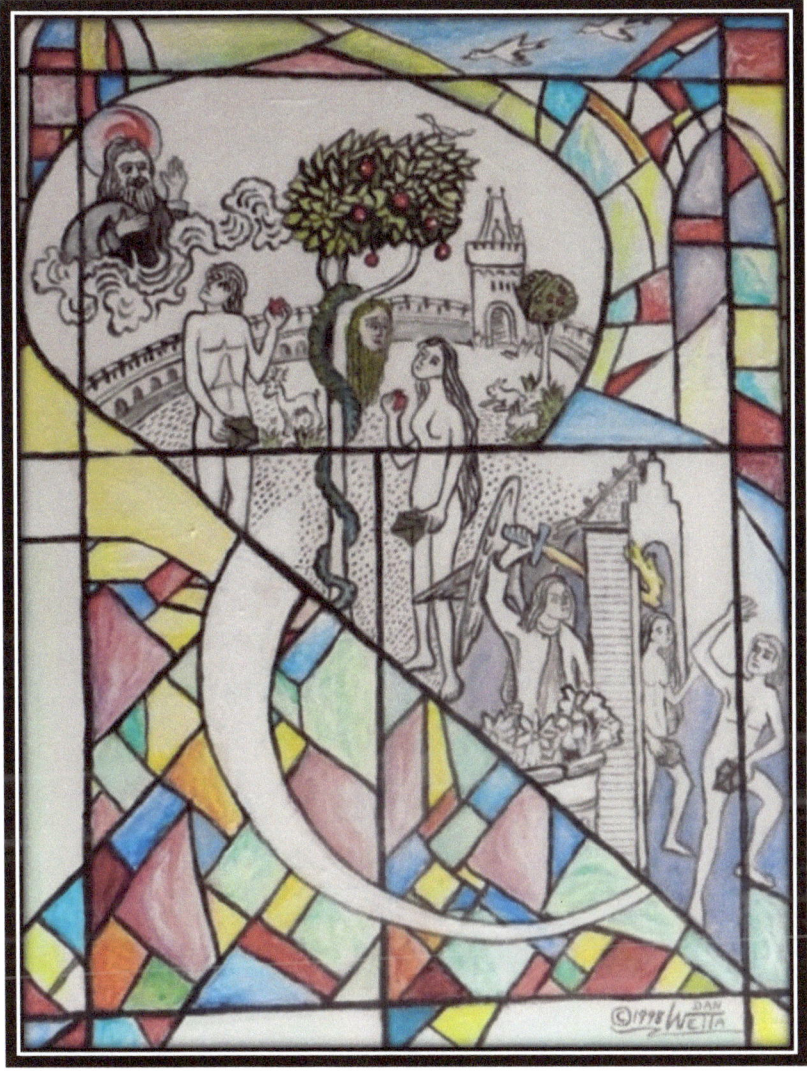

Title: Adam and Eve Expelled From Eden
Size: 16x20 inches
Medium: Acrylic on canvas
Copyright by Dan Wetta 1998

In "Adam and Eve Expelled From Eden," there is a time portal in the lower right hand corner of the design showing the angel driving Adam and Eve out of Eden. That time portal is important, because the first book of Genesis states that in the beginning, God created 'humankind'.

There is no mention of Adam and Eve or the Garden of Eden until the second book of Genesis.

NOTE: This design for a stained glass window and several of the following designs are also based upon 15th-century-block-print-bible illustrations.

The designs are not exact copies because I have also taken some artistic liberties by adding stained glass touches. Also, the original illustrations were not colored.

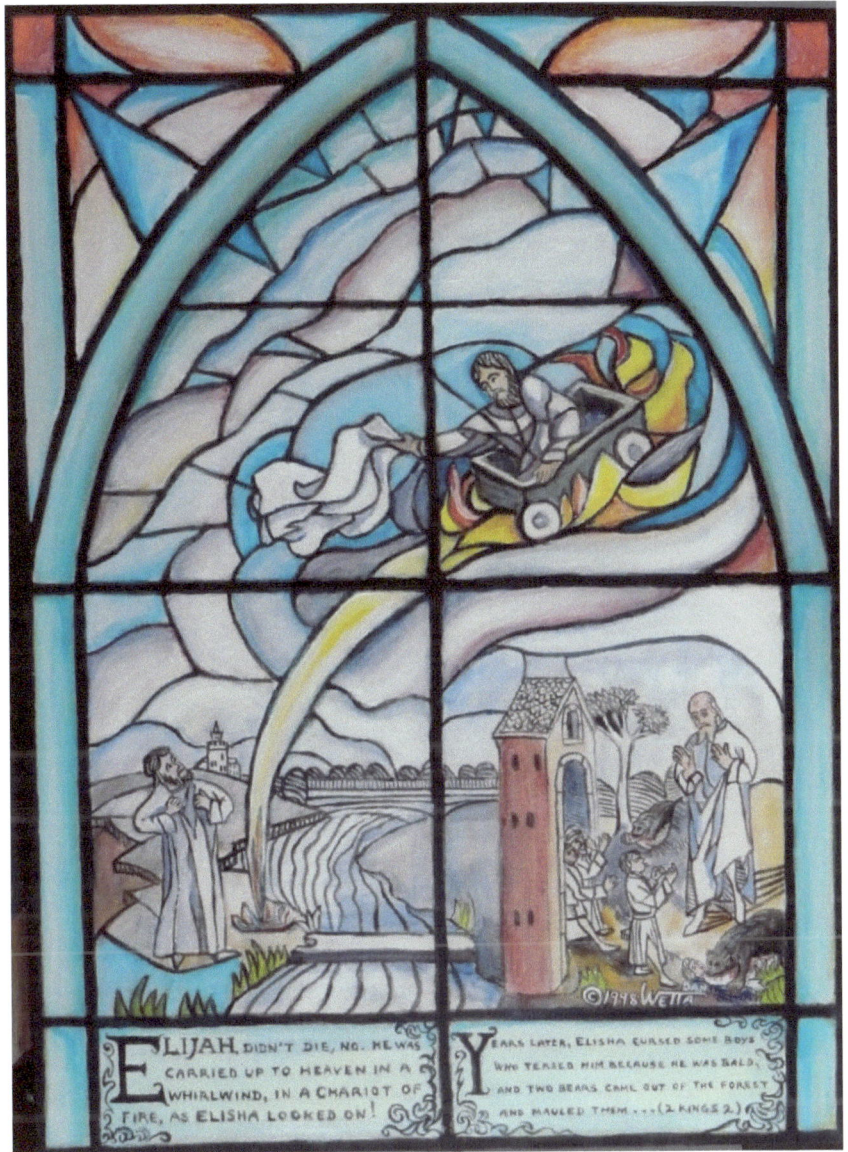

Title: Elijah Didn't Die
Size: 18x24
Medium: Acrylic on canvas
Copyright by Dan Wetta 1998

Elijah was carried to heaven in a chariot of fire as Elisha looked on!

The time portal in the lower right corner of "Elijah Didn't Die" projects the scene into the future when some boys teased Elisha about his bald head. (See the following cartoon.)

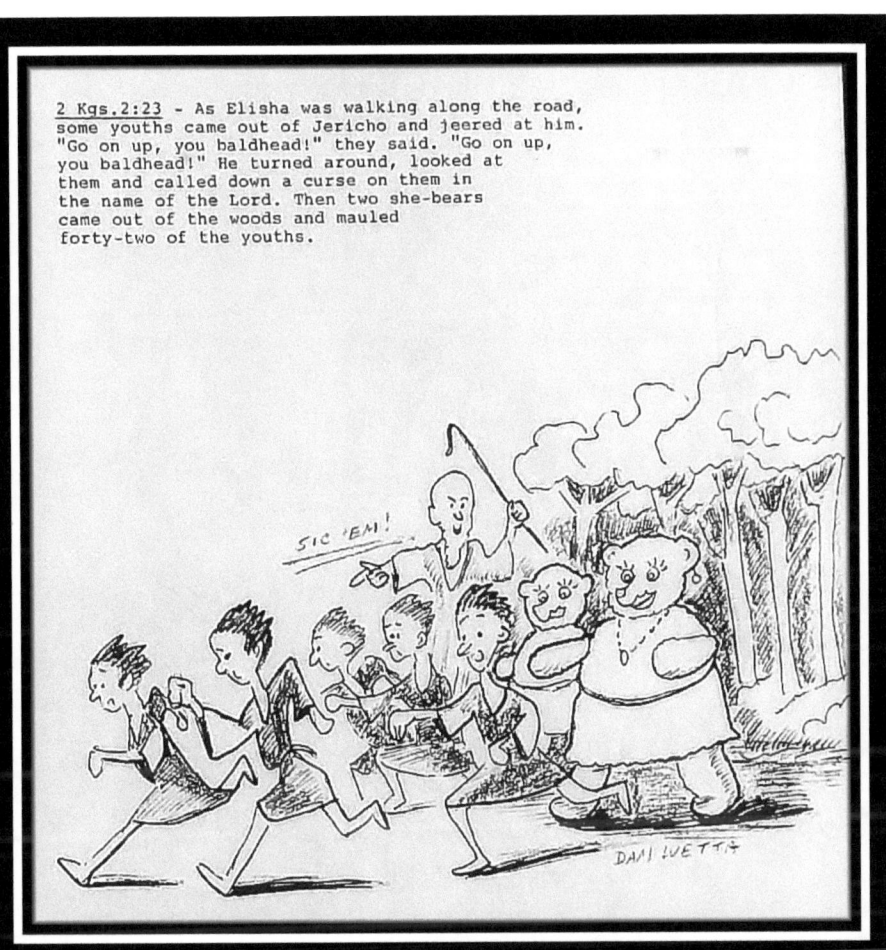

Title: cartoon Elisha
Copyright by Dan Wetta

Never tease a man about his bald head.

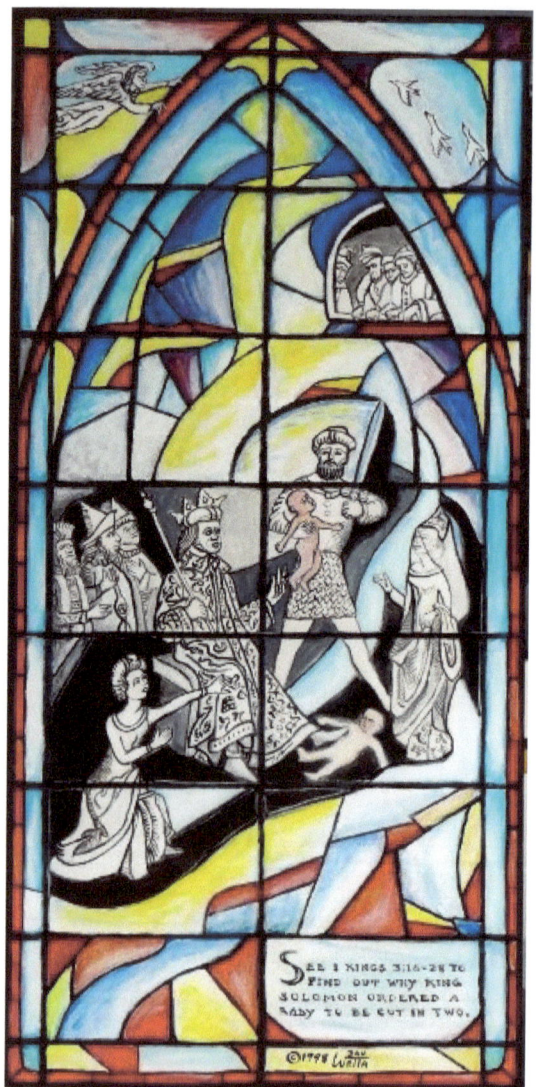

Title: King Solomon's Verdict
Size: 18"x36"
Medium: Acrylic on canvas
Copyright Dan Wetta 1998

The "King Solomon's Verdict" design for a stained glass window is fashioned after the block-printing style of 15th-century-illustrated bibles.

They called King Solomon wise because he ordered a baby to be cut in half – but this statement is misleading because it is taken out of context, so don't believe everything you read in the news since the news media often slants a story by omitting part of the facts.

Therefore, if you want to know why King Solomon was wise, you will have to read the bible story at: 1 kings 3:16 – 28.

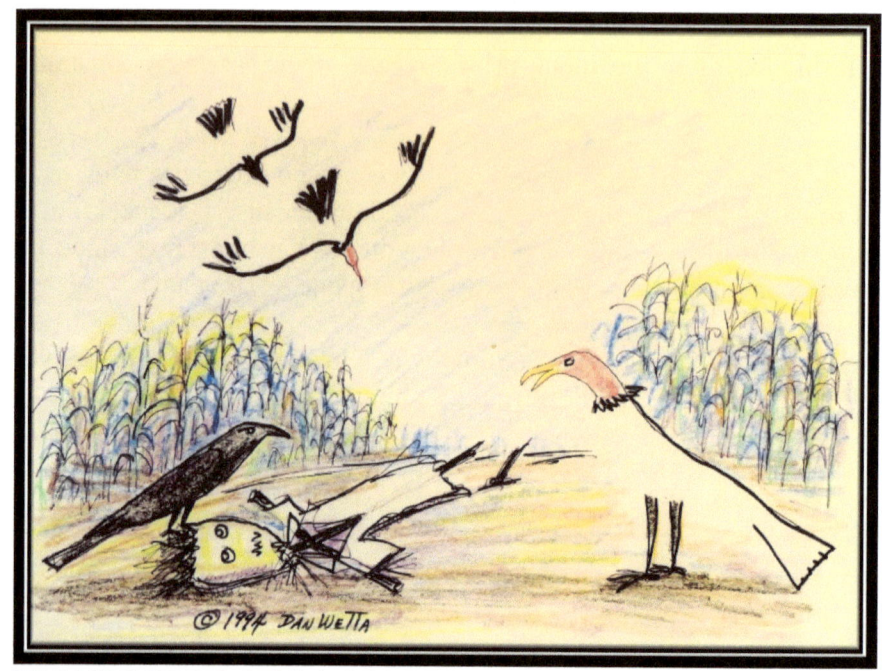

IT'S NOT FOOD, IT'S A SCARECROW, YOU DUMB CROW!

Title: Dumb Crow
Copyright by Dan Wetta 1994

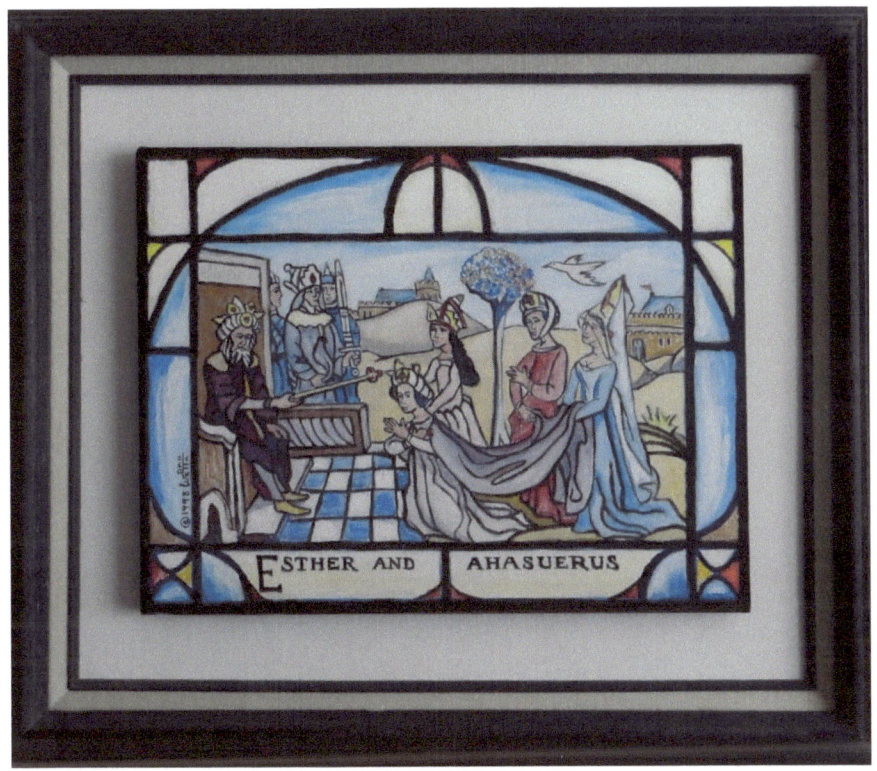

Title: Esther and Ahasuerus
Size:12"x20" on 16"x20" canvas panel
Medium: Acrylic on canvas
Copyright by Dan Wetta1998

This painting is rendered in the block-printing style of 15th-century-bible illustrations.

Esther is the heroine of the biblical book of Esther. She became the Jewish queen of King Ahasuerus. If you are interested in heroines, read the book of Esther in the Old Testament.

If you are interested in spelling, go the book of Esther and practice spelling King Ahasuerus.

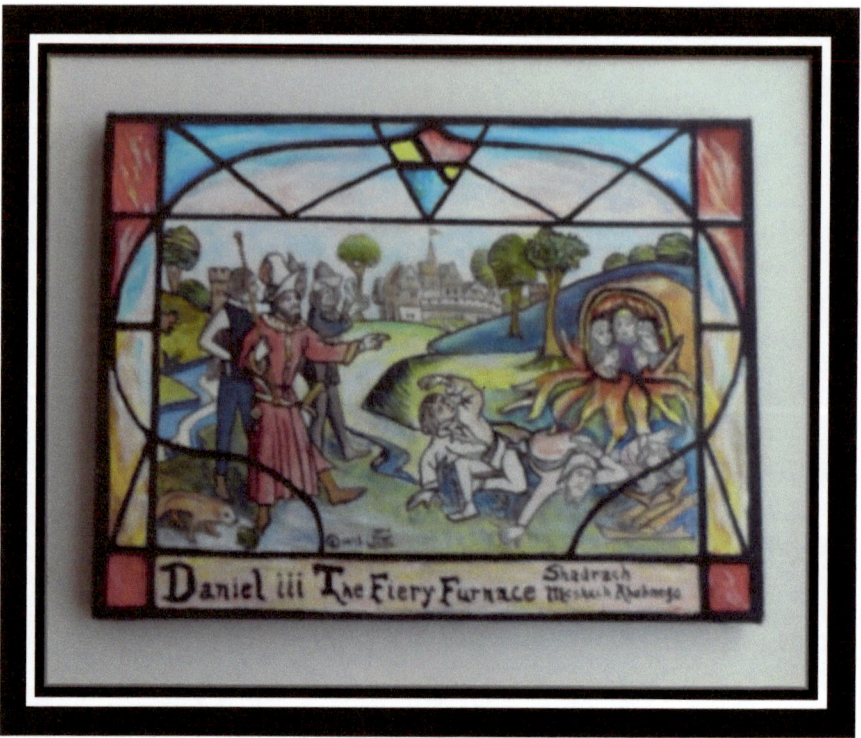

Title: Backfire
Size: 12"x16" canvas mounted on 16"x20" board
Medium: Acrylic on canvas
Copyright by Dan Wetta 1998

This is an interesting story in the Old Testament.

King Nebuchednezar had Shadrach, Meshach and Abed-Nego thrown into a very hot furnace. The flames were so hot that they burned the King's servants to death.

Only three men were thrown into the fire, but the King saw four.

PS If you look up the story in Daniel 3, you can check to see how many names I misspelled.

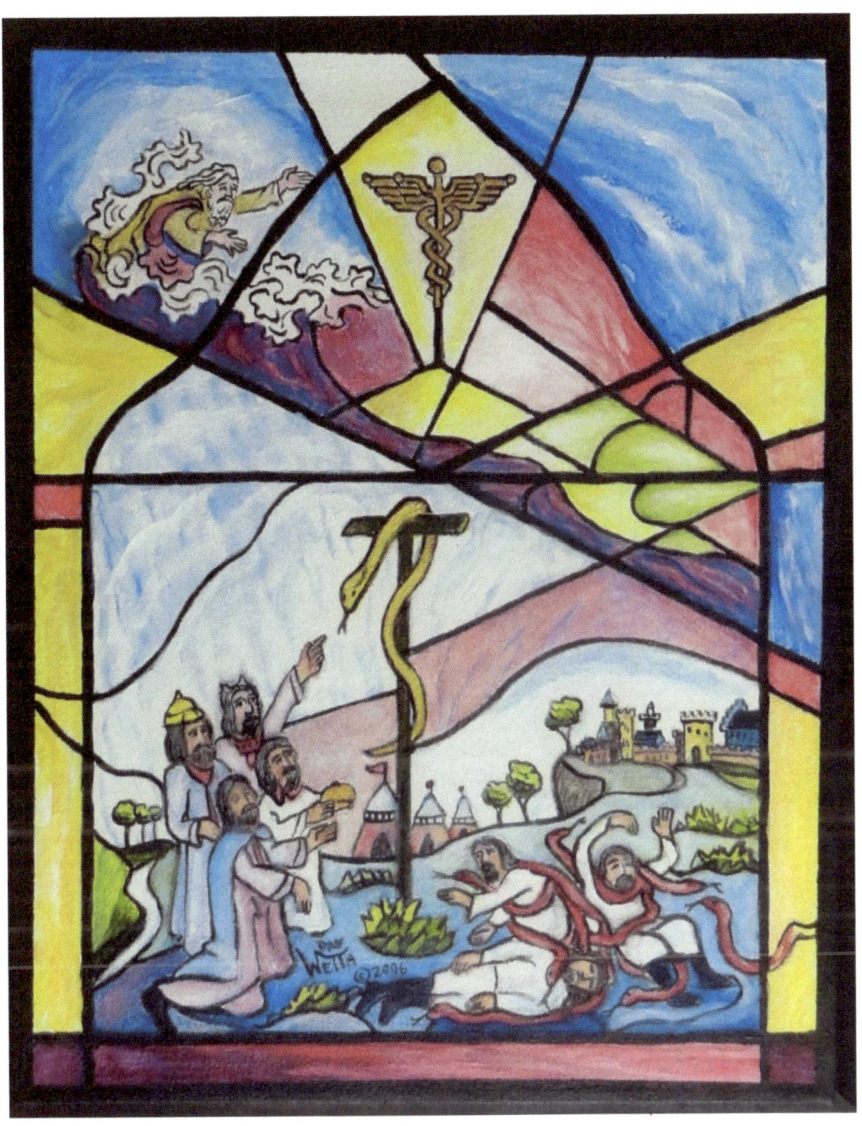

Title: Caduceus
Size 16"x20"
Medium: Acrylic on canvas
Copyright by Dan Wetta 2006

The Lord said to Moses, "Make a bronze snake and put it up on a pole; anyone who is bitten by a snake can look at it and live." So Moses made a bronze snake and put it up on a pole.

Then when anyone was bitten by a snake and looked at the bronze snake, he lived.

See Numbers 21 for the full story if you're not squeamish about snakes.

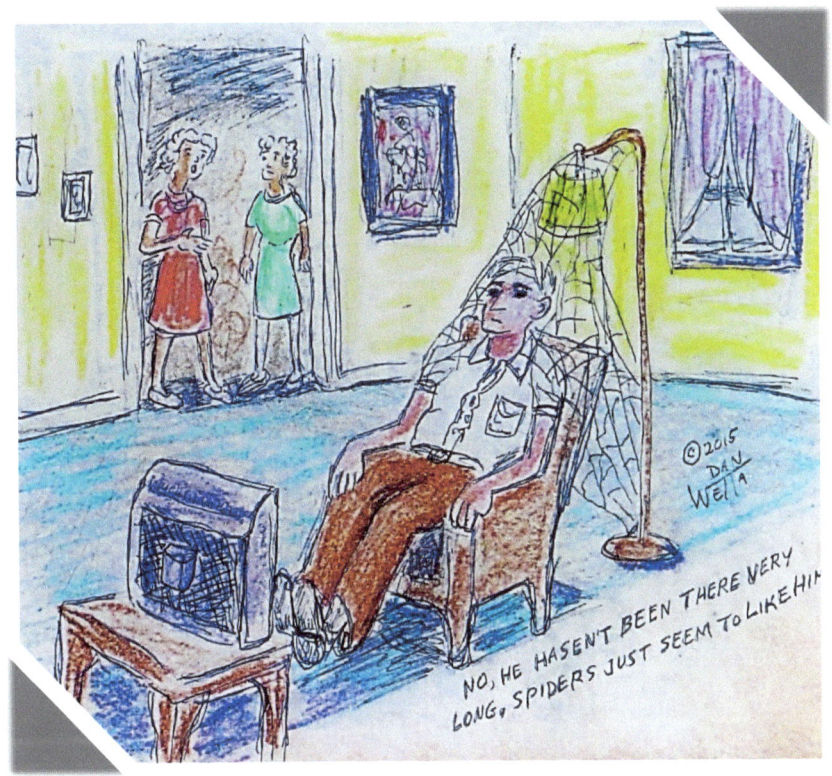

Title: Spider-web Man cartoon
Medium: Mixed media on paper
Copyright 2015

My experience is that spiders will take over any place where there has been no human activity for a long time.

Years ago, an elderly man who lived next door was going to do some work on his yard. He went out to his tool shed in the spring and put on his old work shoes which had been left there all winter long.

A black-widow spider in a shoe bit him, and he nearly died.

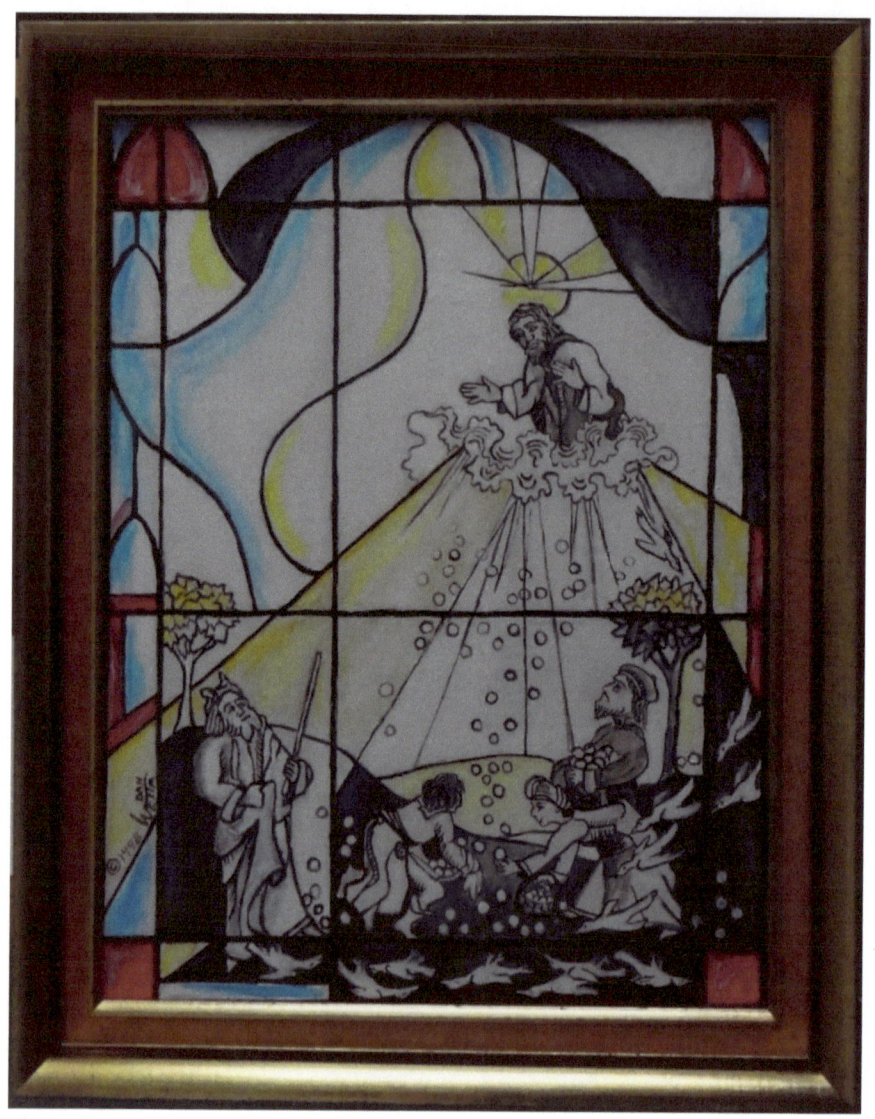

Title: Manna and Quail
Size: 14"x18"
Medium: Acrylic on canvas
Copyright by Dan Wetta 1998

This is a design for a stained glass window in the block print style of illustrations in l5th century bibles.

Exodus 16 - "During their forty year exodus in the desert, the Israelites complained to the Lord that they were hungry, so the Lord sent them manna, and thousands of quail fell from the sky."

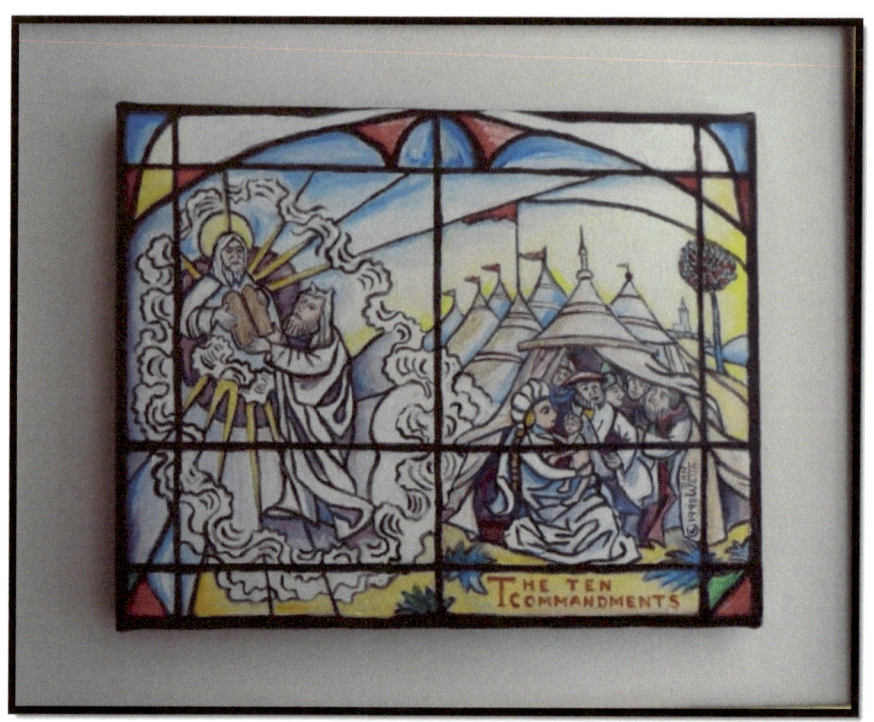

Title: Ten Commandments
Size:11x14 inches on 16x20 inch canvas panel
Medium: Acrylic on canvas
Copyright by Dan Wetta 1998

This design for a stained glass window is based upon the block-printing illustrations in 15th-century bibles.

Nobody has been paying much attention to the Ten Commandments for the last fifty years or so, although they have been posted everywhere, in public places, court houses, schools, parks and churches.

But lately, some people think if they can get the government to repeal the Ten Commandments, nobody will be able to accuse them of doing anything wrong or immoral.

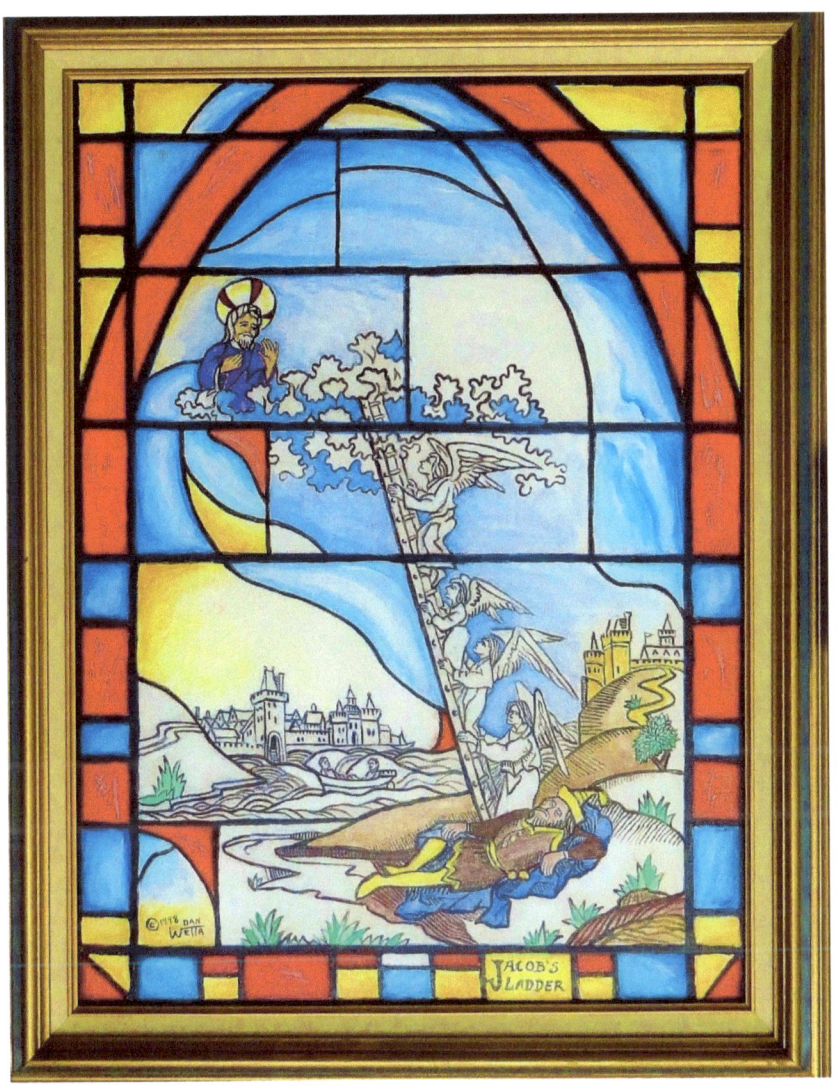

Title: Jacob's Ladder
Size: 18 x 24 inches
Medium: Acrylic on canvas
Copyright by Dan Wetta 1998

Jacob was resting his head on a stone when he had this dream about the ladder. I think I would awaken with a headache if I had a stone for a pillow.

This is one of the more interesting stories in the Old Testament, so you might want to read it at Genesis 28:15.

Chapter 5: If God Wanted Man to Fly, He Would Have Given Him Wings

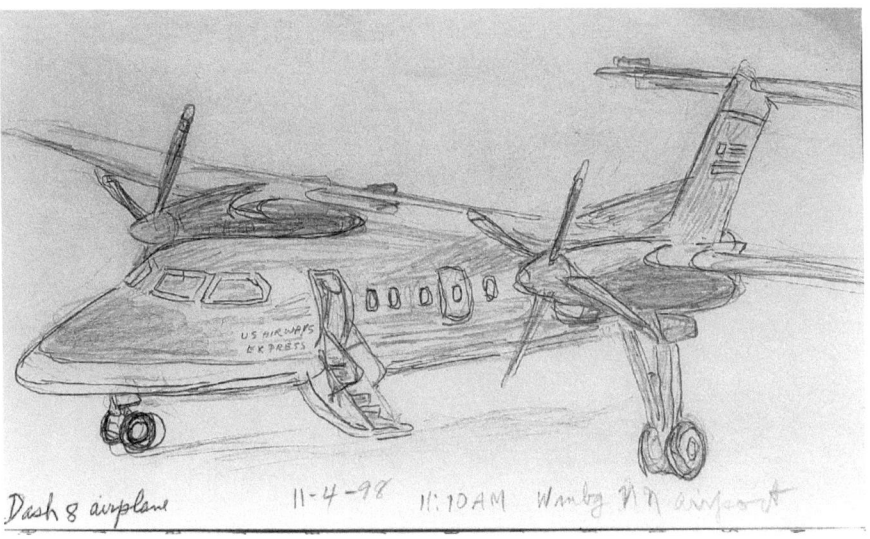

Title: Airplane – Dash 8
Medium: Pencil on paper

I used to fly several times a year with no problem, until one day I took a good look at an airplane and the thought entered my mind that there was no way anything that big and heavy could ever get off the ground. I became a proponent of the philosophy that says, "If God wanted man to fly, he would have given him wings." I developed a fear of flying, but my fear was limited to take-off. Once the plane got safely off the ground, I was okay.

I tried praying as we were taking off, but that only made the fear worse. I then decided to try sketching, and that worked. Not that I have anything against praying. However, praying made me concentrate on the problem.

Instead, when I was sketching, I was concentrating on the subject of my drawing and totally unaware of how the plane was doing on takeoff.

The following pages contain some of those sketches.

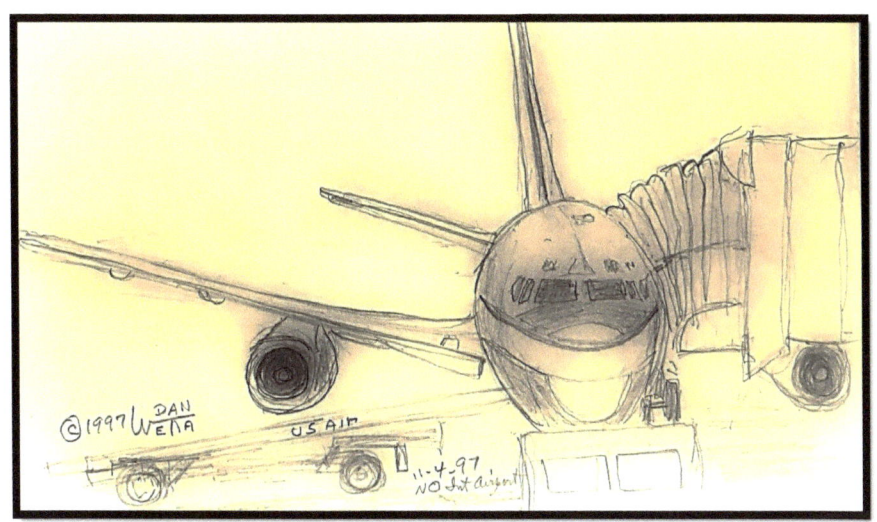

Title: Airplane – New Orleans
Medium: Pen and pencil on sketch pad paper

How can something like this get off the ground?

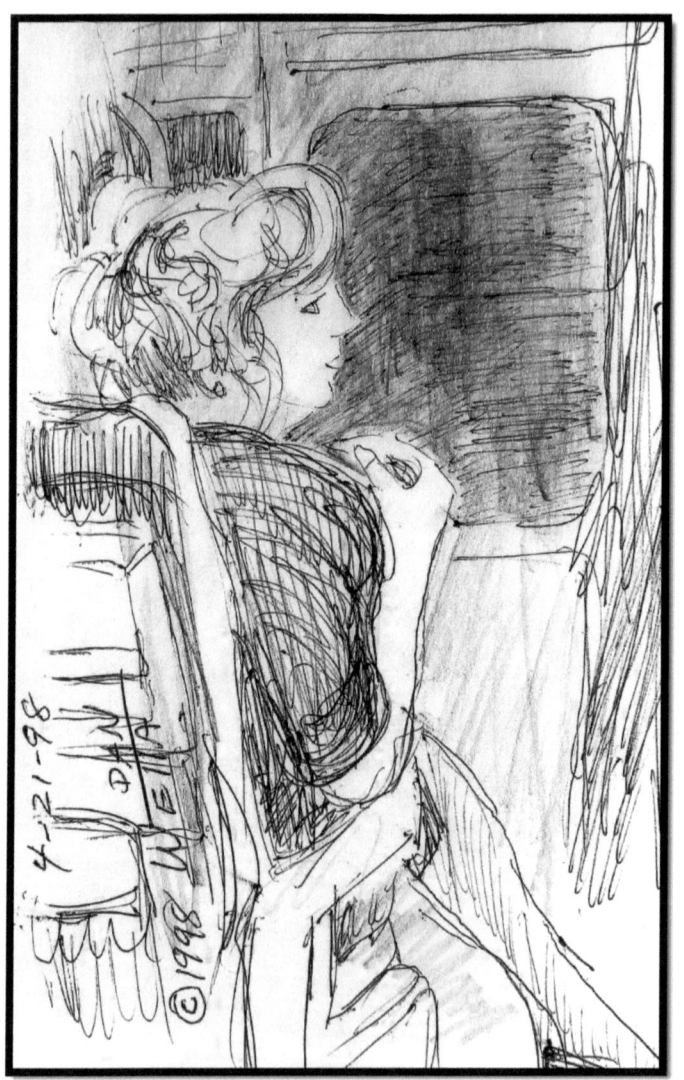

Title: Airplane – Woman Daydreaming
Medium: Pen and pencil on note book paper

Did you ever notice how your mind goes blank when someone interrupts your daydreaming with the query, "A penny for your thoughts?"

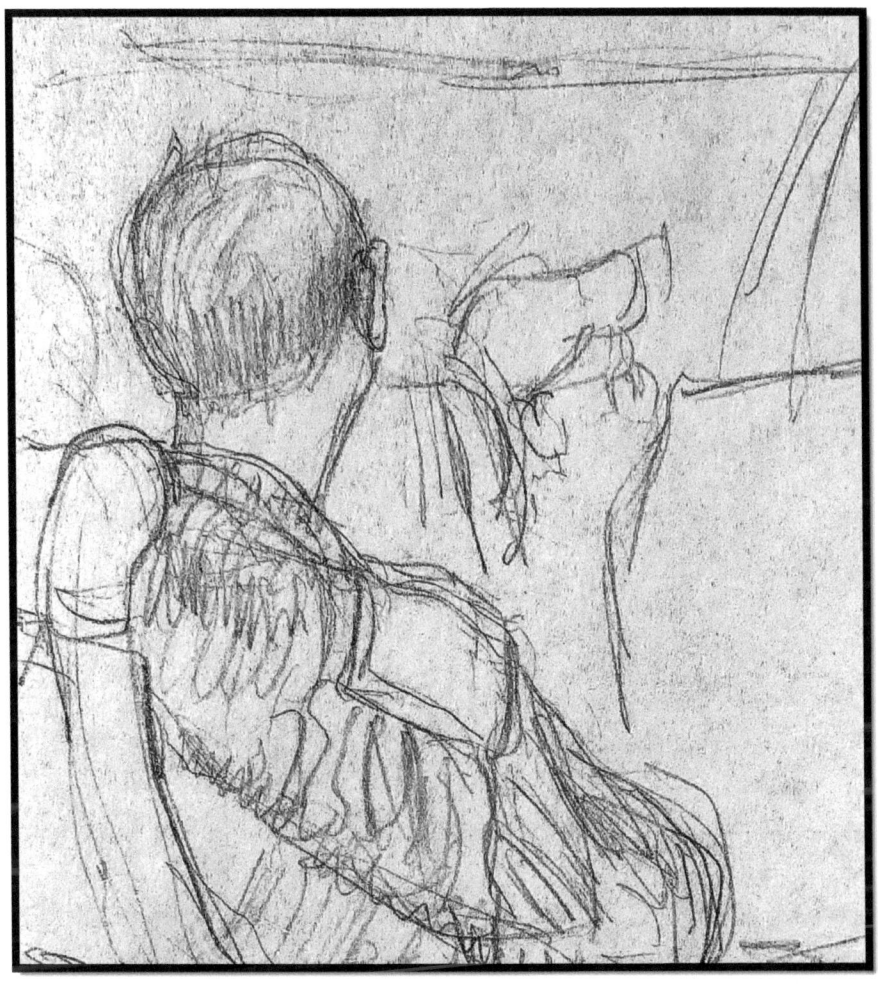

Title: Airplane – Man Cleaning Eyeglasses
Medium: Pen and pencil on note book paper

This is the best I could do, because the man's hands were moving rapidly as he was cleaning his glasses.

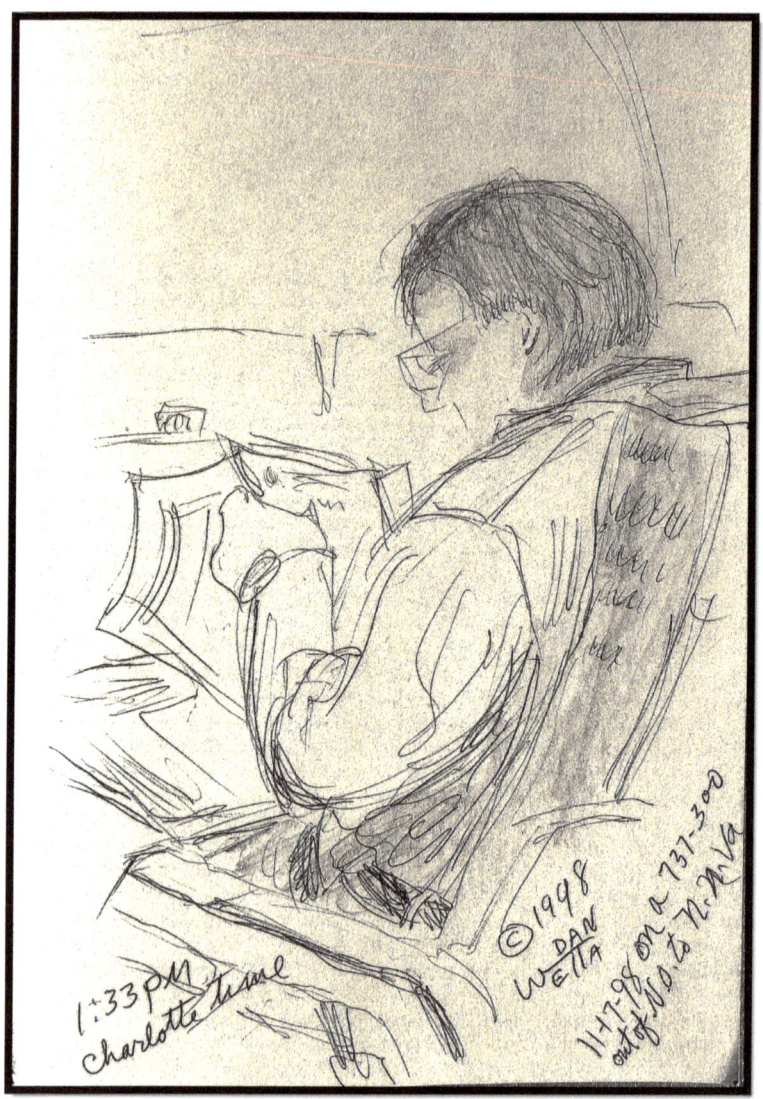

Title: Airplane – Man Reading
Medium: Pen and pencil on sketch book paper

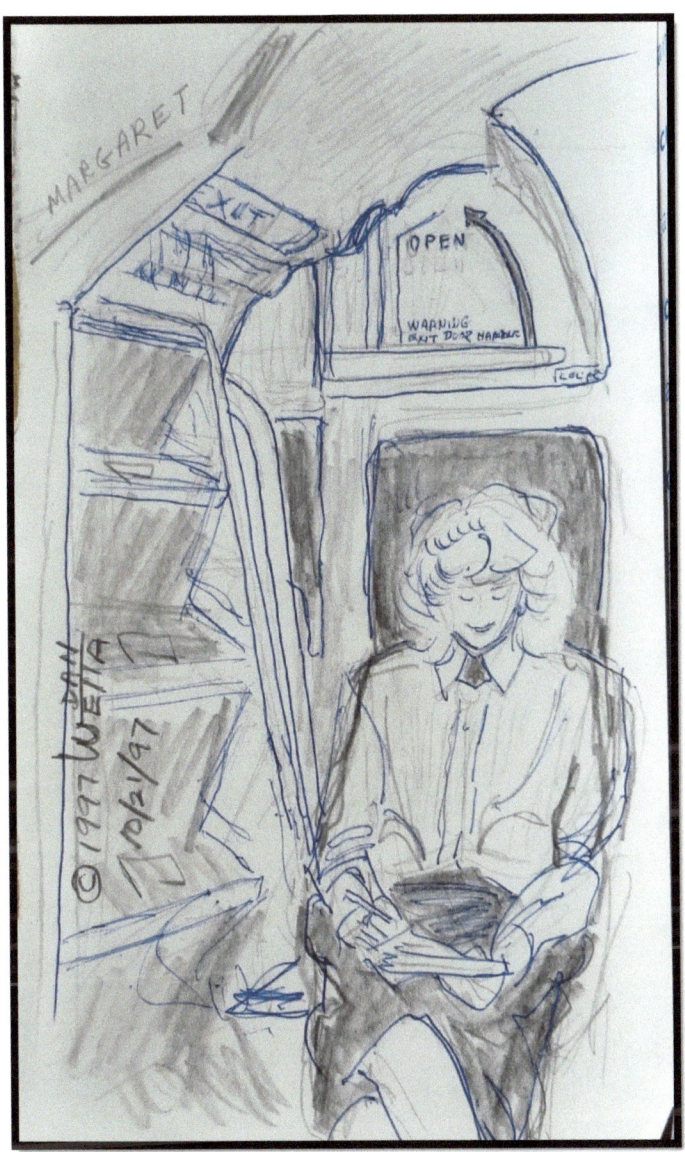

Title: Airplane – Margaret
Medium: Pen and pencil on sketch book paper

Margaret was a stewardess on a two-motor-propeller plane. She walked to my seat when she noticed me sketching her, and she was very pleasant. She even told me her name. I was going to give her the sketch, but she was not at the door when we passengers were disembarking, so I still have the sketch. But some stewardesses look with suspicion upon artists, as I will demonstrate in the following page.

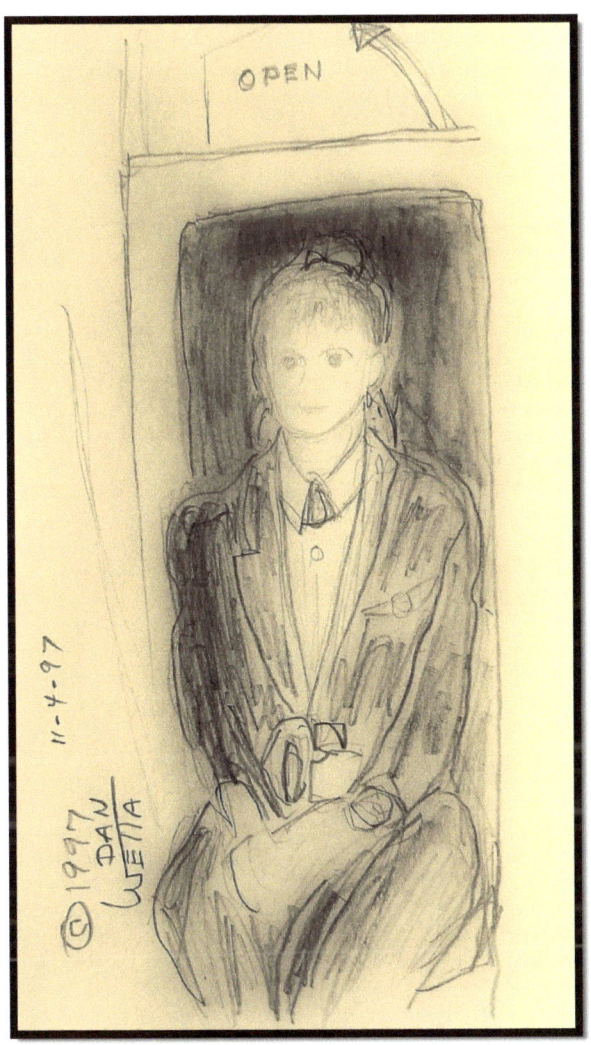

Title: Airplane – Suspicious Flight Attendant
Medium: Pen and pencil on sketch pad paper

When this flight attendant noticed me sketching, she came to my seat and wanted to know what I was doing - like I was some sort of pervert!

I thought she was going to report me to airport security.

Chapter 6: Sketching At The Art Gallery

In the early 1990's, I was a member of an art gallery in Williamsburg. The gallery is a two story Sears and Roebuck pre-fab house.

I also volunteered to man the front desk, and when visitors were few and far between, I might have become very bored. However, there was an old wind-up, tick-tock clock on the front desk which kept me busy. Busy sketching, that is.

So, here are some of those sketches.

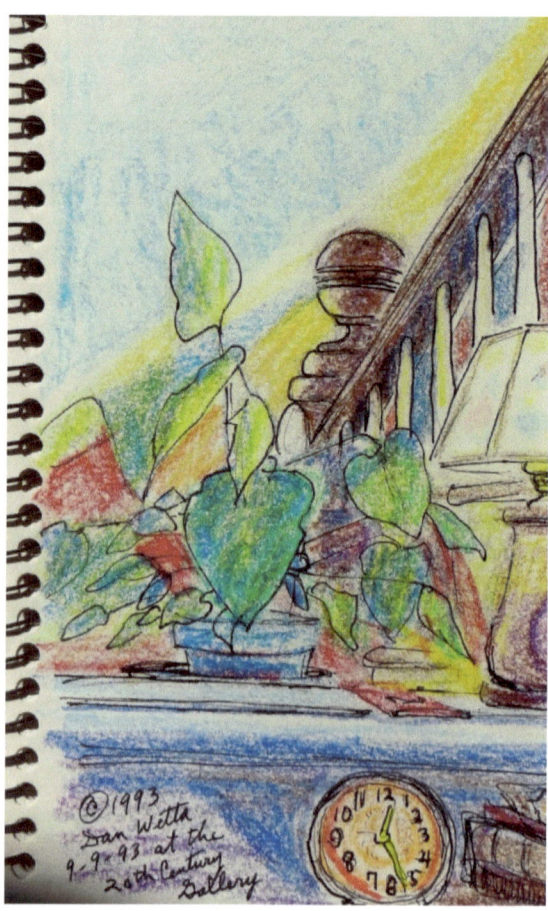

Title: Art Gallery – Clock Clock
Medium: Mixed media on sketch book paper

When I began manning the front desk at the art gallery, I began sketching my surroundings, and that old-time wind-up clock looked like it needed some attention, so I gave it a prominent place at the bottom of my sketch.

But at that time, I did not realize how important this old-time clock would become.

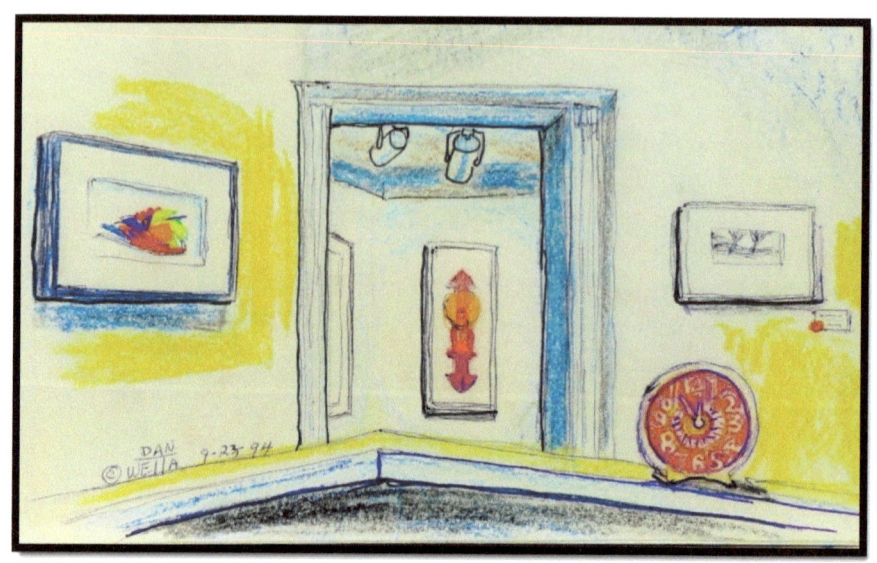

Title: Art Gallery – The Clock
Medium: Mixed media on paper

When I was a member of this gallery, I volunteered to be on the front desk during the day, when we did not get a lot of visitors. So I had a lot of time on my hands, and a clock was there to remind me that idleness is the devil's workshop.

So what can an artist do to keep busy? Sketch, of course. And that's what I did, beginning with the clock.

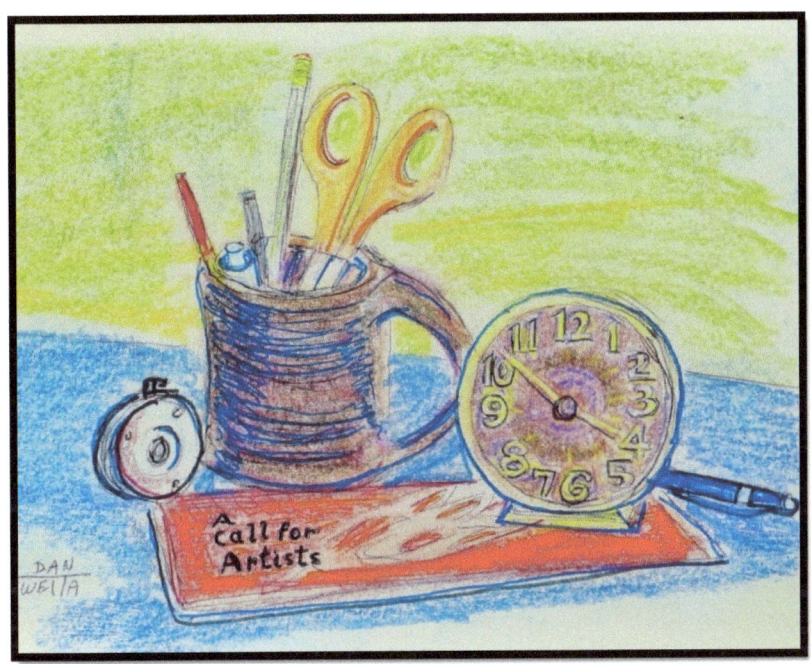

Title: Art Gallery – Clock Keeps Ticking
Medium: Mixed media on paper

Here's that clock again. I heard a preacher say, "We only live a split second at a time." And the way I see it, he is right.

Since we cannot travel back in time, and since we cannot project ourselves into the future, then we are always in the present.

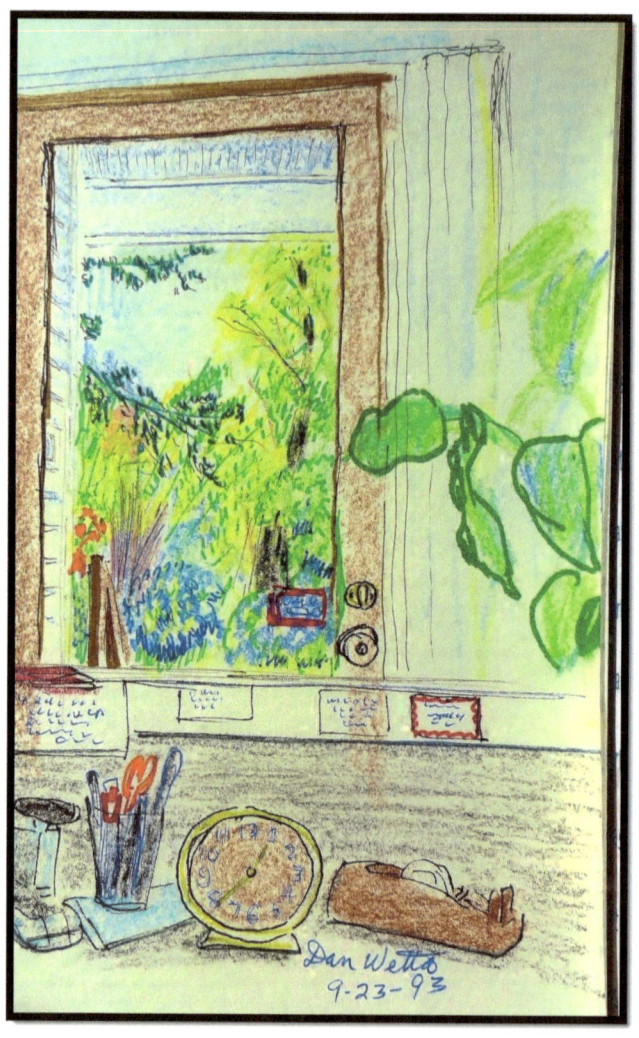

Title: Art Gallery – Clock Wants to Tell Me Something
Medium: Mixed media on paper

That is an old-fashioned-wind-up clock, and it acts old fashioned. It doesn't like people who waste time. Maybe it will stop bugging me if I can convince it that sketching is not a waste of time – it is what artists do.

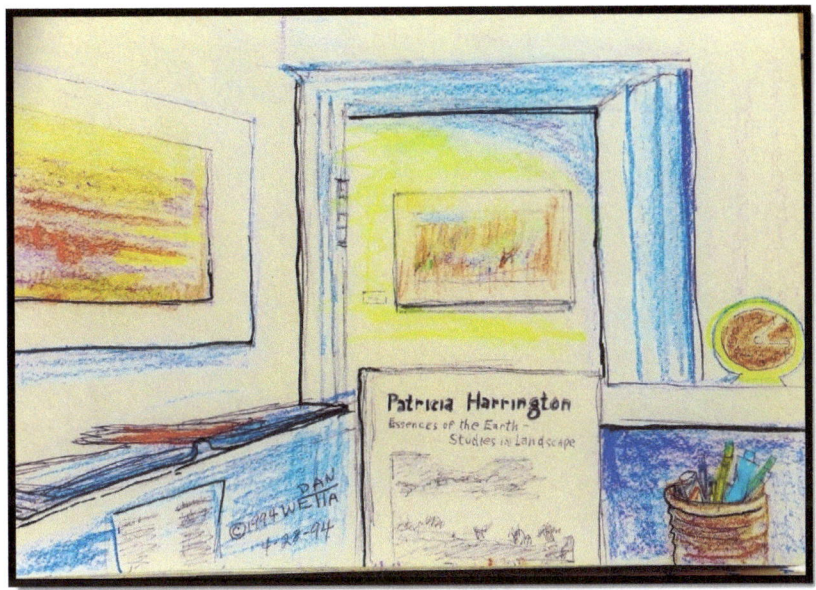

Title: Art Gallery – Clock is Persistent
Medium: Mixed media on paper

I have never seen such a persistent clock. Is it trying to tell me that time is running out?

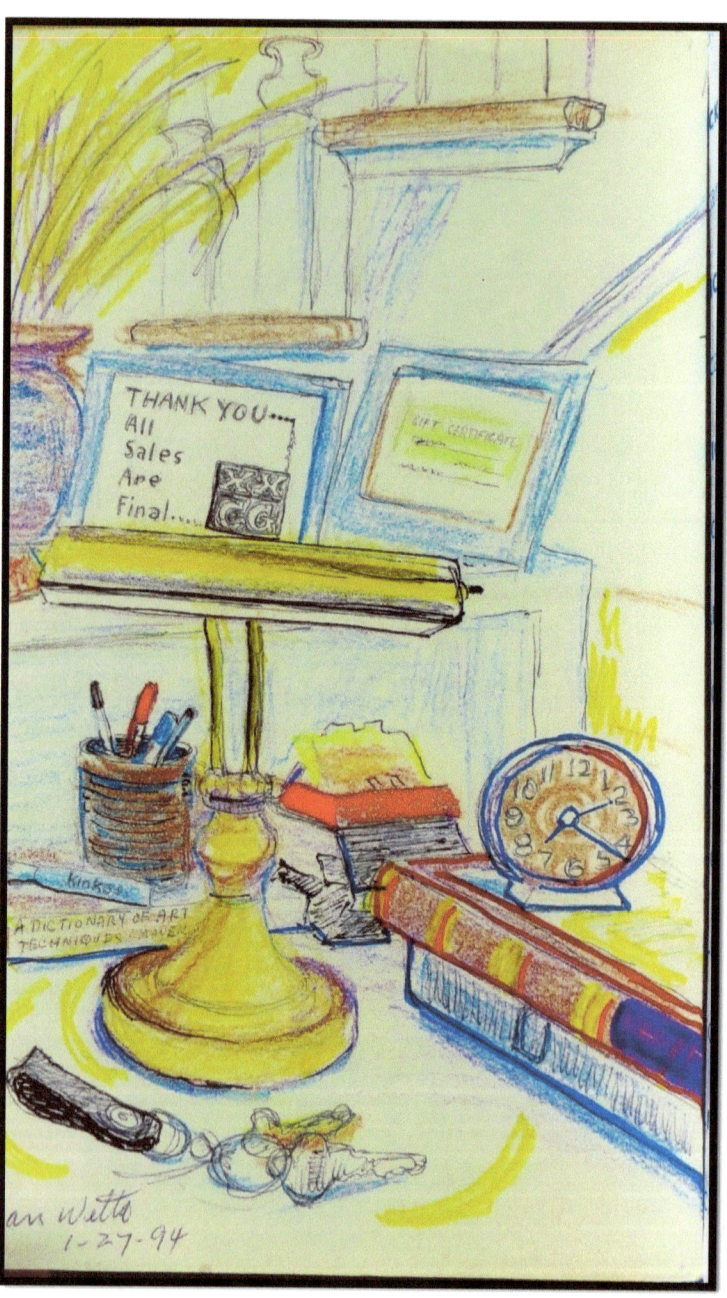

Title: Art Gallery – Ticking Clock
Medium: Mixed media on sketch book paper

That ticking clock just won't go away. Each tick is to remind you that you are always in the present, not in the past, not in the future.

As soon as you hear a tick, it disappears into the past, and then a tick from the future takes its place.

This old-time clock is warning us, "Do not waste time. You are born with a limited number of clock ticks."

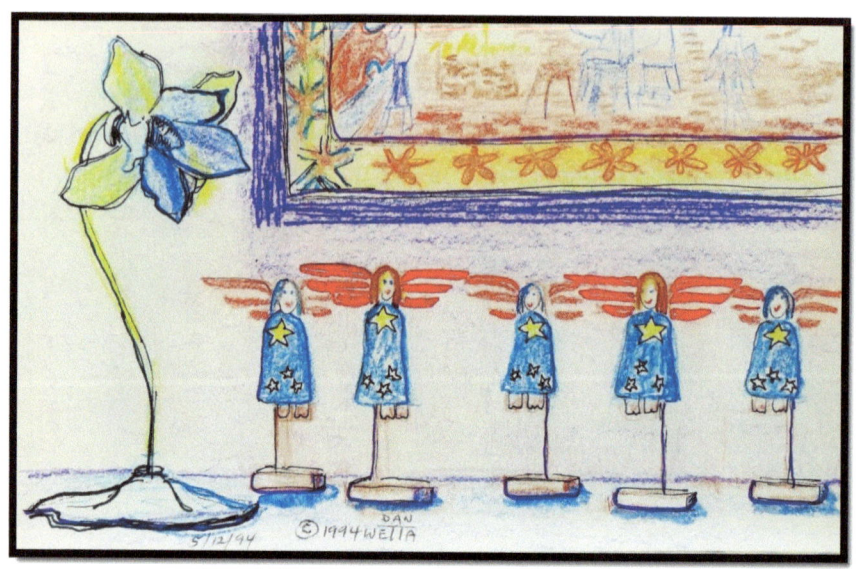

Art Gallery – Angels on Guard

We even had angels to watch over the paintings.

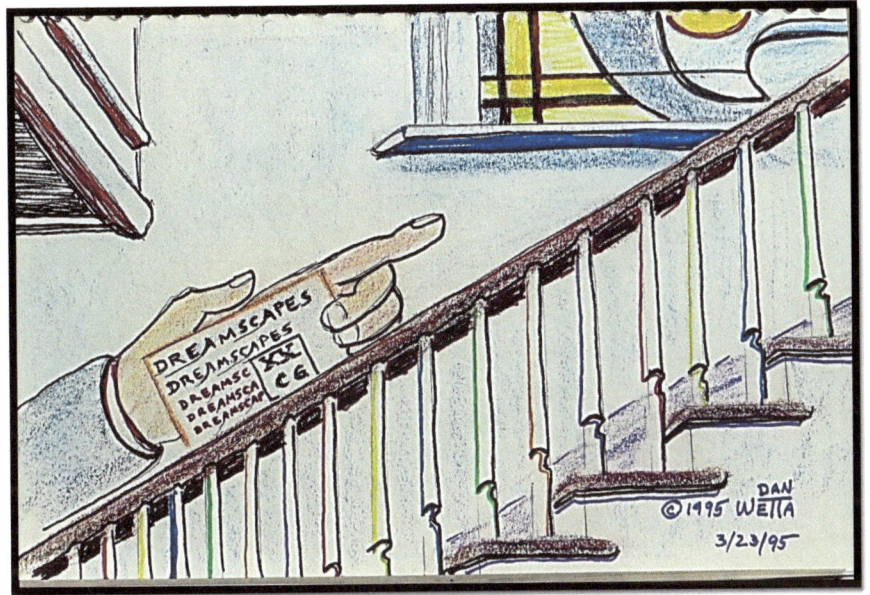

Title:Art Gallery - Dreamscapes
Medium: Mixed media on paper

How does an artist horse around?

This is the way I horse around. I drew an elongated hand to draw attention to my dreamscape paintings, which were on exhibit upstairs in the art gallery.

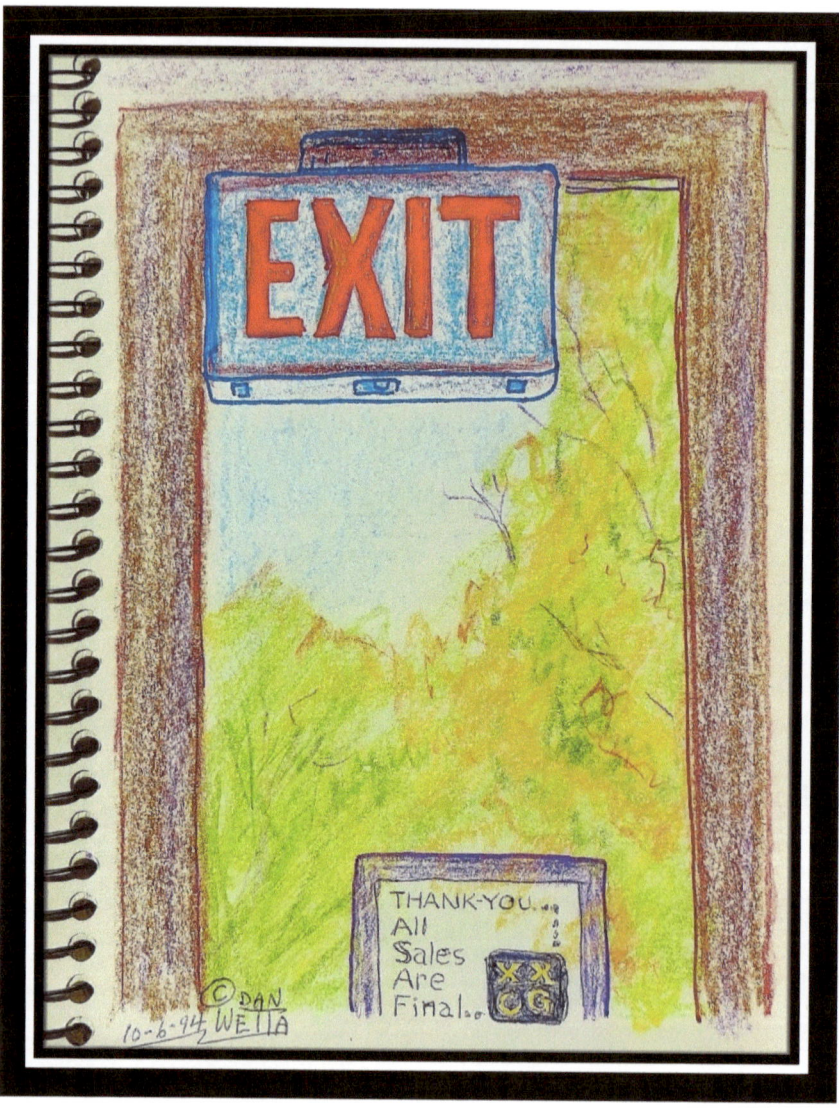

Title: Art Gallery – Exit
Medium: Mixed media on art note book paper

There's the EXIT sign on the front door. Let's get out of here
before time runs out!

Chapter 7: Miscellaneous Paintings and Cartoons

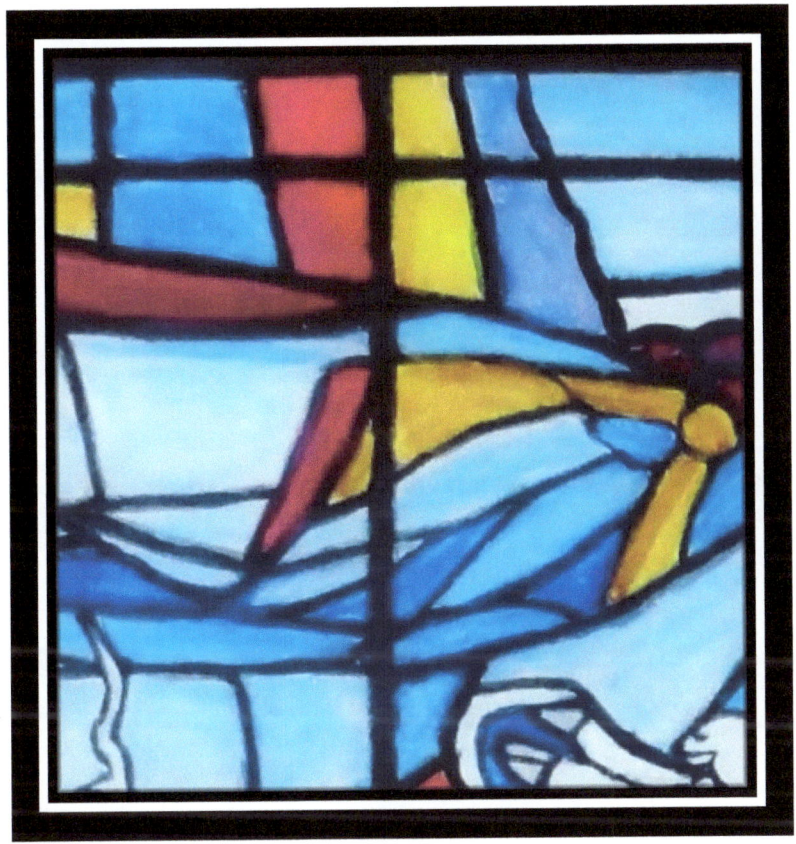

Abstract Lost Lamb
Copyright by Dan Wetta 1997

This was taken from my painting, "Lost Lamb."

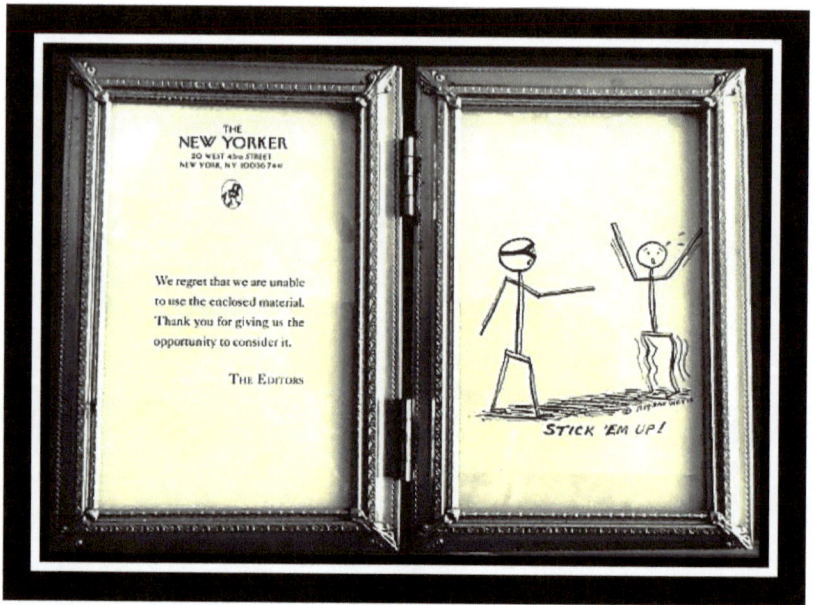

Title: Cartoon Award!

Now You Can't Say I Didn't Warn You About my Cartoons!
(This notice has been posted in all my books.)

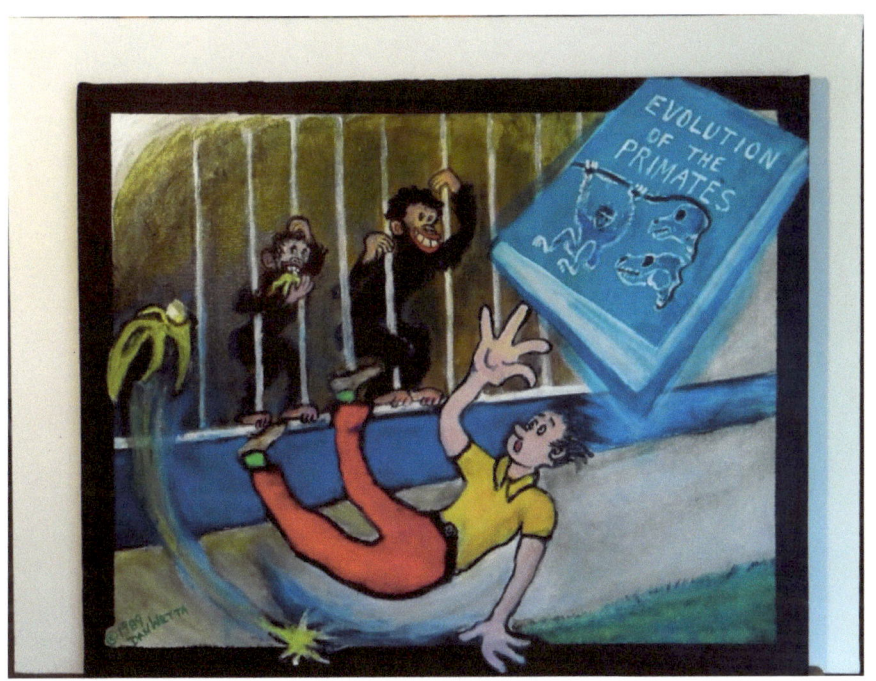

Title: Evolution of Monkeys
Size: 14 x 18 inches
Medium: Acrylic on Canvas
Copyright by Dan Wetta 1989

We humans have at least one thing in common with monkeys: We both get a kick out of pratfalls.

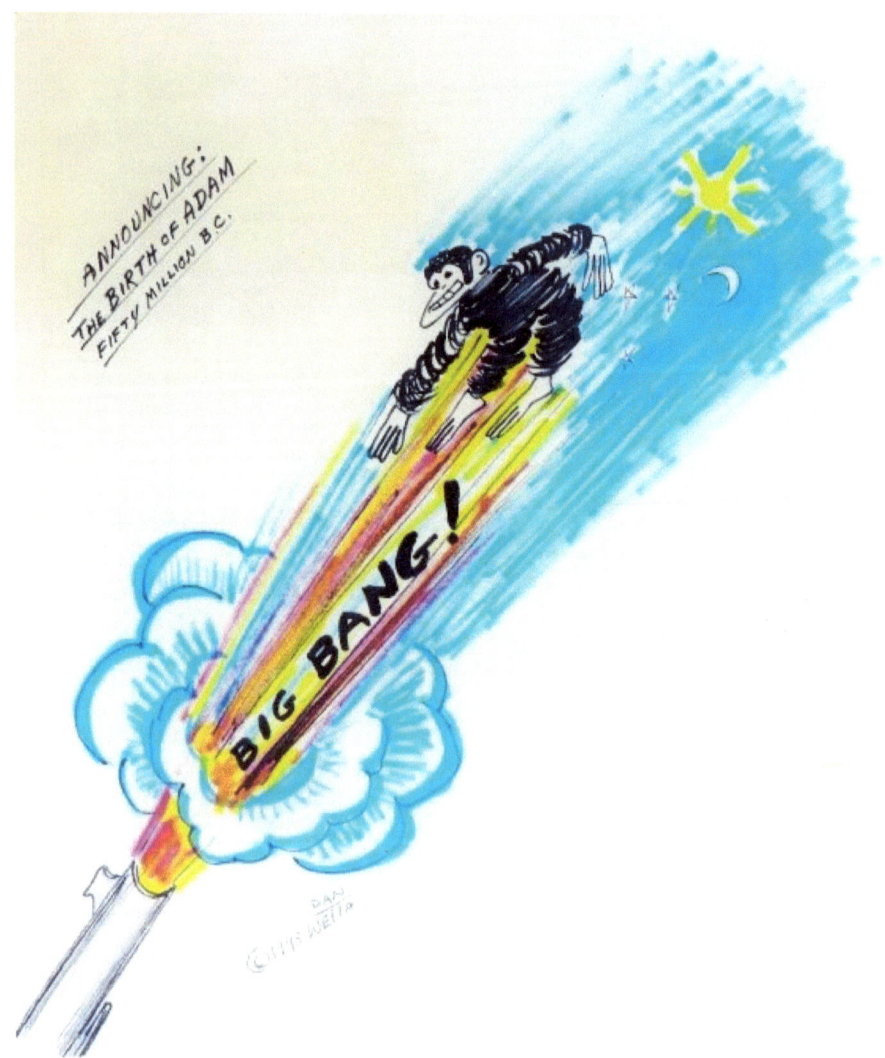

Title: Big Bang
Copyright 1995 by Dan Wetta

If there were a Big Bang, certain things were created immediately, no evolution required:
Light
Shadow
Speed of Light
Sound
Speed of Sound
Fire
Heat
Cold
Space
Gravity
Anti-gravity
Infinity
Ice/water

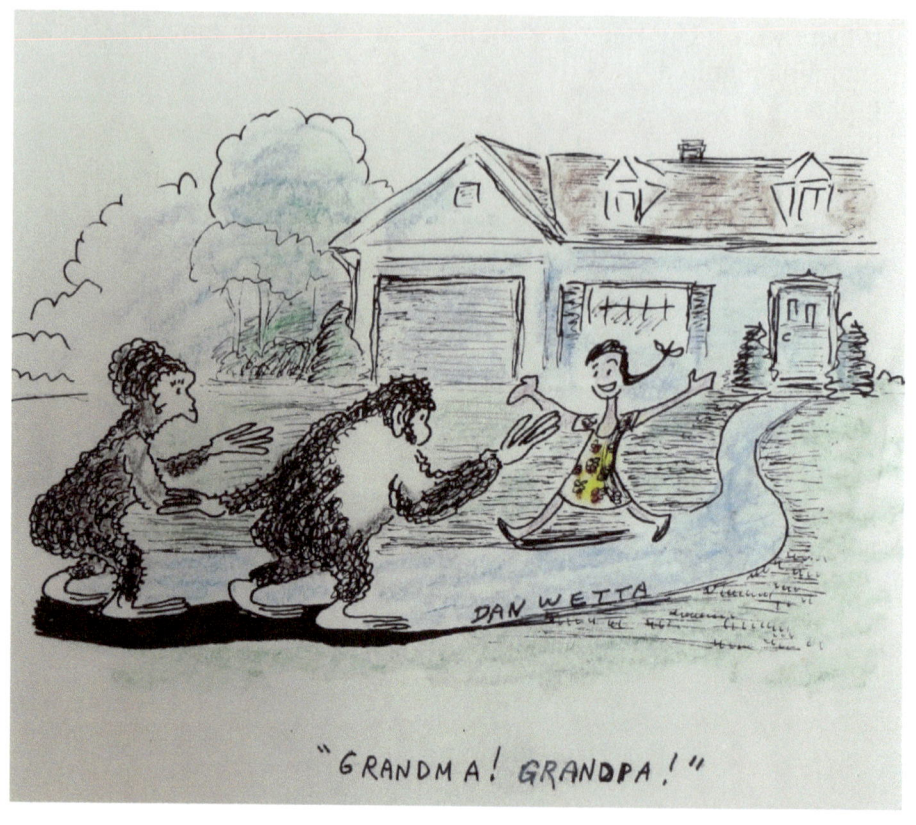

"GRANDMA! GRANDPA!"

Title: Evolution, "Grandma! Grandpa!"
Copyright by Dan Wetta

Archaeologists don't have the faintest idea how the Egyptians built the pyramids a few thousand years ago, but scientists know how the world was formed a billion eons ago?

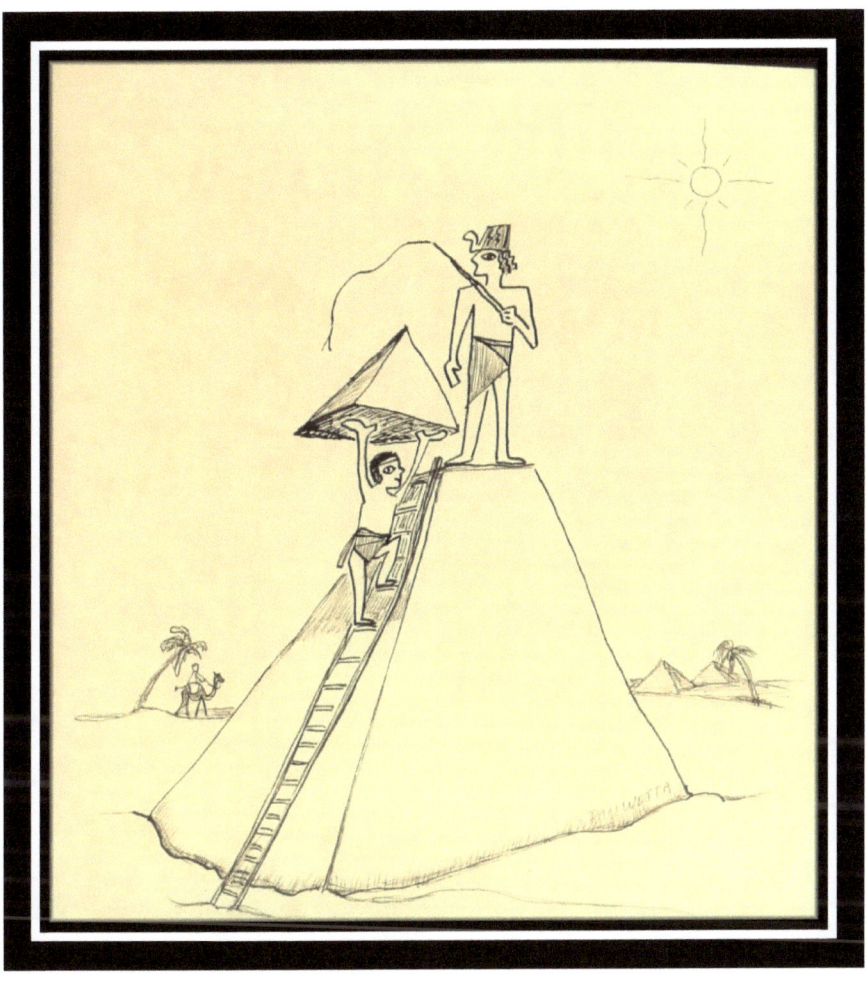

Title: Pyramids and Monuments cartoon
Copyright by Dan Wetta

Scientists don't know how the ancient Egyptians built the pyramids, yet they claim to know that the universe was formed by a Big Bang.

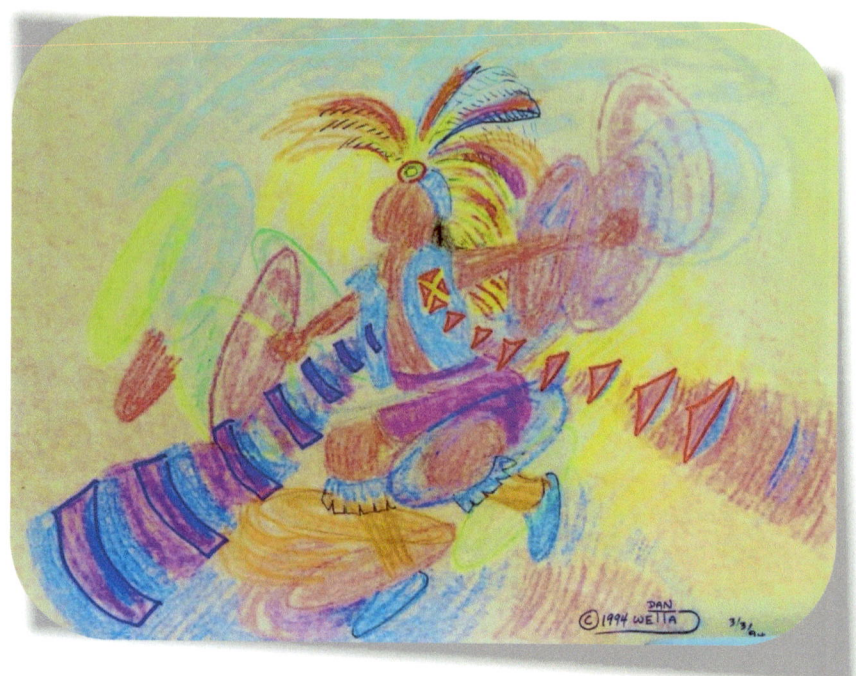

Title: Indian Dancer
Medium: Mixed media on paper
Copyright 1994

This is an impression I got from watching an Indian dancing in a Virginia pow-wow. Some Virginia tribes are serious about keeping their traditions alive.

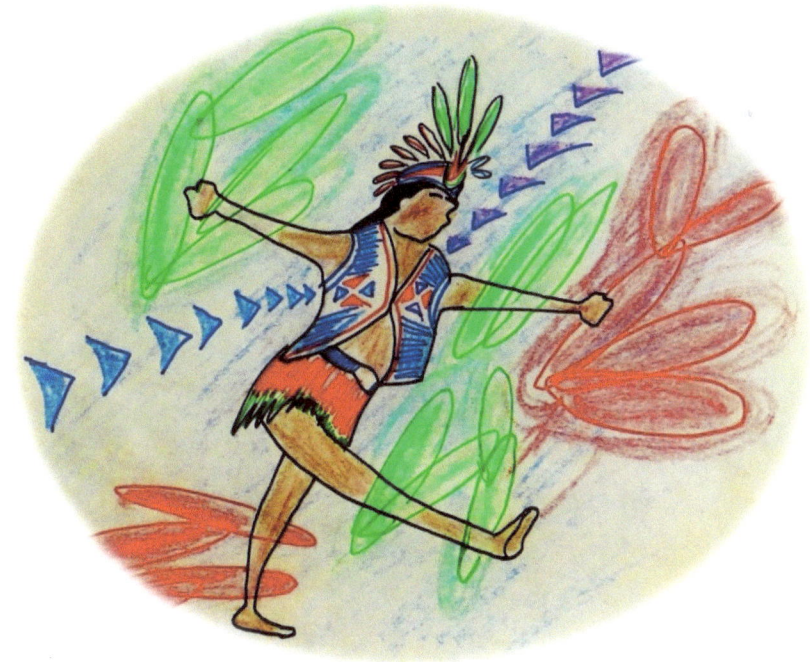

Title: Indian Dancing
Medium: Mixed media on paper

This is another memory sketch I did of an Indian who was dancing in a Virginia pow-wow several years ago. Each one of us gets a different impression of the people we see, and this is my artistic vision of an Indian who seemed to have been dancing with ancestors of yesteryear.

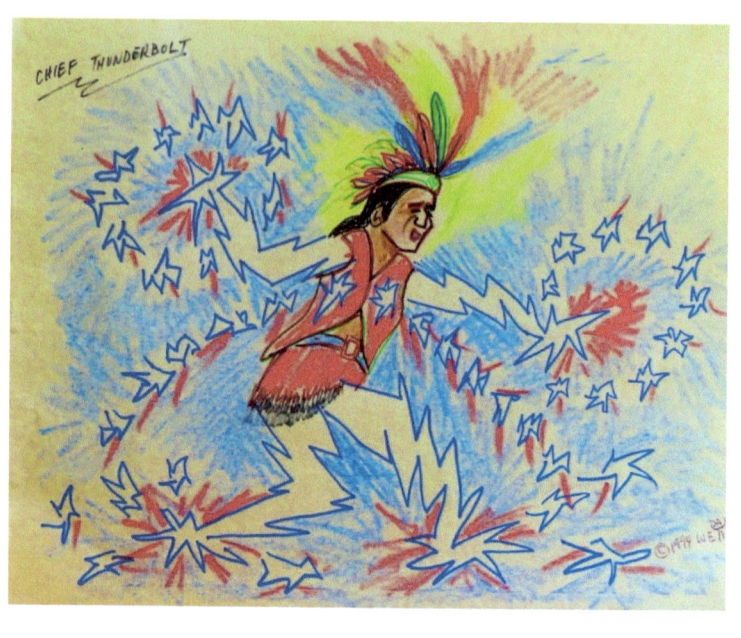

Title: Indian Thunderbolt

Speaking of the impressions we get of people we meet in life, this sketch depicts one of the strongest I ever had of a person. It is my impression of an Indian whom I saw dancing at a pow-wow in Virginia several years ago.

Surely he is the great-great-grandson of some powerful Indian Chief.

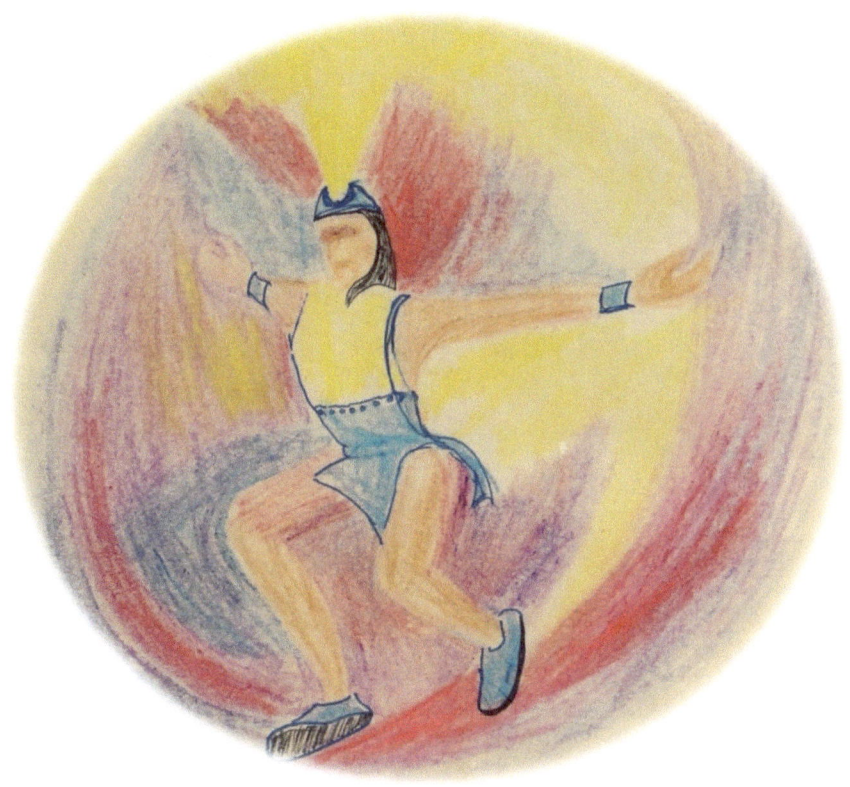

Title: Indian colors
Medium: Mixed media on paper

These visits to some Indian pow-wows in Virginia years ago inspired me to do several sketches of the Indian dancers. This one is a computer-enhanced version of one of my sketches.

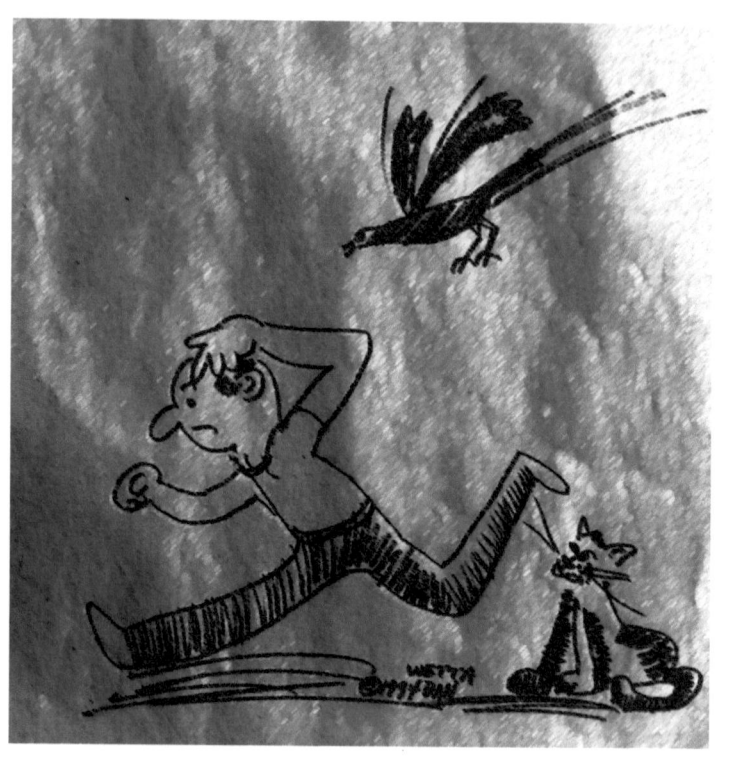

Title: Look Out – Here Come the Birds
Copyright 1994

Introduction to the birds!

Any reader of my other volume of books knows I have always
been fascinated with birds and have depicted them in cartoons,
sketches, and paintings. The next pages contain a few more.

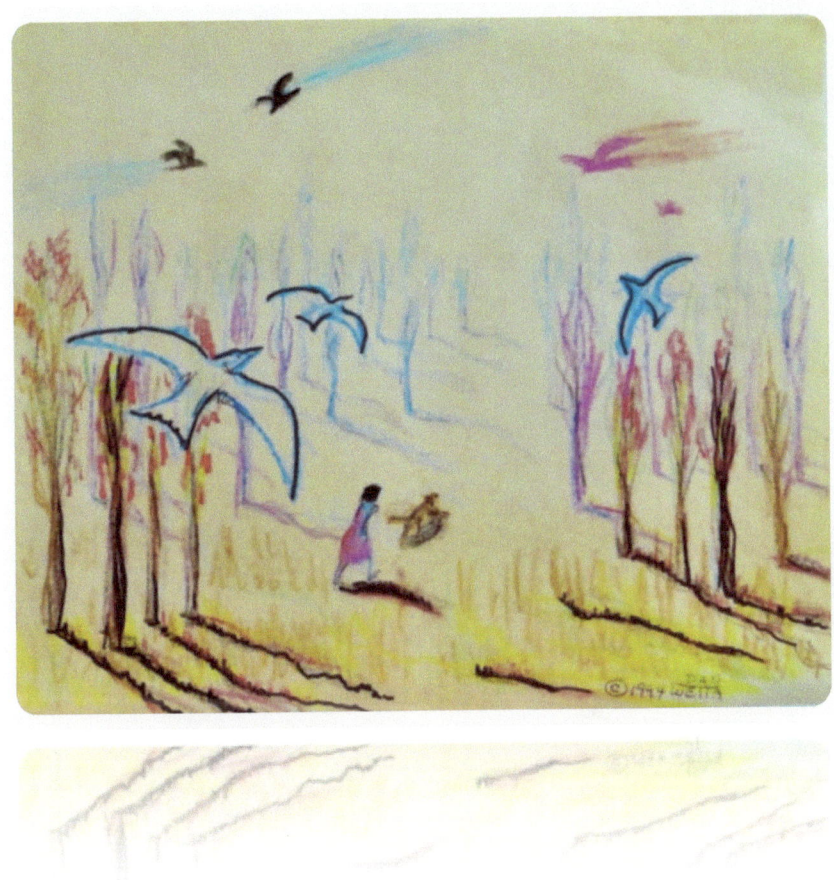

Title: Lost in Bird Land
Medium: Mixed media on paper

If you ever get lost in Bird Land, just follow the birds. They will show you the way home.

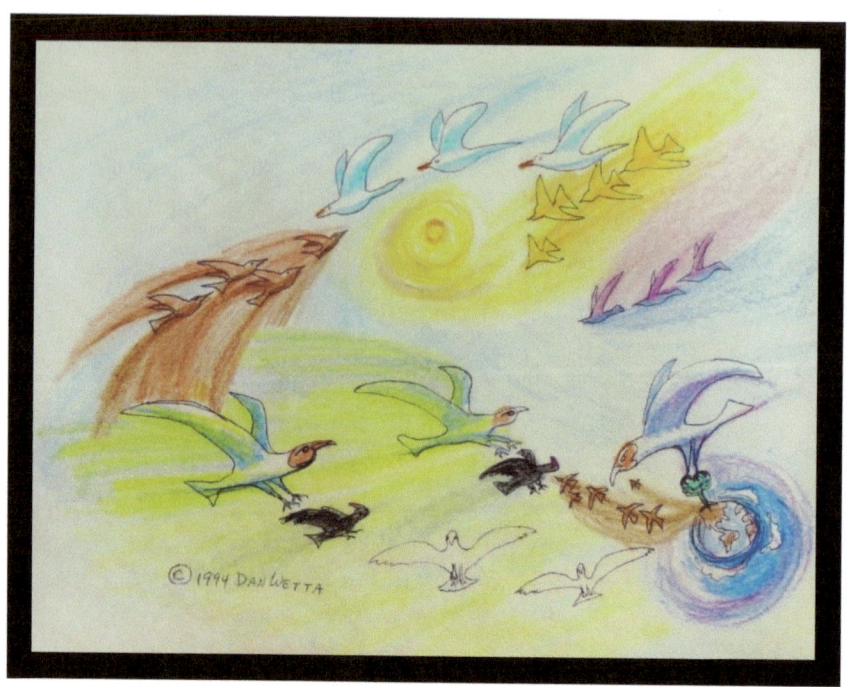

Title: Between Sun and Earth
Medium: Mixed media on paper
Copyright 1994

Air is to birds as water is to fish.

Whenever I look up at the sky and don't see any birds, or even buzzards, I am disappointed.

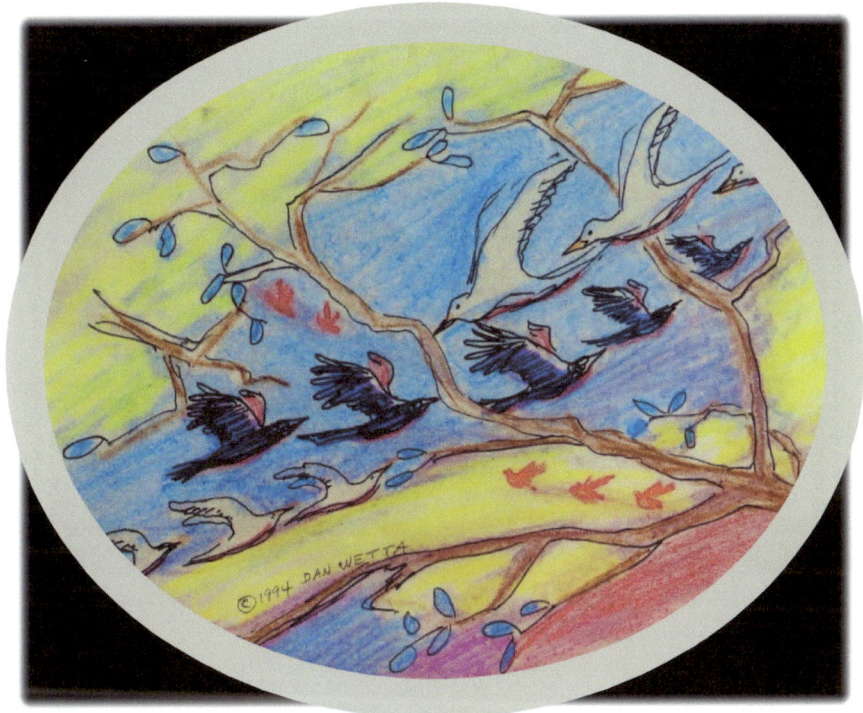

Title: Birds Fly, Birds Glide
Copyright 1994 by Dan Wetta

Birds fly and glide, but never collide,
And they live in trees that sway in the breeze.

I hope you can finish this poem,
Because I sure can't do it.

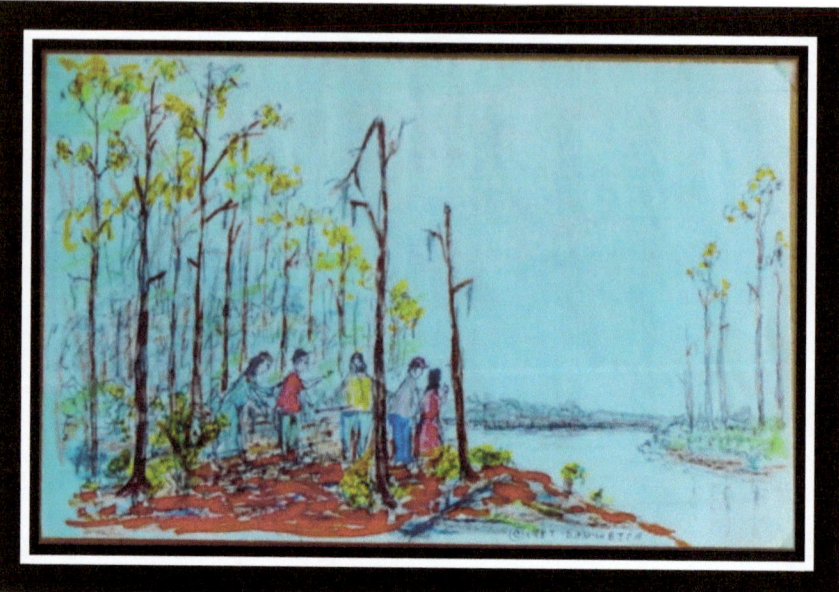

Title: What Now?
Medium: Mixed media on paper
Copyright 1987 by Dan Wetta

This is a "What Now?" sketch.

What do you do when you come to a river?
Two of those people can't swim.

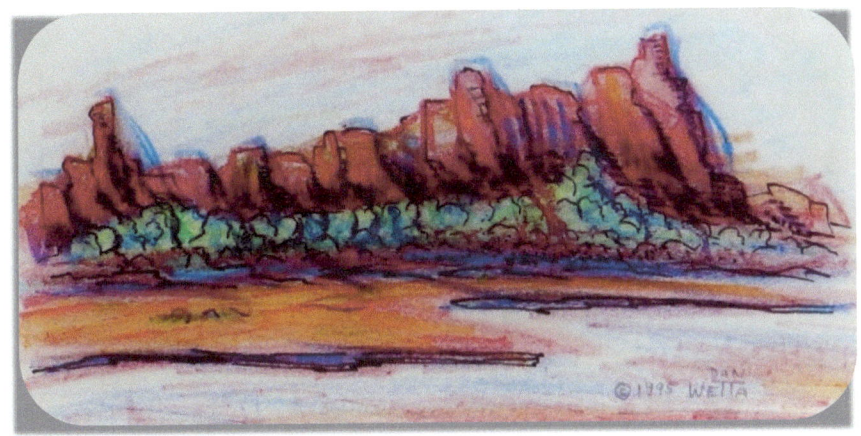

Title: Somewhere Out West
Medium: Mixed media on paper
Copyright 1995 by Dan Wetta

If you stare at this sketch for 60 seconds, then gently close your eyes, you will see that the mountains have changed color. They will be a green/blue, and the trees and shrubbery at the base of the mountains will be reddish.

Your brain sees the complementary color of whatever you are looking at.

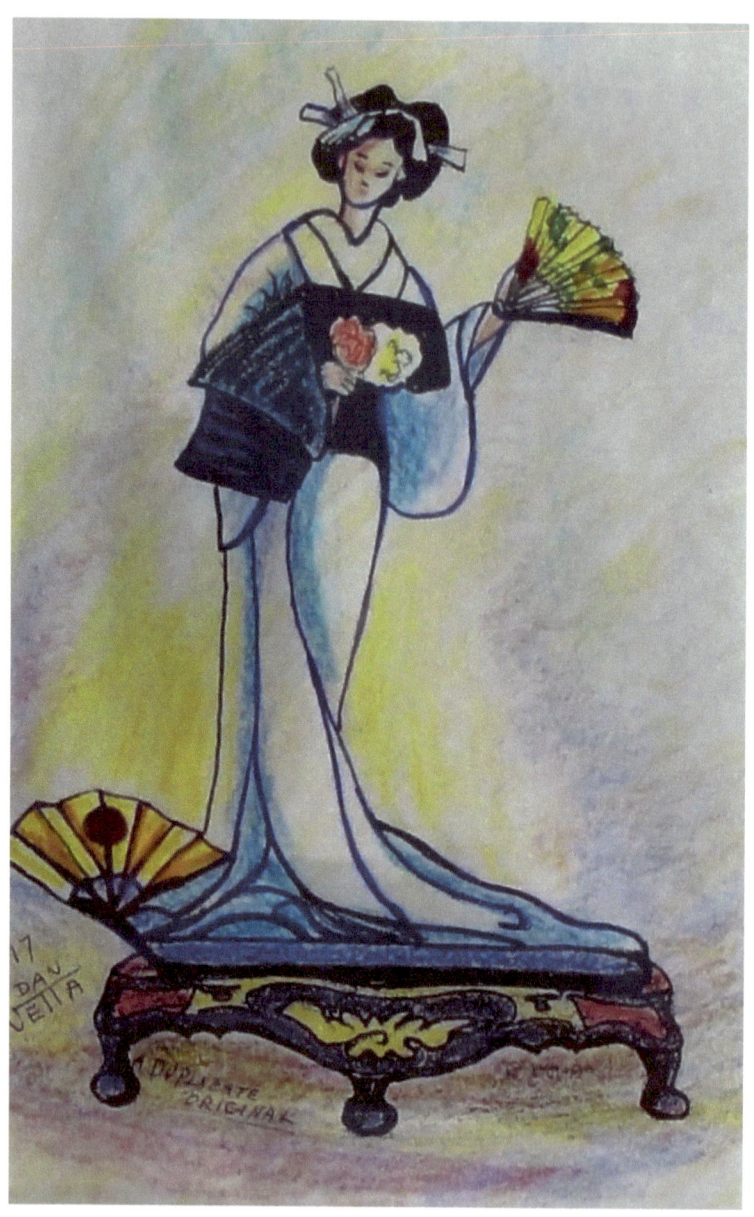

Title: Antique Lady with Fan (doodle)
Copyright 1997 by Dan Wetta

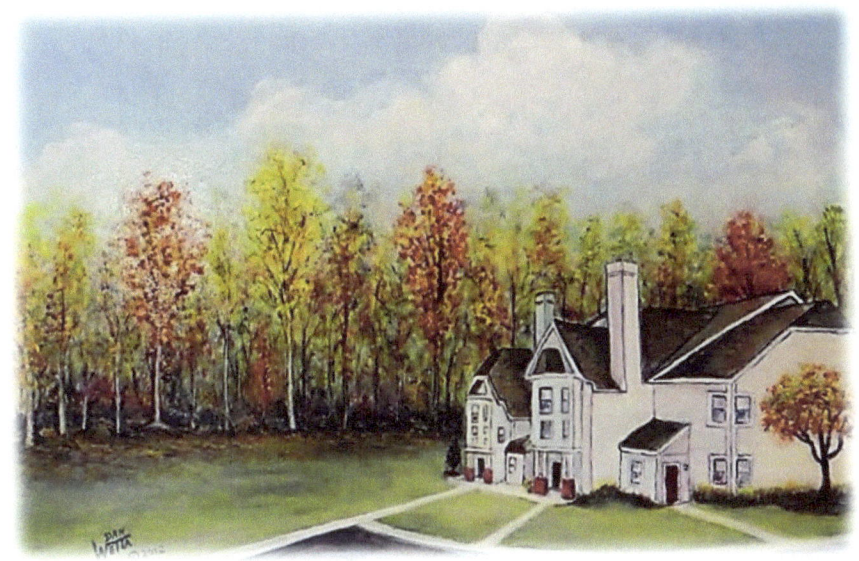

Title: Autumn in Williamsburg Commons
Size: 20"x30"
Medium: Acrylic on Canvas
Copyright by Dan Wetta 1992

Some people say that a dry summer creates a beautiful autumn, while others say that a wet summer creates a colorful autumn, but Mother Nature does as she pleases.

One thing for sure: - I do not have to rake autumn leaves because the condominium association has a yard maintenance crew to take care of that.

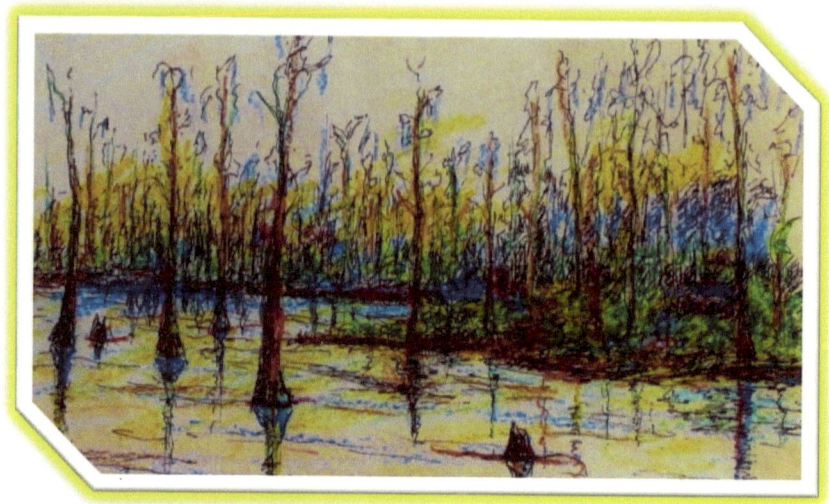

Title: Bayou Sketch
Medium: Mixed Media on paper

Most of us prefer the conveniences and comforts of city living, but my brother, JJ, used to visit the alligators, mosquitoes and water moccasins two or three times a year at his camp house in the marsh lands surrounding the city of New Orleans, but it was destroyed by Hurricane Katrina.

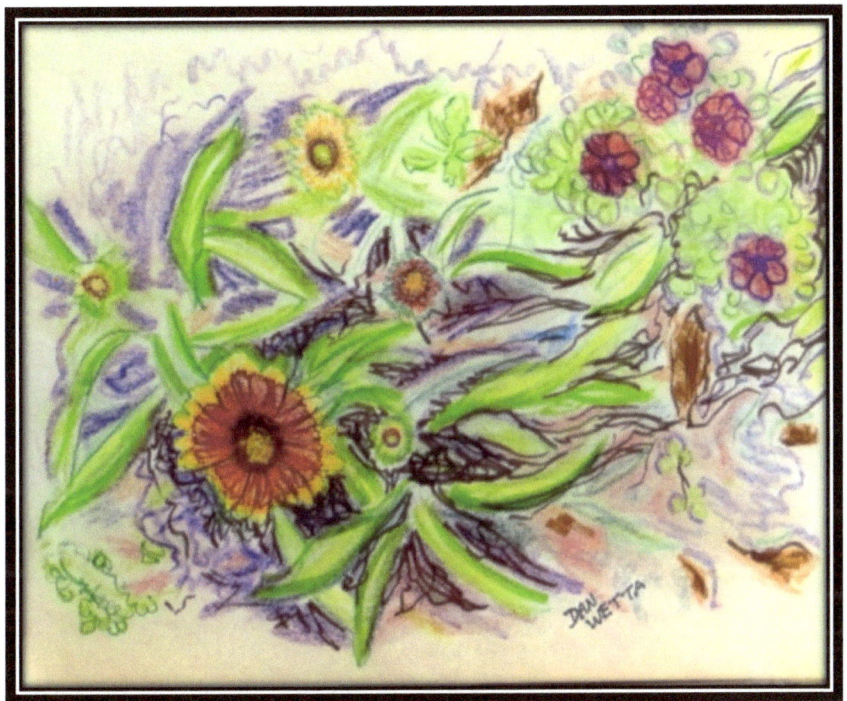

Title: Wild Sand Flowers
Medium: Crayon and Markers on paper

I am just beginning to realize that most of our world is wild. There are wild flowers as well as wild animals, and all of the woods and forests are wild. If you look at the cracks in the cement of sidewalks, you will see wild weeds. Human beings can suppress the wild for a while, but it is only hiding – just waiting for a chance to make a comeback.

I just happened to look down one day and was surprised to see these flowers growing in the sand along the Outer Banks of North Carolina. I also did an acrylic painting from this original sketch. But how could anything grow in sand? Then I remembered that cactus also grows in sand.

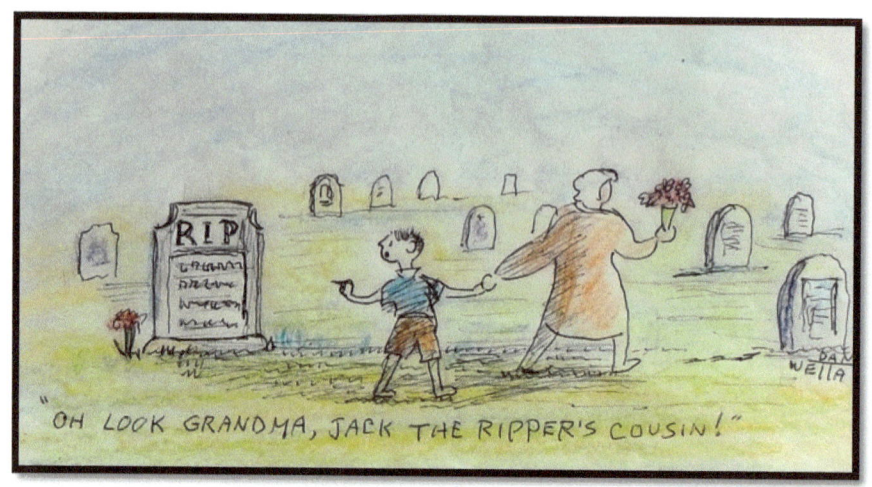

Title: Jack the Ripper's Cousin

This is just another graveyard cartoon. Do you ever wonder why graveyards become spooky during the night?

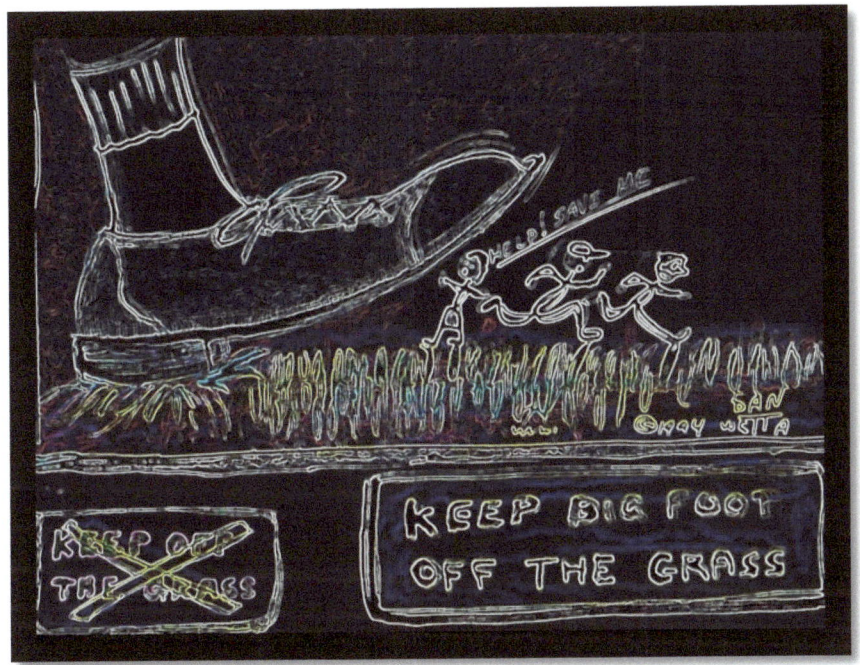

Title: Keep Off the Grass
No, Keep Big Foot off the Grass

Medium: Mixed media on paper
This is a computer-enhanced version of Big Foot.

Why do TV people think that the best time to look for Big Foot is at night? Squish!

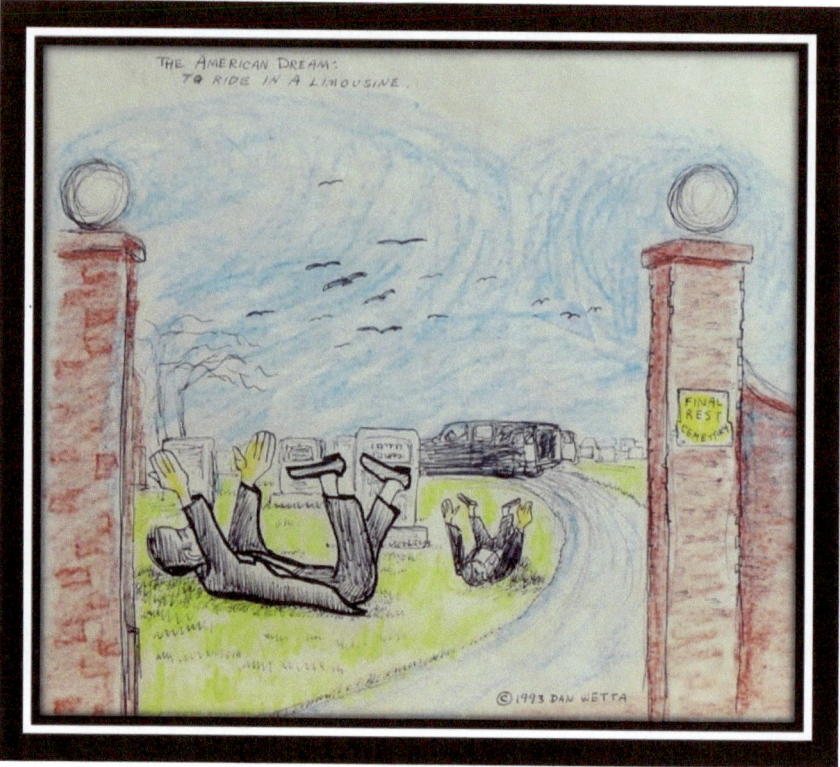

Title: Why You Wanna Ride in a Limousine?
Medium: Mixed media on paper

Look at those vultures up in the sky.
Why do you think those vultures are following that limousine?

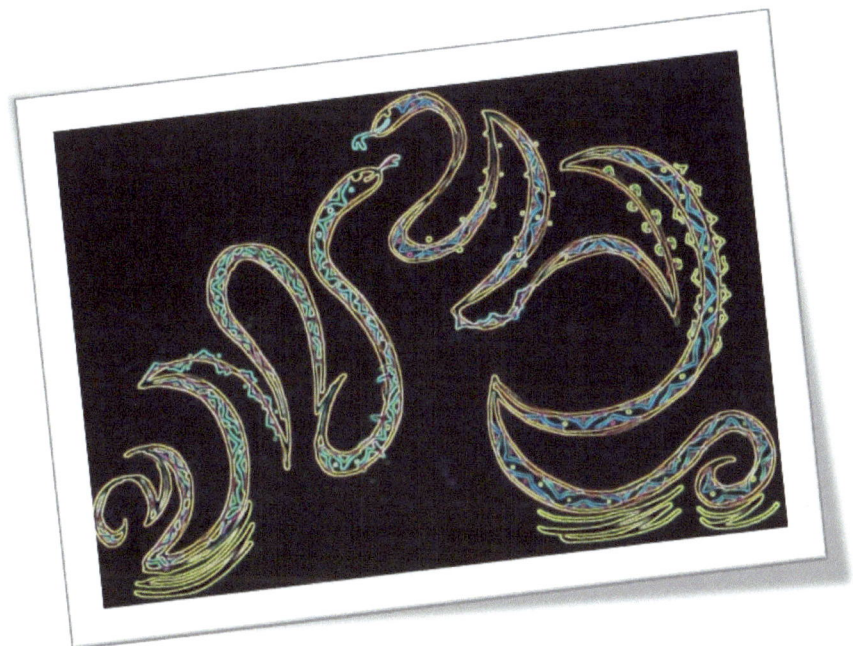

Title: Snakes Cuttin Up cartoon
Medium: Mixed media on paper

This is a computer-enhanced artistic version of my original sketch. I wanted to do something different, because snake lovers are few and far between. I hope you like the colorful patterns on these two snakes.

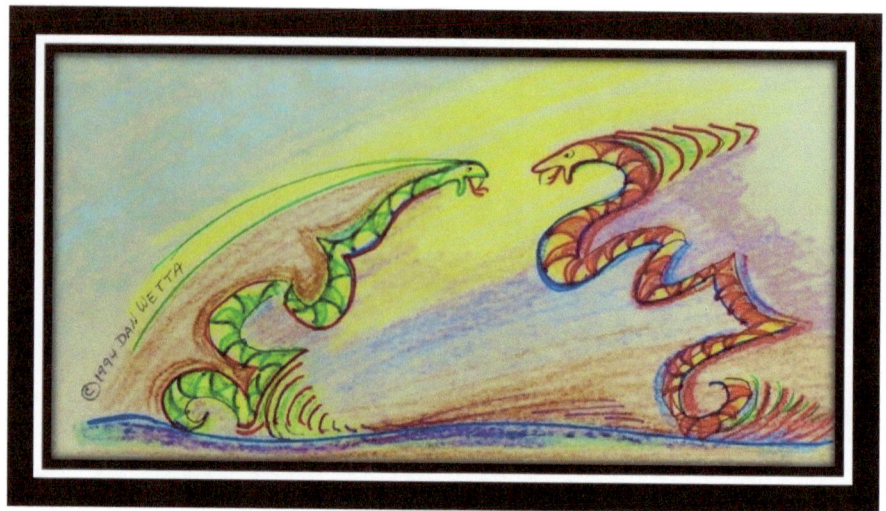

Title: Snake Fight cartoon
Medium: Mixed media on paper

Does this really look like a snake fight?

I admitted that I had never been to a snake fight when my son told me that these snakes have a surprised look on their faces instead of an angry look.

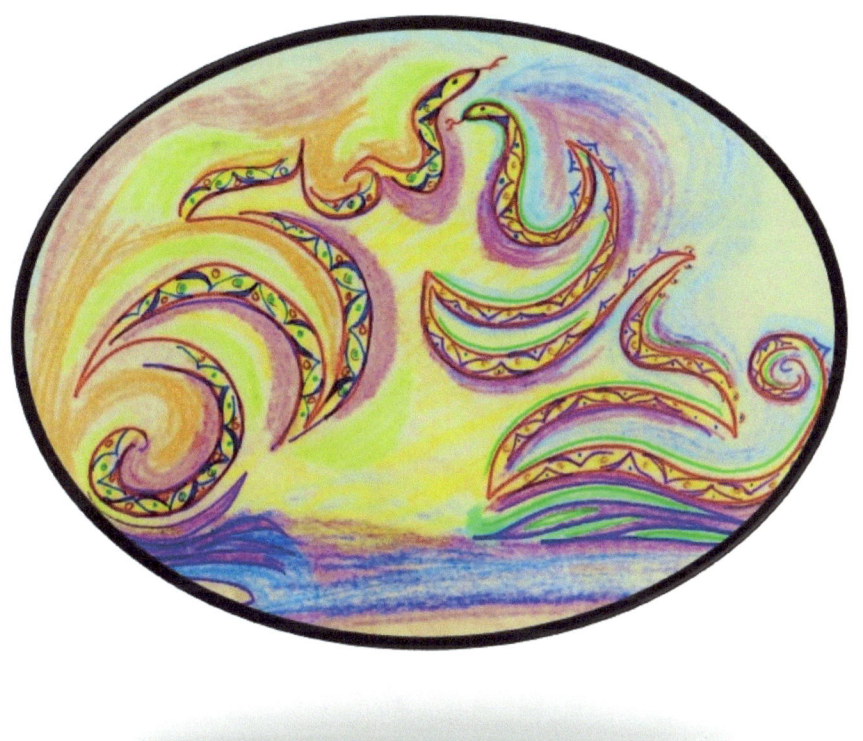

Title: Snake Lover cartoon
Medium: Mixed media on paper

Only a snake lover would hang a picture like this on her living room wall. She would oooh and aaah about the colorful pattern on the snake bodies, and she would tell you that snakes won't bother you if you don't bother them.

Chapter 8: A Skinny Bible

(The Bible As Seen Through The Eyes Of A Cartoonist)

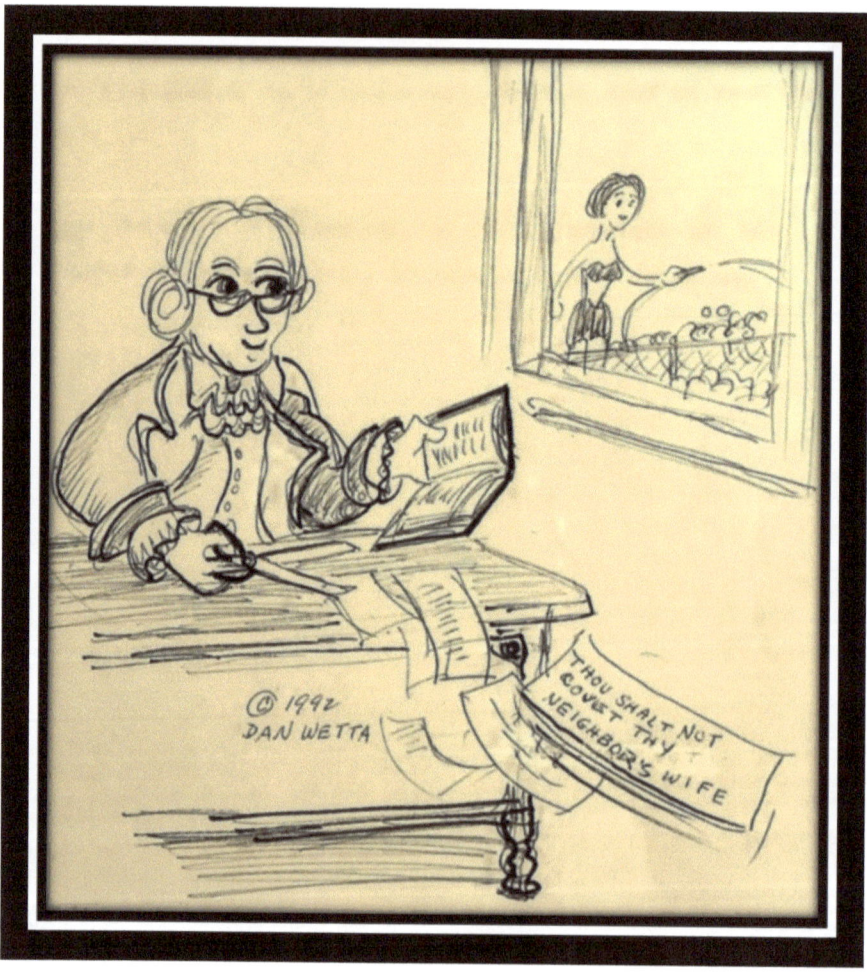

Title: A Skinny Bible by Thomas Jefferson
Copyright by Dan Wetta 1992

When I retired, I thought my auditing experience would help me to find errors in the bible, but I soon found out that learned bible scholars had already done a thorough job of dissecting every passage of the bible.

What I did find out, though, is that the problem is not with the bible. The problem is the interpretation of it. Ten or twelve bible scholars will interpret each passage differently; hence, the reason for so many different denominations.

Also, when I was auditing the bible, I didn't cut out passages like Thomas Jefferson did. He did this, and then he rearranged the remaining pages into a version of the bible that was more to his own personal beliefs. Although he was the third President of the United States, his bible did not catch on because *it was too skinny*.

As an artist, my interpretation of scripture is done in the form of cartoons and caricatures that emphasize human nature rather than spirituality, and I don't think you will find my sketches to be profane or irreverent.

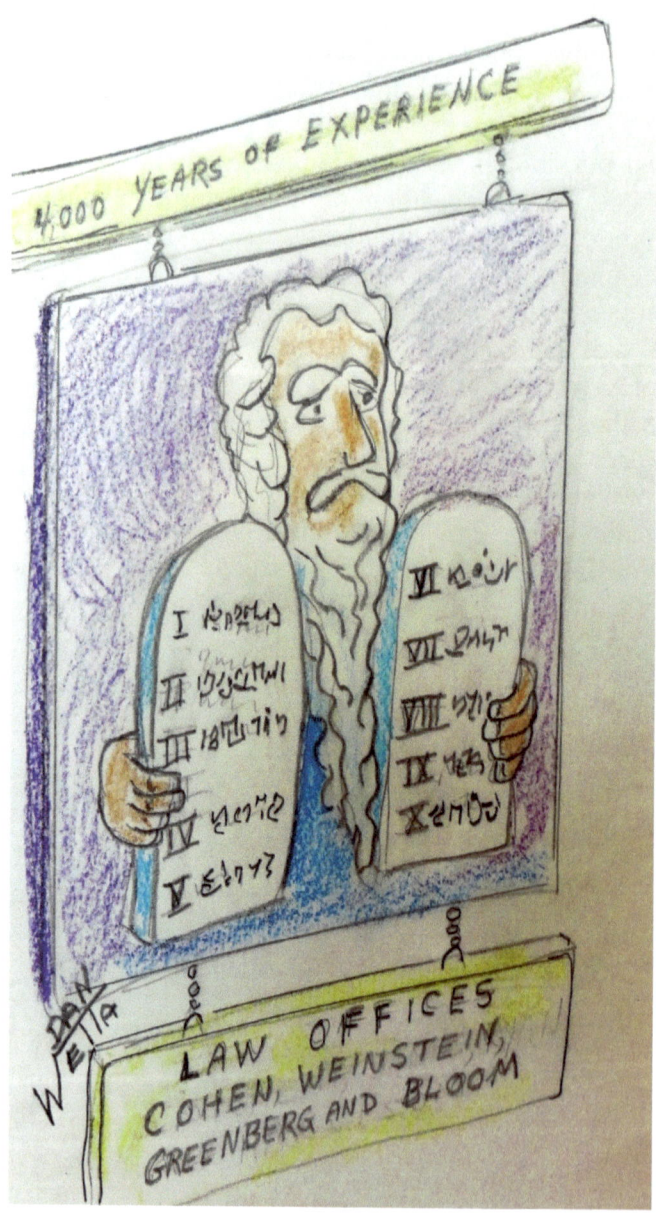

Title: Law Offices
Copyright by Dan Wetta

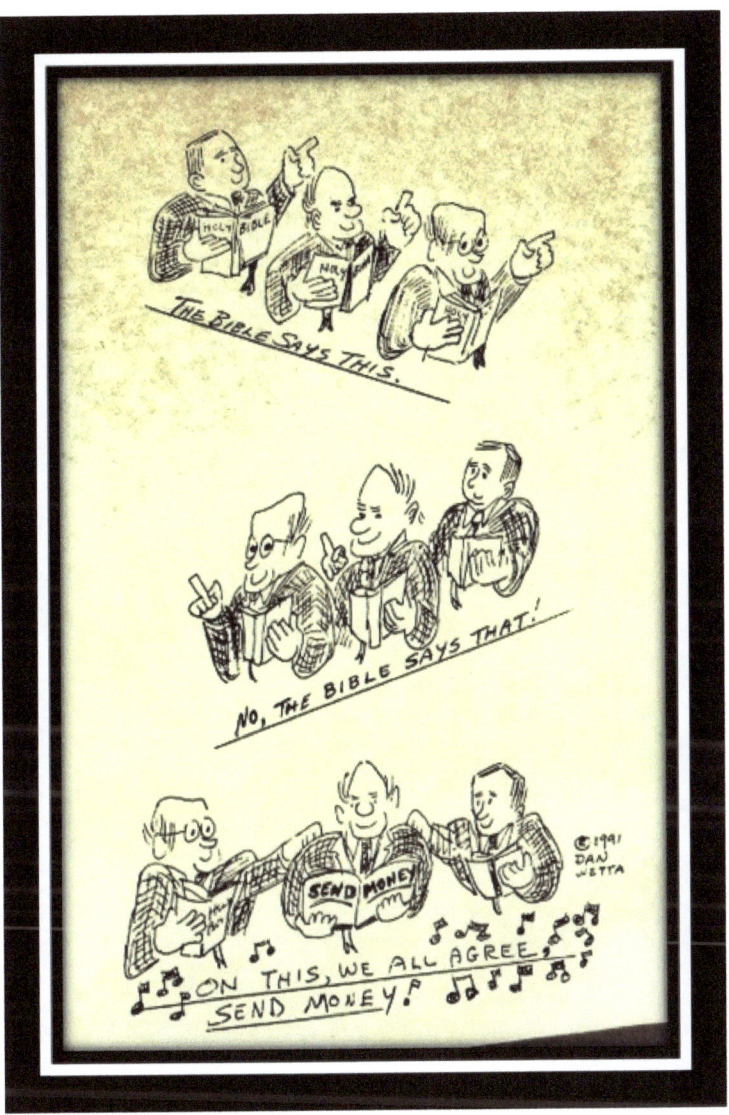

Title: What the Bible Says

Although I did not find anything wrong in the bible, I did find that five bible scholars can read the same passage in the bible and come up with five different interpretations.

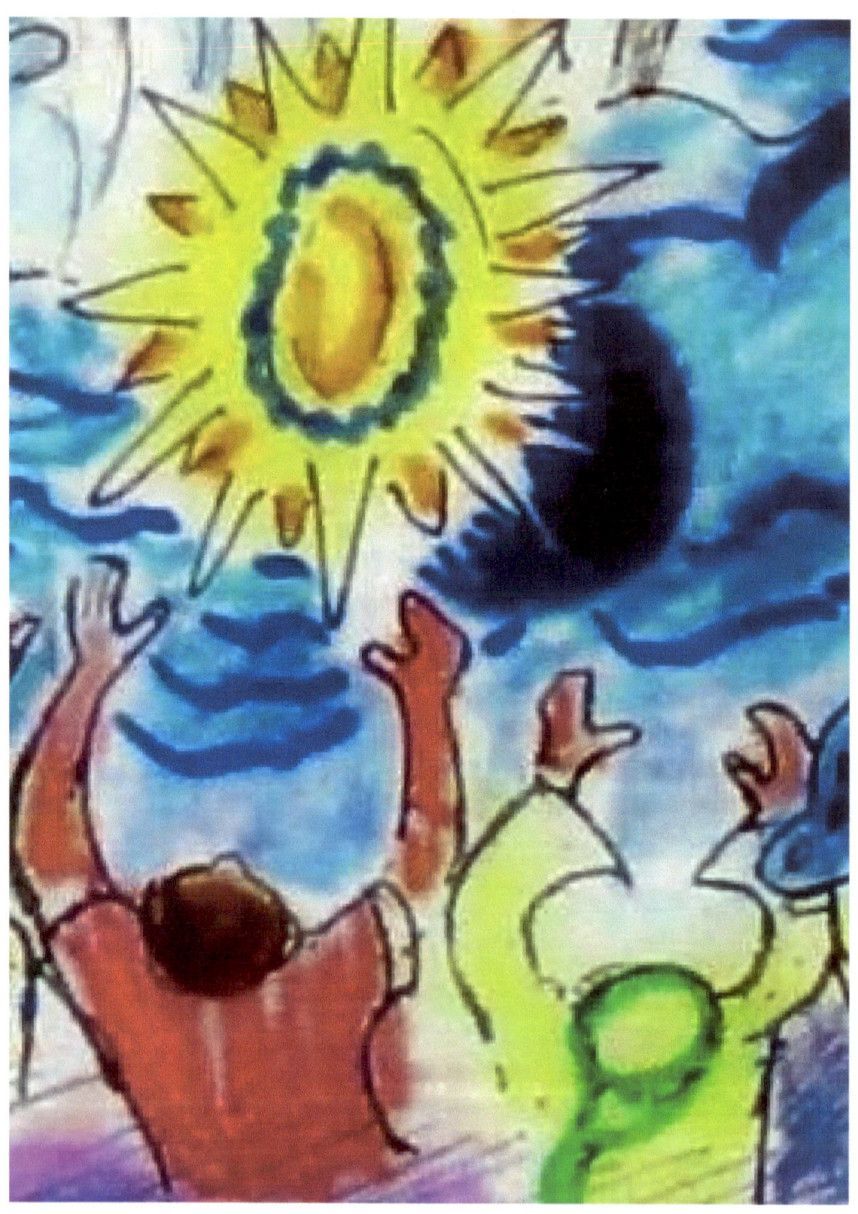

Title: Orbiting The Sun

How old is the earth?

A year to us is one orbit of the earth around the sun, but the Lord is not bound by our view of time, because 2 Peter 3:8 and psalm 90.4 say that, in the eyes of the Lord, a thousand years are as a passing day. In that case, the earth is only six days old.

Furthermore, the Lord can stop the earth from orbiting anytime he wants to. See Joshua 10:13 where the Lord stopped the orbit for a whole day.

Therefore, do not squabble with scientists about how old the earth is. Only the Lord knows.

Summary: The problem is not what the bible says, but rather man's interpretation of it. Since my bible cartoons reflect human nature rather than the spiritual meaning of bible verses, I hope I am not adding to the confusion.

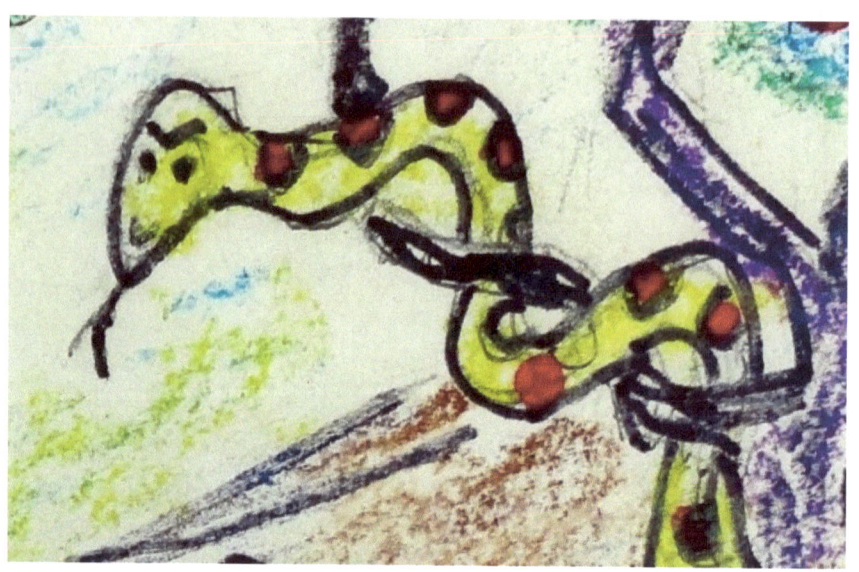

Title: Snake Handlers cartoon

If you take every passage of the bible literally, you might wind up dead.

Mark 16:18 says: "They will be able to pick up serpents with safety."

You see what happened to this preacher: "Feb 18, 2014: The snake handling pastor of a church in Kentucky died after being bitten by a rattle snake during a weekend church service."

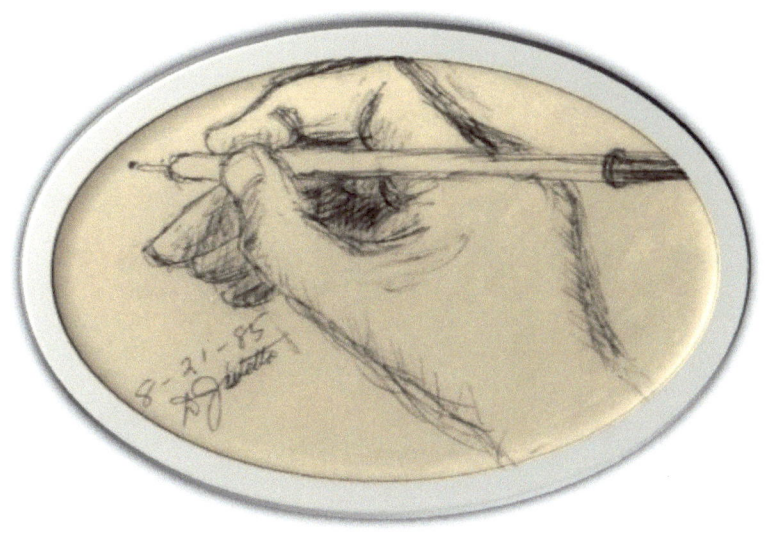

Title: My Right Hand
Copyright by Dan Wetta 1985

Matthew 5:20 says: If your right hand is an occasion of sin, cut it off. It is better to lose one part of your body than for your whole body to go into hell.

Even the snake handlers do not take this verse literally. In other words, bible thumpers are inconsistent.

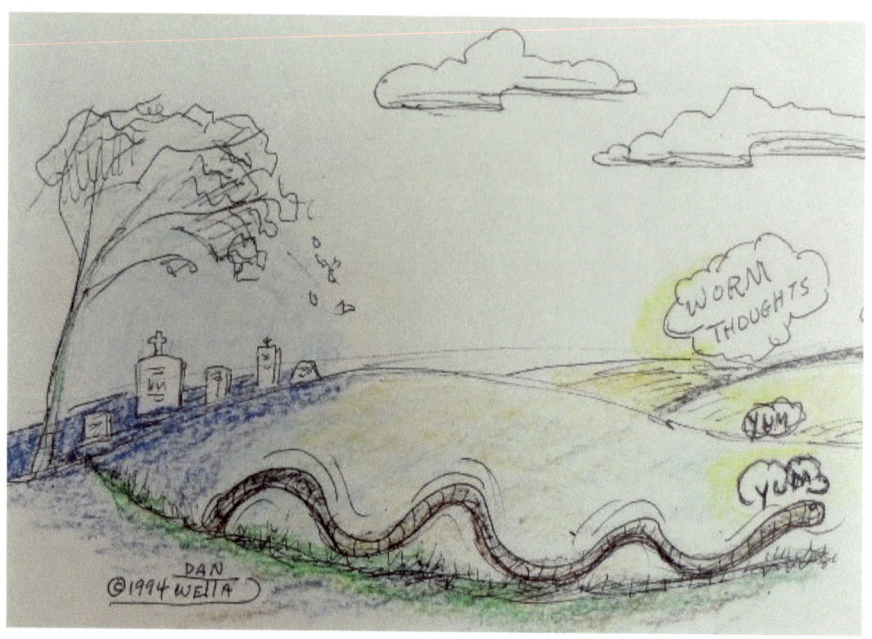

Title: cartoon Worm Thoughts
Copyright by Dan Wetta 1994

This guy has been to worm heaven!

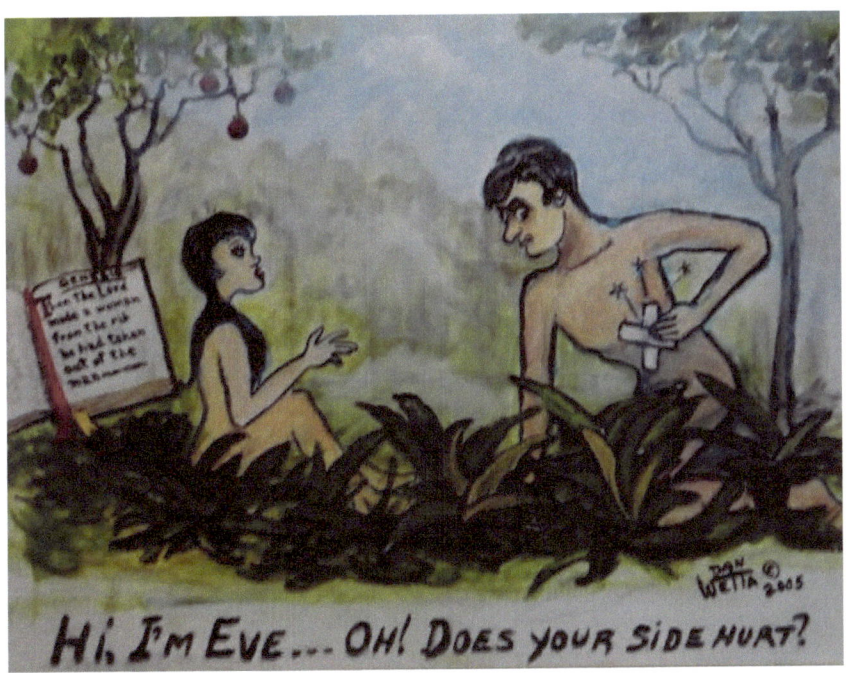

Title: Adam Meets Eve
Size: 18x24 inches
Medium: Acrylic on canvas
Copyright by Dan Wetta 2005

The only problem with the infallible word of God is man's interpretation of it.

There are thousands of Christian denominations with differing interpretations of the word of God.

This is my interpretation of the creation of Eve, which is probably not the impression most readers would get from reading Genesis 2:18-20

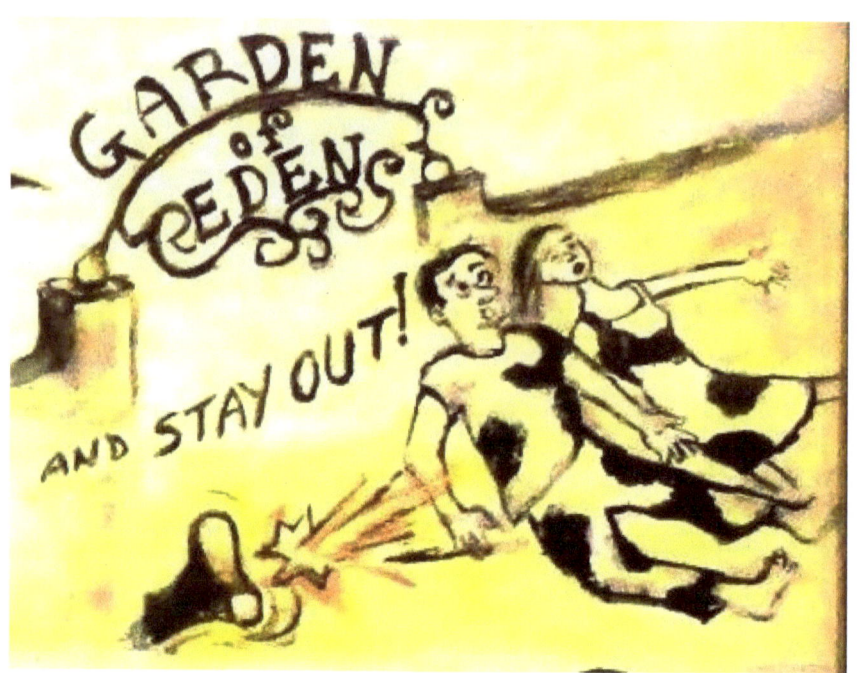

Title: Get Out and Stay Out!
Copyright by Dan Wetta

Just to show how a cartoonist thinks: - this cartoon leaves no doubt that Adam and Eve were expelled from the Garden of Eden.

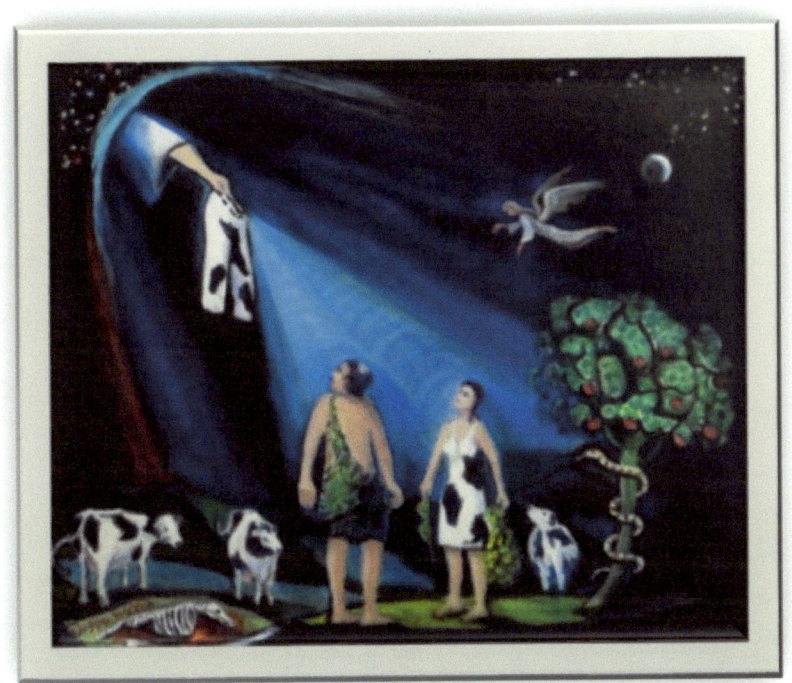

Title: Try These On For Size
Size: 16"x20"
Medium: Acrylic on canvas
Copyright by Dan Wetta 1994

This is my version of Adam and Eve being clothed in skins.

I believe they were given garments of skin after they were expelled from the Garden of Eden, so the serpent does not belong in this illustration.

Maybe I will paint it out of the picture. That's the advantage of acrylic paint over water color. With water color, you have to get it right the first time.

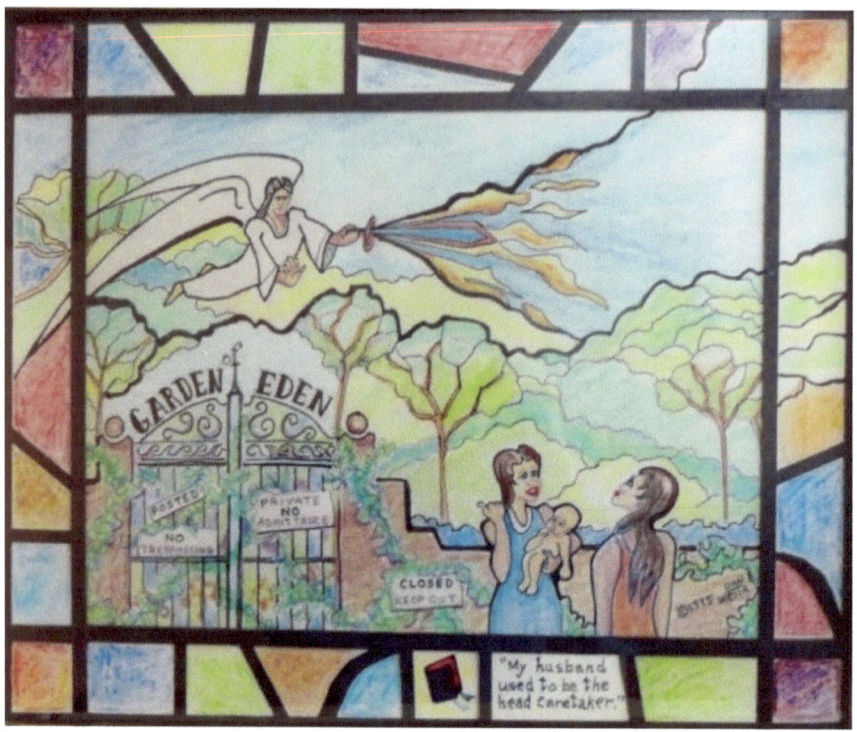

Title: Eve Reminiscing About the Good-Ole Days
Size: 16x20 inches
Medium: Acrylic on canvas
Copyright by Dan Wetta 1995

"My husband used to be the head caretaker."
This is another example of my interpretation of scripture.
I tried to humanize the expulsion from the Garden of Eden, but so far, no one has shown any interest in using this design for a stained glass window in his church.

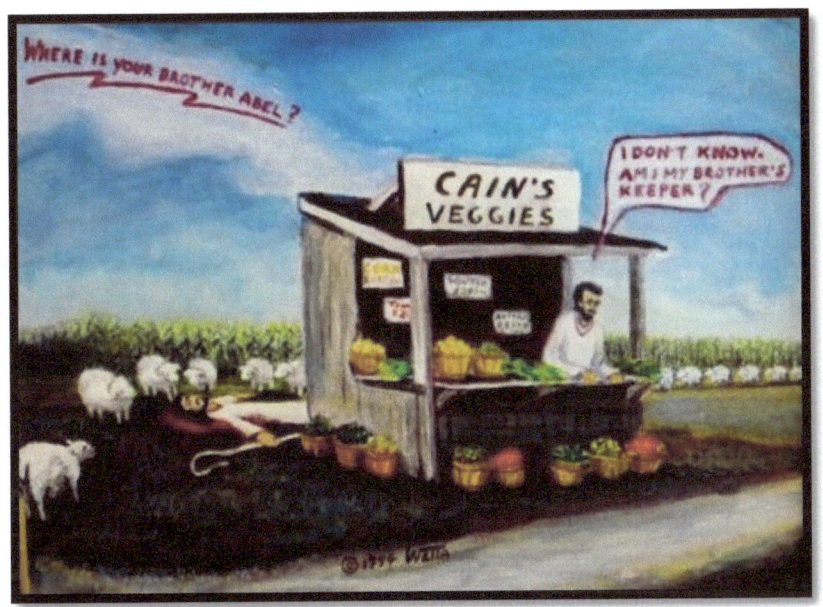

Title: Cain's Veggie cartoon
Size: 14x 18 inches
Medium: Acrylic on canvas
Copyright by Dan Wetta 1994

Cain grew up to be a farmer, and Abel became a shepherd.

There came a time when Cain brought an offering to the Lord God from the fruit of the soil, while Abel brought one of the firstlings of his flock.

The Lord looked with favor on Abel and his offering, but on Cain and his offering, he did not. Cain resented this so much that he slew his brother Abel in a field.

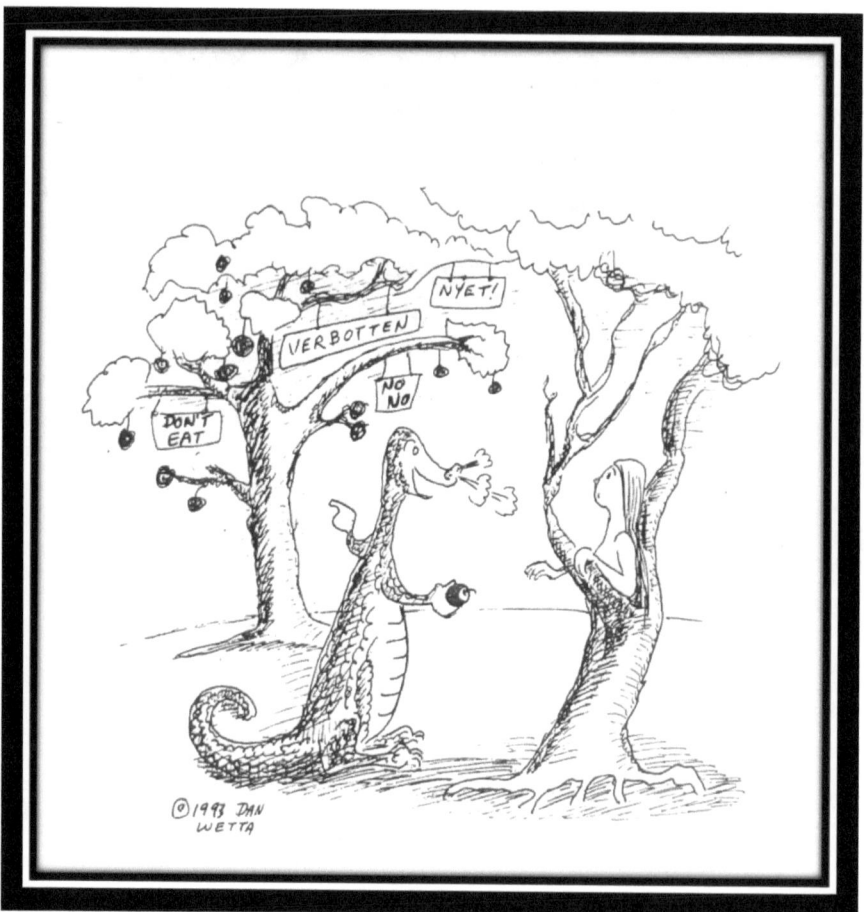

Title: Verbotten
Copyright by Dan Wetta 1993

I did several versions of Eve's temptation.

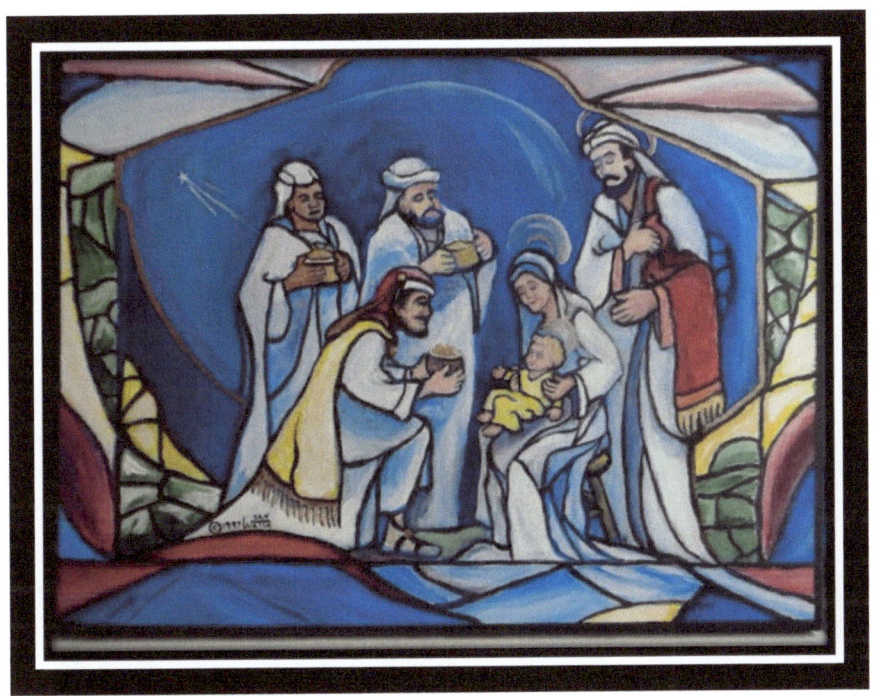

Title: Nativity Scene
Copyright by Dan Wetta 1997

This is a picture of the very first Christmas, sort of like the Big Bang, and then the evolution of Christmas begins.

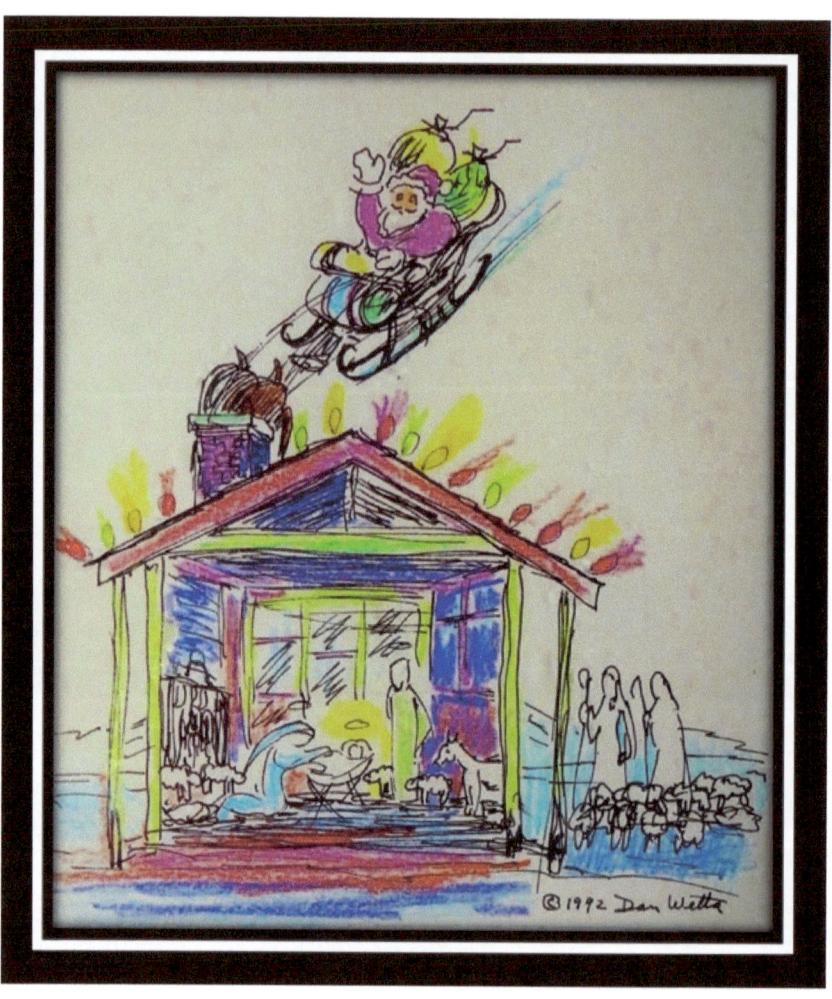

Title: Evolution of Christmas
Copyright by Dan Wetta 1992

If a cartoonist had drawn this cartoon two thousand years ago, in the days of Peter and Paul, it would have been considered sacrilegious.

Today, however, the traditional Nativity Scene has been replaced by Santa Claus decorations and "Happy Holiday" greeting cards. In fact, the Nativity Scene is forbidden in most public places.

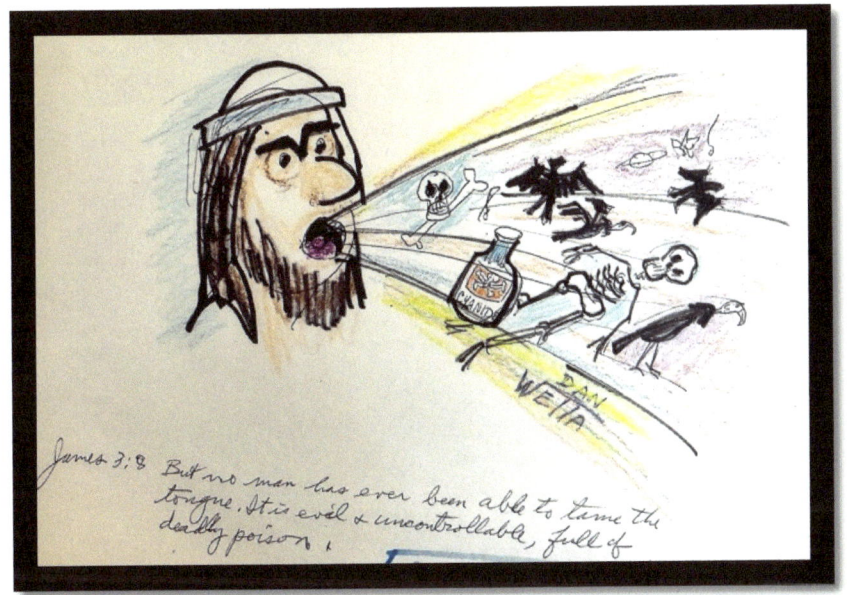

Title: Poisonous Tongue
Medium: Mixed media on paper

This is a quote from James 3:8, and that's my poor handwriting in the bottom of the cartoon, which says:

"But no man has ever been able to tame the tongue. It is evil and uncontrollable, full of deadly poison."

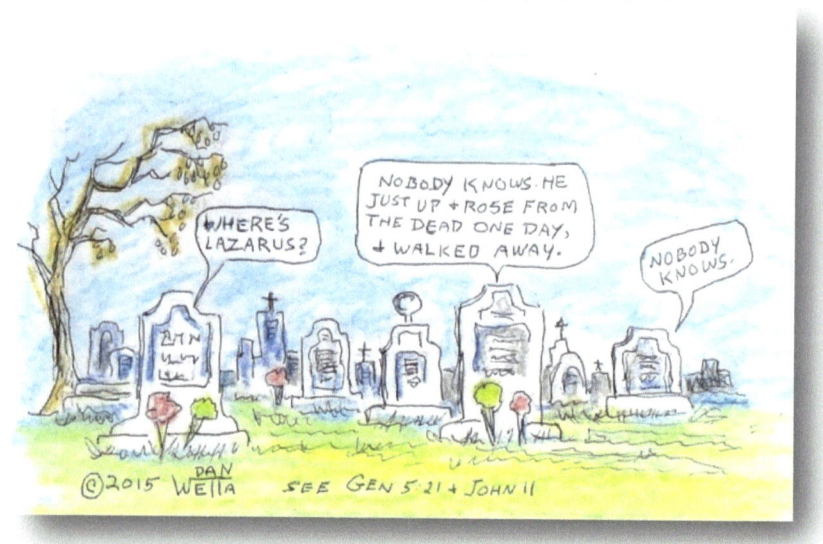

Title: Where's Lazarus?
Copyright by Dan Wetta 2015

DID JESUS RAISE LAZARUS FROM THE DEAD, OR JUST
WAKE HIM UP? - (John 11:11 Jesus said that Lazarus was asleep).

I once read a fictional story about a man who had a terminal
illness for which there was no cure, so his family had him quick-frozen
until a cure could be found. A cure was found a few years later, so they
brought him back to life, and the doctors were able to cure him.

However, he was a man without a soul, because when they froze
him, his soul left his body, and a man without a soul has no
conscience. So this man who came back to life without a conscience
did many evil things.

I think Lazarus was just sleeping, as John said in John 11:11.

When I did this doodle, I was feeling
   Down in the Dumps
Woe is me, and oh my aching back,
Where are the days of yesteryear?

GONE, GONE, GONE, GONE, GONE

Oh me, it's so
dark down here
in the dumps.

But then I read John 6, and felt better.

Studios In Richmond & Williamsburg, Virginia,
And New Orleans, Louisiana

Title: Q text John 6
Copyright 1987 by Dan Wetta

When I did this doodle, I was feeling down in the dumps. Woe is me and my aching back, I thought. Where are the days of yesteryear? Gone, gone, gone! It felt so dark down in the dumps. But then I remembered the quote from John 6:57: "So the man who feeds on me will have life because of me." I remembered a doodle I had done a couple years before. (It follows.)

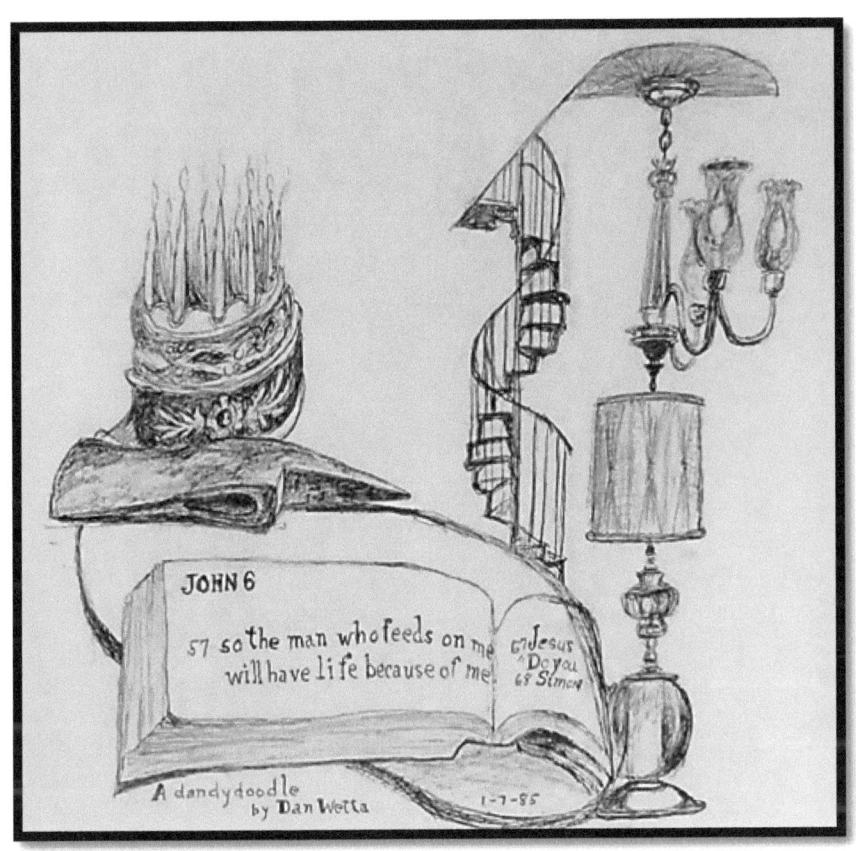

Title: John 6
Copyright by Dan Wetta 1985

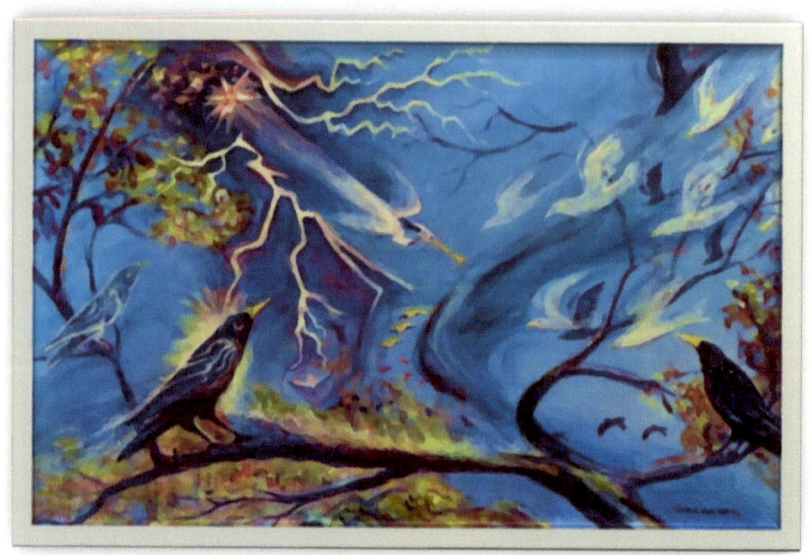

Title: Angel Gabriel
Size: 20x30 inches
Medium: Acrylic on canvas
Copyright by Dan Wetta 1995

This painting is on the cover of my first paper back book entitled *An Artist's Life, New Orleans Framed.*

The painting is my impression of the biblical prophecy about the Angel Gabriel blowing his horn on the last day. The birds of the air will be the first to see him coming.
If you want to know the real story, read: 1 Thessalonians 4:16-17

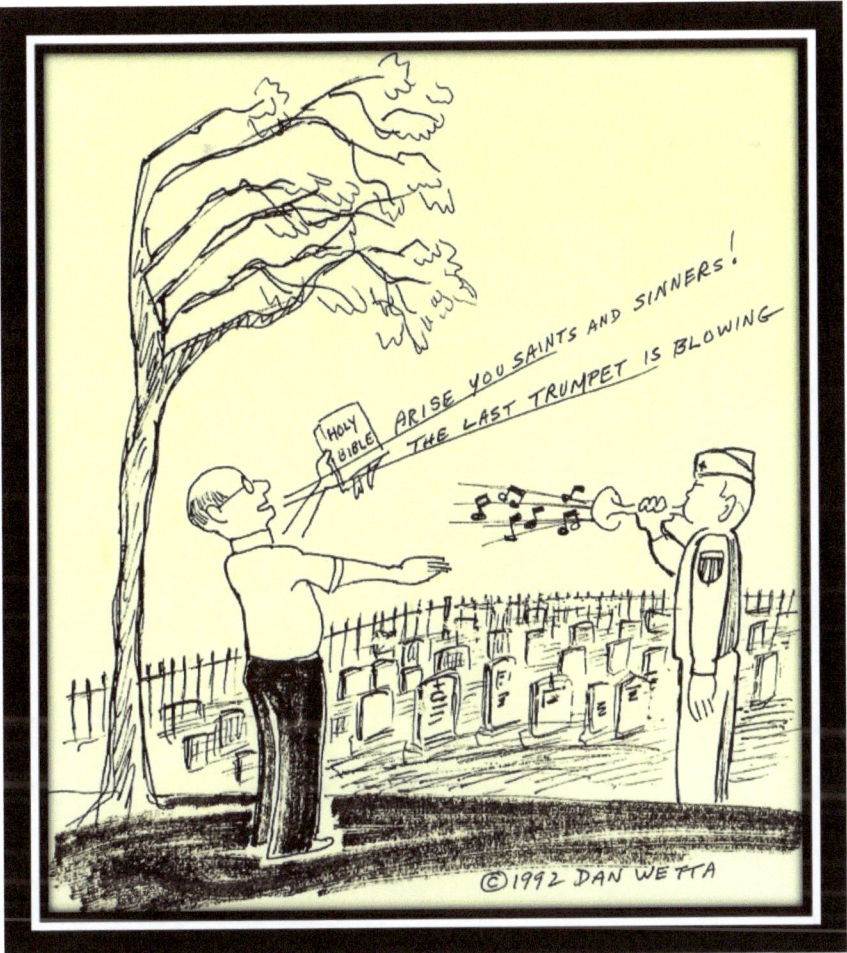

Title: Arise
Copyright by Dan Wetta 1992

Just to show how some preachers go to extremes.

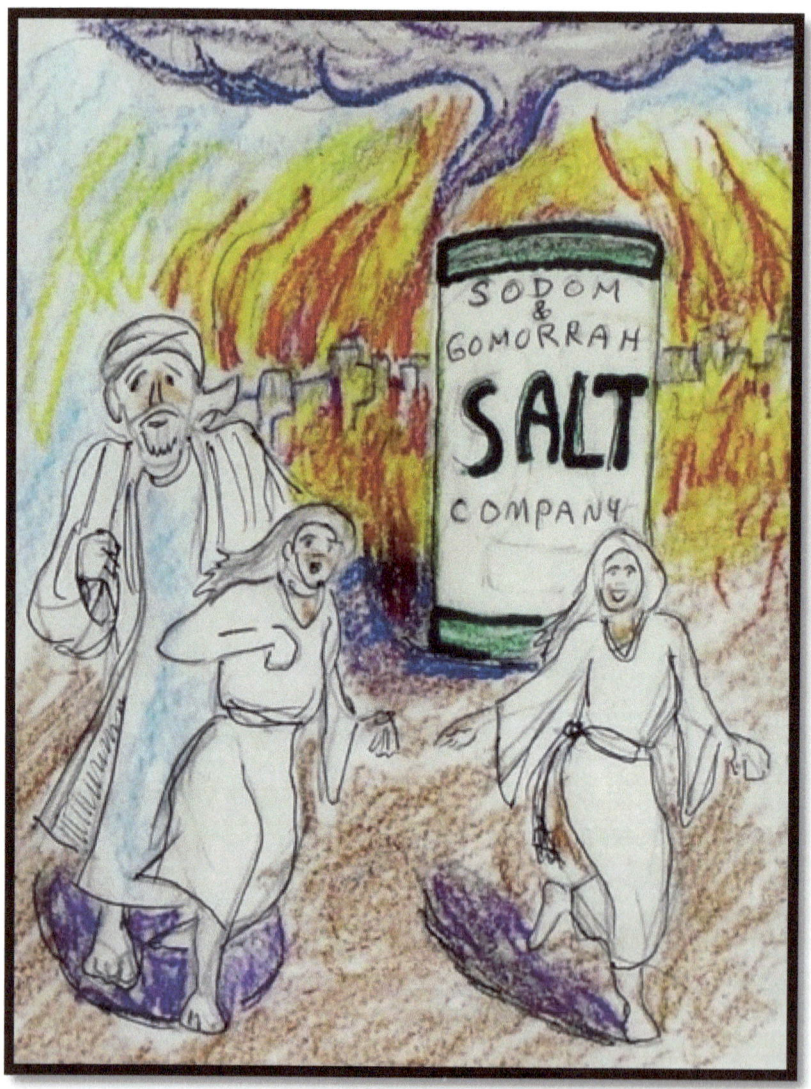

Title: Sodom & Gomorrah Salt Company
Copyright by Dan Wetta

I used this illustration as the cover of my second e-book, entitled *High Blood Pressure.*

Every time I eat too much salty food, my feet swell up so much that I have trouble putting on my shoes and socks.

If you want to know where high blood pressure and hypertension came from, read the story about Sodom and Gomorrah in Genesis 19.

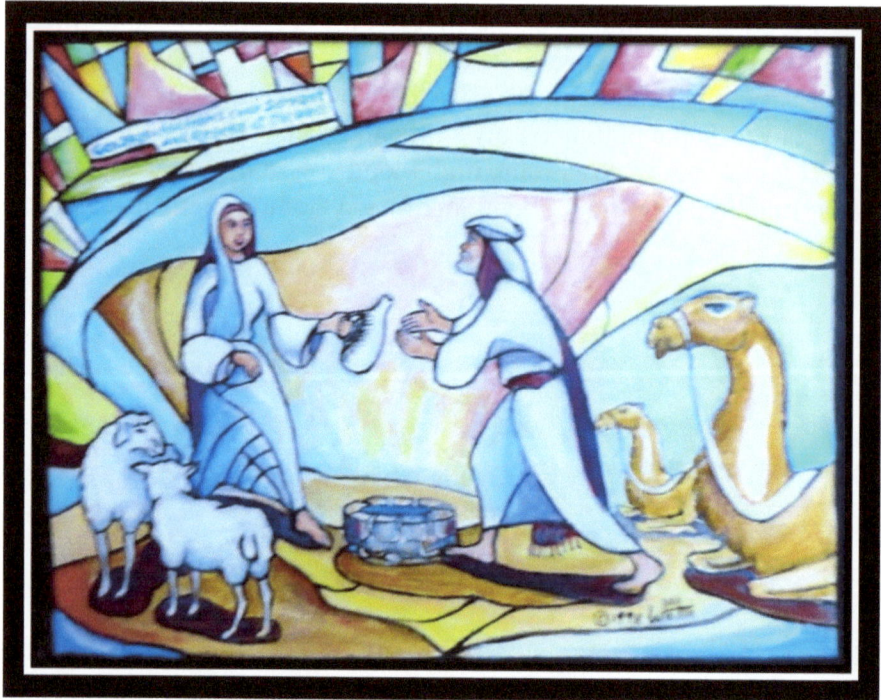

Title: Rebecca
Size: 14x18 inches
Medium: Acrylic on canvas
Copyright by Dan Wetta 1998

Several incidents in the bible occurred around water wells in the desert.

This scene takes place just before Abraham's chief servant takes out a gold ring weighing half a shekel, and... if you want to know the rest of the story, go to Genesis 24:22.

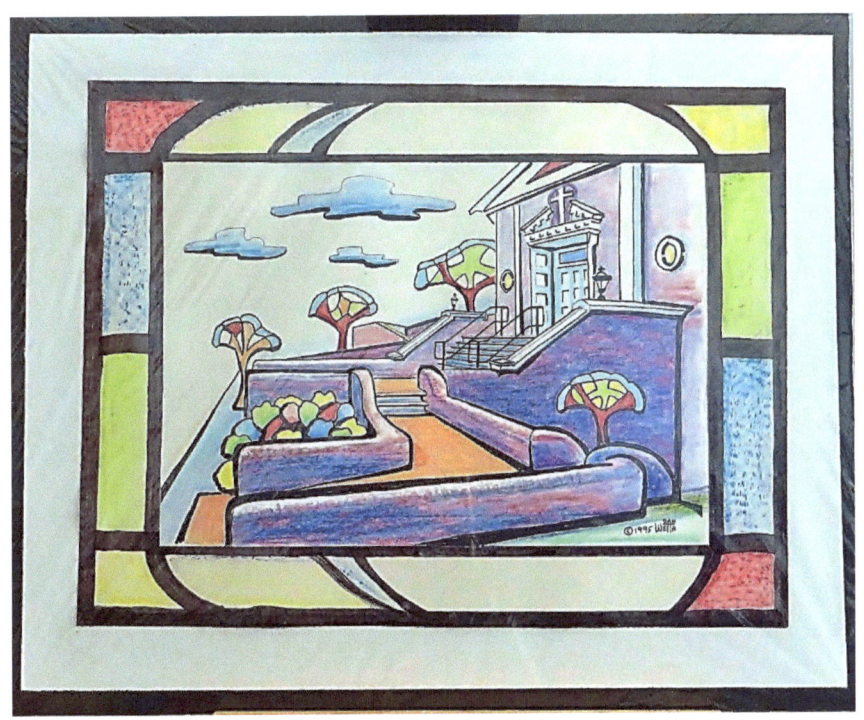

Title: Stairway to Heaven
Size: 22 x 28 inches
Medium: Mixed media on paper
Copyright by Dan Wetta 1995

When I saw the elaborate entrance way to this old church, it reminded me of a stairway to heaven.

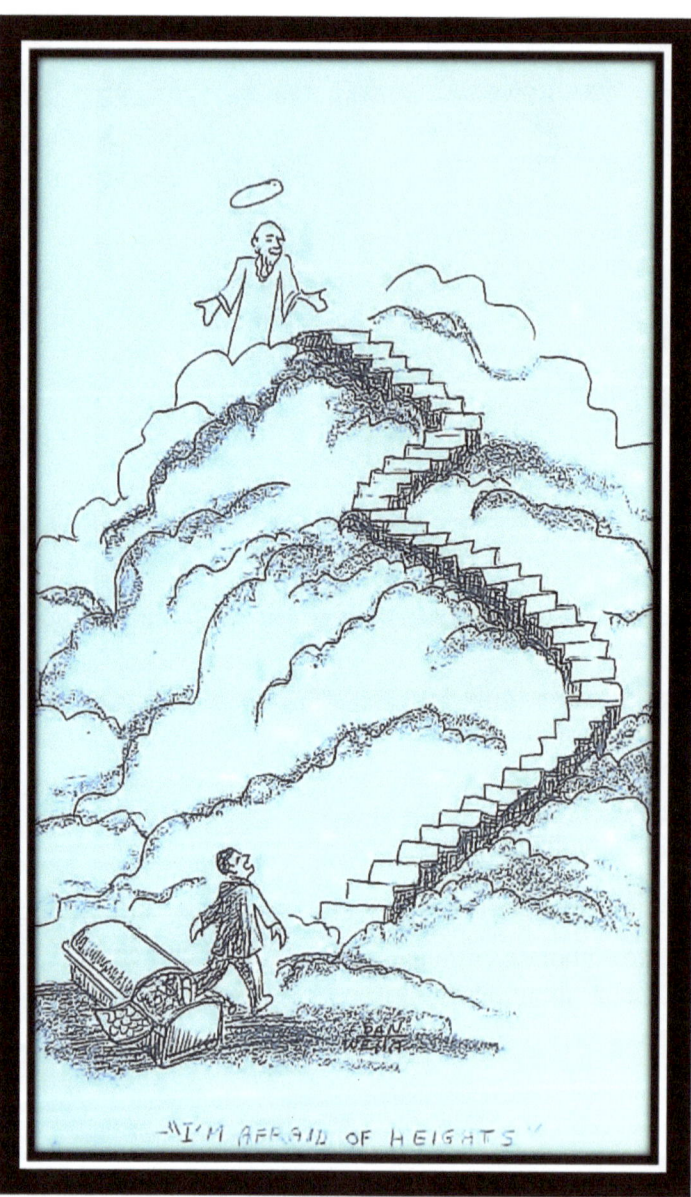

I'M AFRAID OF HEIGHTS

Title: Afraid of Heights
Copyright by Dan Wetta 1992

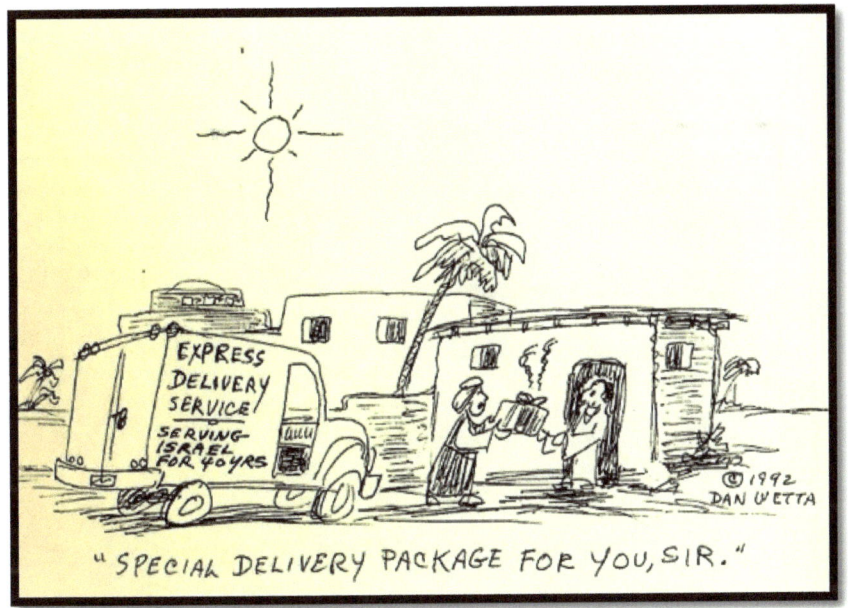

Title: Levite and his Concubine cartoon
Copyright by Dan Wetta 1992

This is one of the goriest stories in the Old Testament. Poor concubine! See Judges 19 on the next page.

Judges 19:22-29 & 21:25

While the old man and his Levite guest were
enjoying their meal, some of the wicked men
of the city surrounded the house. Pounding
on the door, they shouted to the old man who
owned the house, "Bring out the man who came
to your house so we can have sex with him."

The owner of the house went outside and said
to them, "No, my friends, don't be so vile.
Since this man is my guest, don't do this
disgraceful thing."

But the men would not listen to him. So the
Levite took his concubine and sent her outside
to them, and they raped her and abused her
throughout the night, and at dawn they let her
go. At daybreak the woman went back to the house
where her master was staying, fell down at the
door and lay there until daylight.

When her Levite master got up in the morning and
opened the door of the house and stepped out to
continue on his way, there lay his concubine,
fallen in the doorway of the house, with her
hands on the threshhold. He said to her, "Get up,
let's go." But there was no answer. Then he put
her on his donkey and set out for home. In those
days Israel had no king; everyone did as he saw fit.

When he reached home, he took a knife and cut up
his concubine, limb by limb, into twelve parts and
sent them into all the areas of Israel.

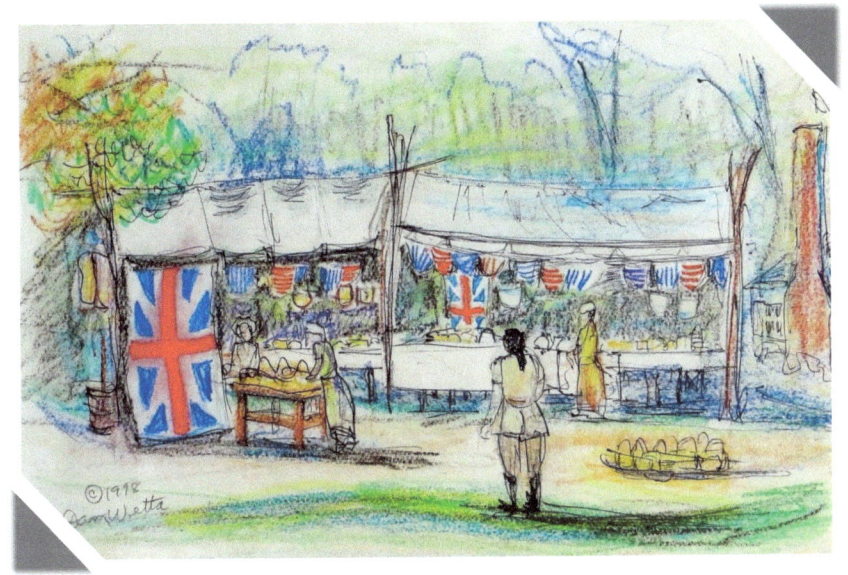

Title: Flags Come and Go

Flags come and go. Nations come and go. People come and go. Leaders come and go. Governments come and go.
We call it history.

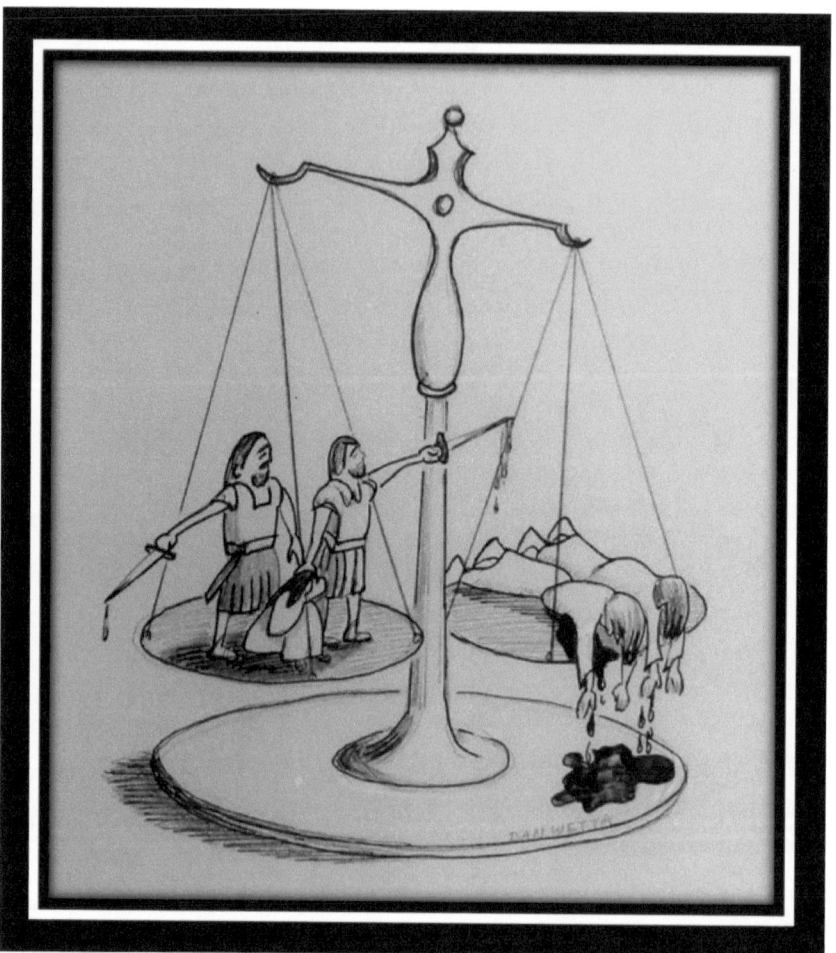

Title: Dinah means Justice
Copyright by Dan Wetta

Dinah and her brothers are on one side of the scale.
Shechem, and his father, Hamor, are on the other side.

Sechem had raped Dinah, and Sechem then asked his father, Hamor, to get Dinah for his wife.

So when Hamor asked Jacob to let Shechem marry Dinah, Jacob's sons said: "Only if you let all your males be circumcised."

So every male in Hamor's city was circumcised, and while they were still in pain, Dinah's brothers took revenge and killed every male in Hamor's city.

The full story is at Genesis 34:4-31.

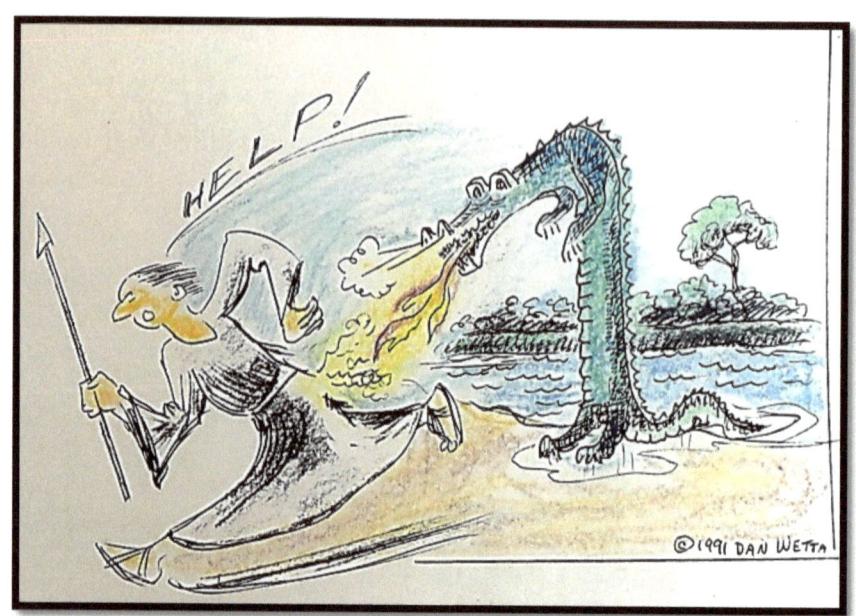

Title: Job's Leviathan
Copyright by Dan Wetta 1991

Job 3:8:
"May those who curse the sea,
Curse the day of my birth,
Those who are ready to rouse Leviathan."

Job 41:19, 20, 21
"When he opens his mouth fire comes out.
Smoke pours out of the nostrils of his nose like steam rising out of a boiling pot.
His breath alone is so hot that it will start fires, and flames shoot out of it's mouth."

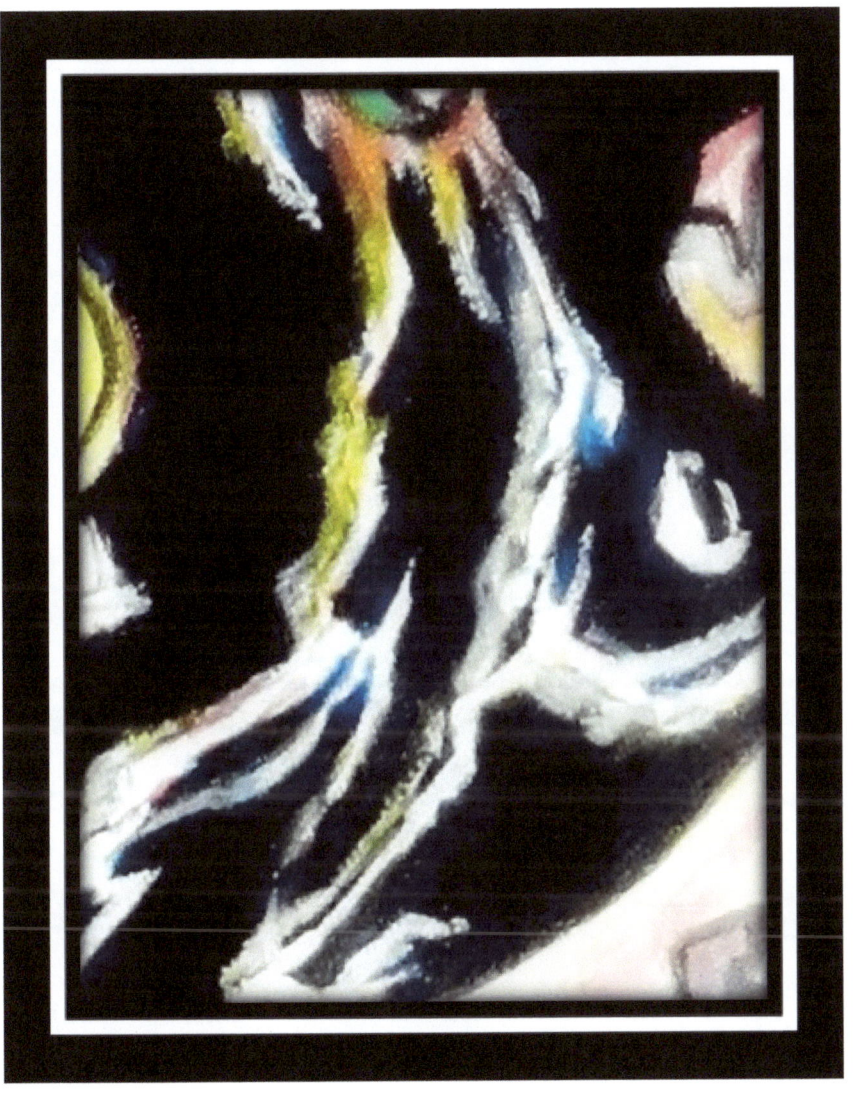

Title: Abstract Twenty-Five
Copyright by Dan Wetta 1995

This creepy abstract was taken from my painting, "Purgatory."

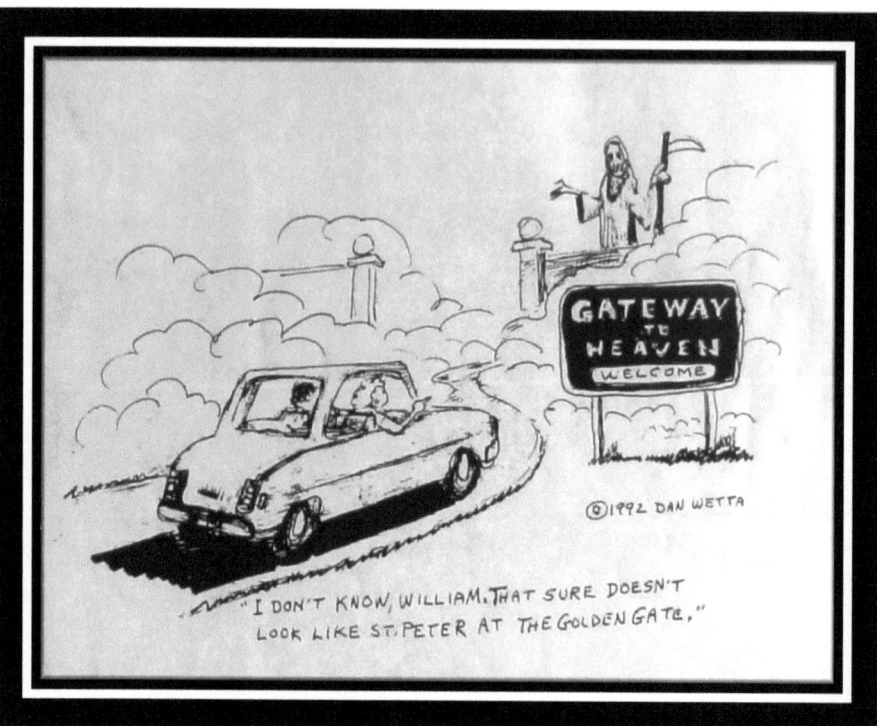

Title: Gateway to Heaven
Copyright by Dan Wetta 1992

This is my interpretation of Job 18:17 which asks the question:
HAVE THE GATES OF HEAVEN BEEN SHOWN TO YOU?

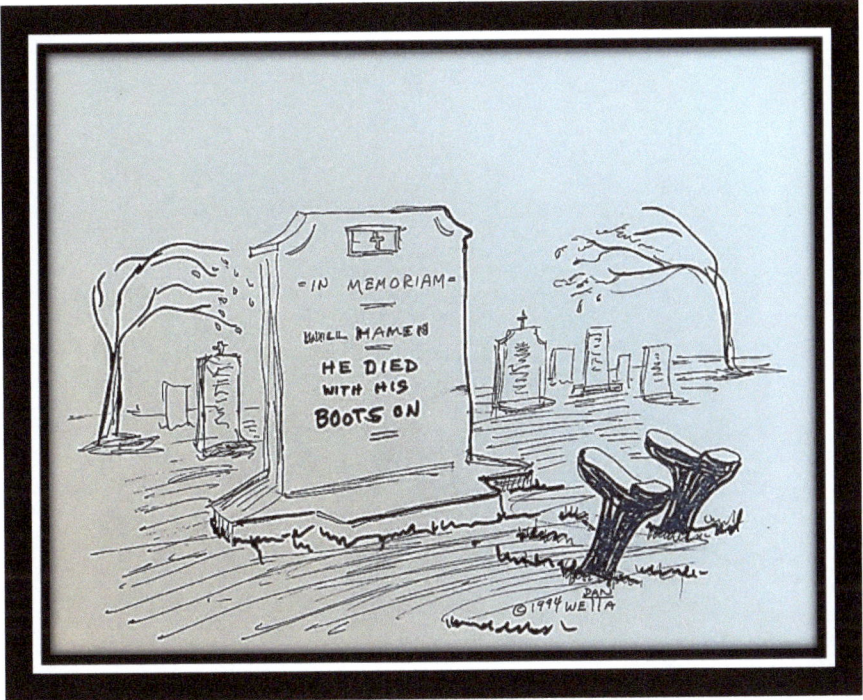

Title: He Died With His Boots On
Copyright by Dan Wetta 1994

"To die with your boots on" is an idiom dating back to the
American Wild West. It can refer to soldiers who died in battle with
their boots on or cowboys who died in a gun fight.

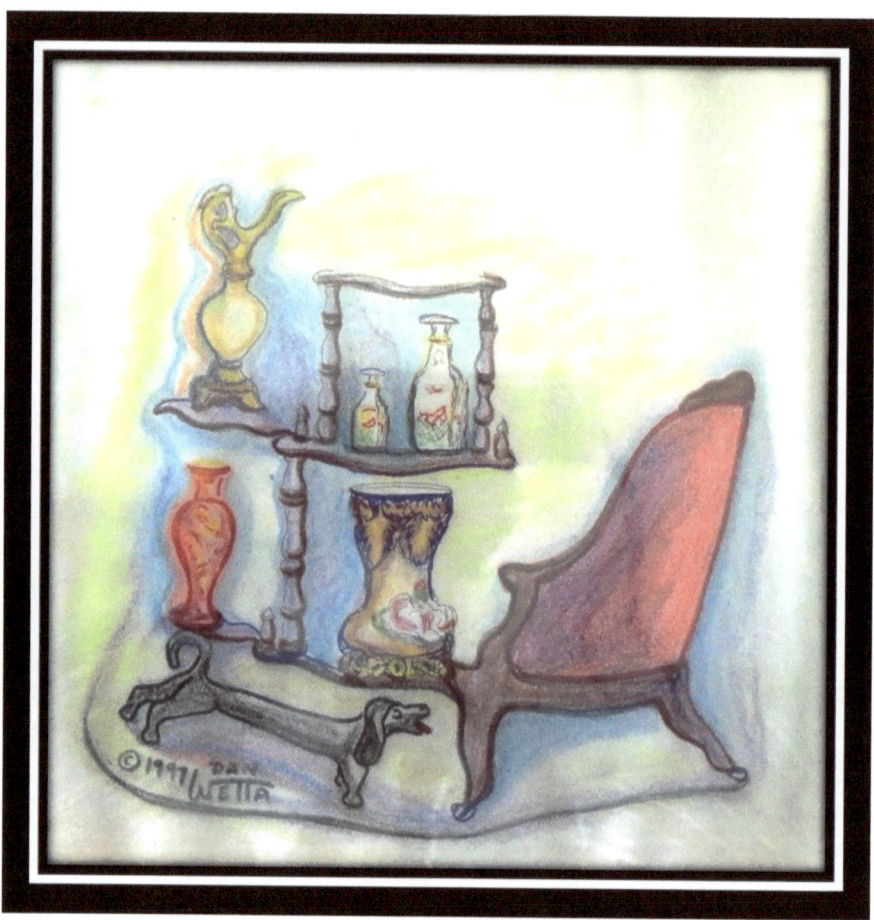

Title: Antique Chair and Weiner Dog
Copyright by Dan Wetta 1997

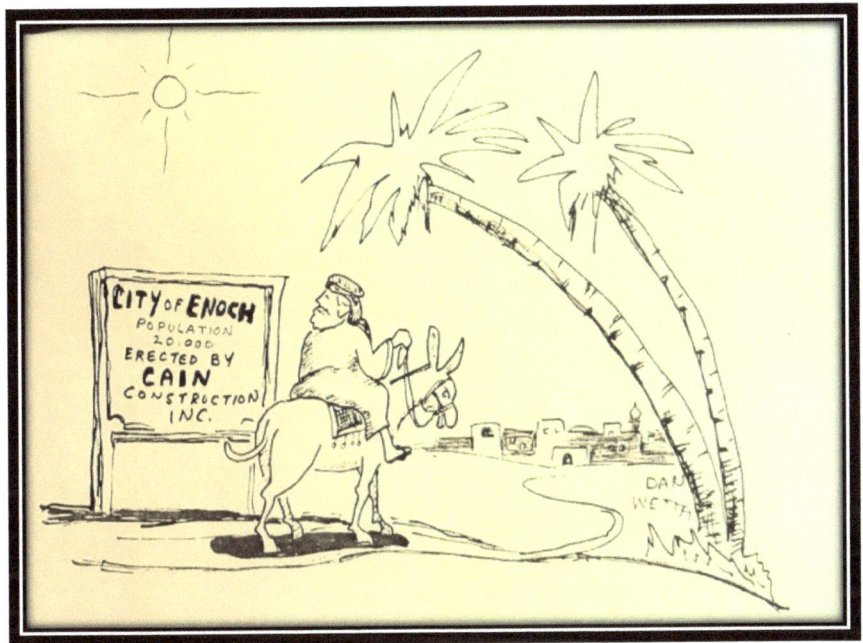

Title: Cain Banished
Copyright by Dan Wetta

When Cain was banished to the land of Nod, people were already there, and he even found a wife in the land of Nod.

My theory is that the people in the land of Nod were the descendants of the "humankind" that God created in the first book of Genesis.

Adam and Eve are not mentioned until eons later, as recorded in the second book of Genesis.

Read the two books of Genesis, and decide for yourself.

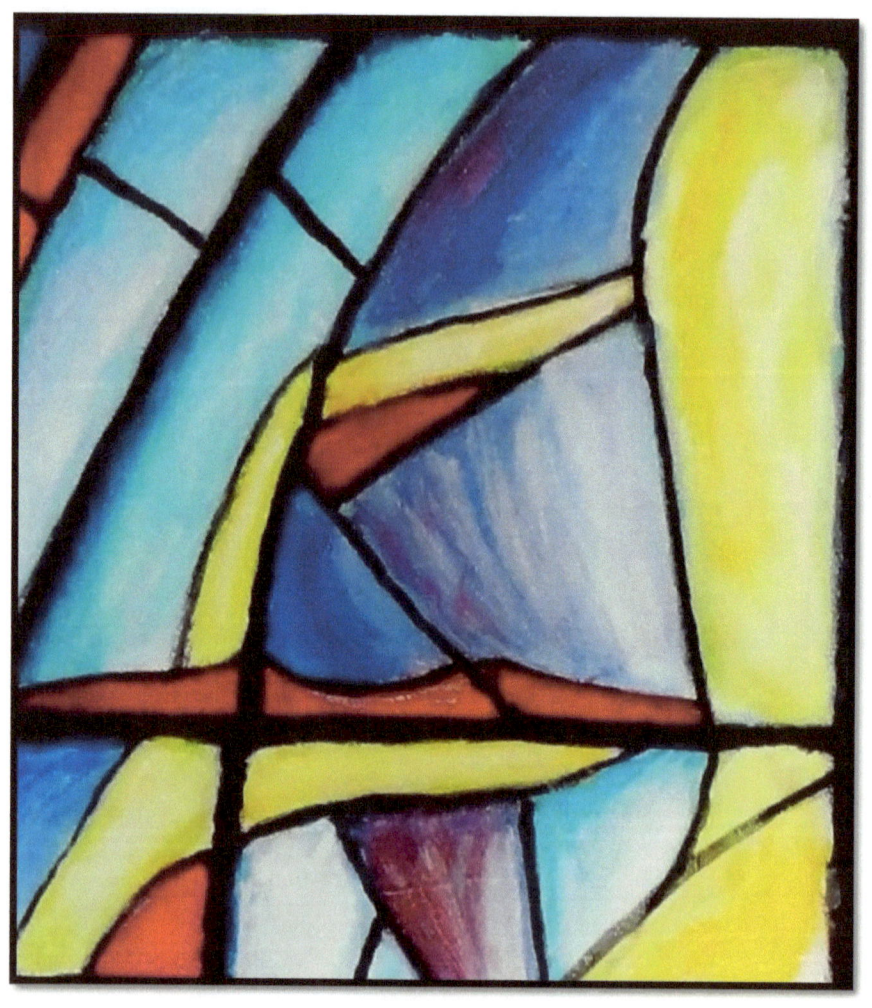

Title: King Solomon's Verdict abstract
Copyright by Dan Wetta

I did not know I could do abstract paintings until I began selecting
small sections of my stained glass designs.

I cropped this abstract from my stained glass design for "King
Solomon's Verdict."

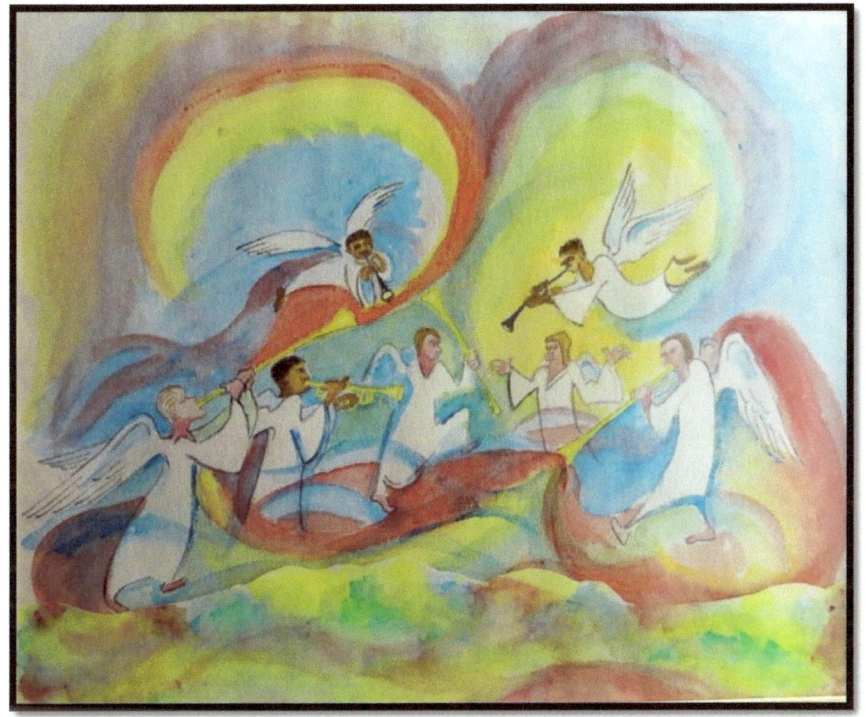

Title: Louis Armstrong's Heavenly Choir
Size: 16 x 20 inches
Medium: Mixed media on paper
Copyright by Dan Wetta

I added some color to the clouds to liven up the heavenly choir, and I hope those angels don't get into trouble for hamming it up with Louis Armstrong – but they will get in trouble for sure if they play "Mack the Knife."

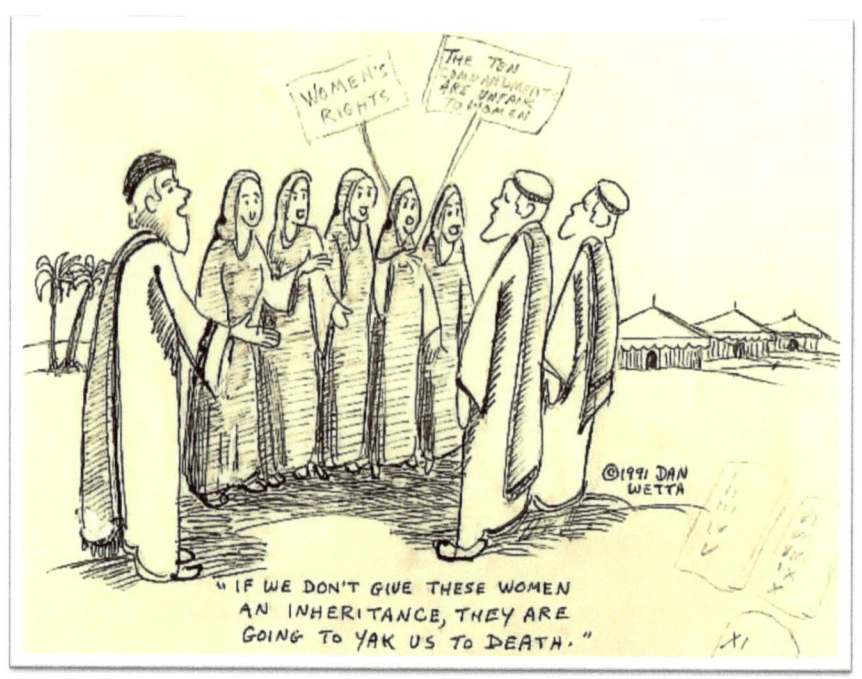

Title: Women's Rights
Copyright by Dan Wetta 1991

```
             Zelophehad's  Daughters
               Num.26.33 and 27.3
Zelophehad son of Hepher had no sons; he
had only daughters, whose names were:
              Mahlah = weak
              Noah   = cheer
              Hoglah = partridge
              Milcah = queen
              Tirzah = pleasure
His daughters said to the leaders of Israel,
"Our father died in the desert and left no
sons. Why should our father's name disappear
from his clan because he had no son? Give us
property among our father's relatives."


Moses consulted the Lord, and the Lord told
him, "If a man dies and leaves no son, turn
his inheritance over to his daughter. This is
to be a legal requirement for the Israelites."

Zelophehad's daughters established a legal precedent for the
women of Israel. That was a long time ago, about 1400 BC.
```

Title: Women's Rights, Text

If you're interested in the history of "women's rights," go to Chapters 26 and 27 of Numbers in the Old Testament.

P.S.: Also note the names of Zelophehad's daughters in the text above.

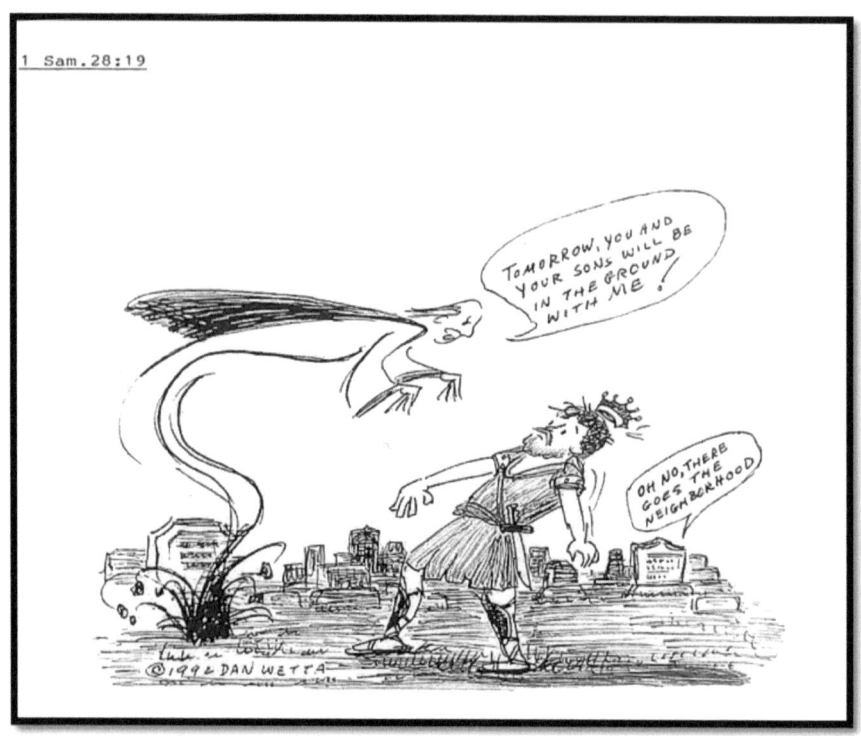

TOMORROW, YOU AND YOUR SONS WILL BE IN THE
GROUND WITH ME!

Title: The Witch of Endor
Copyright by Dan Wetta 1992

See 1: Sam.25:1 – 28:13: "Now Samuel died and all Israel
assembled and mourned for him; they buried him at his home in
Ramah. Saul consulted with a witch in an attempt to contact Samuel.
The witch of Endor said to Saul, 'I see an old man wearing a robe, a
spirit coming up out of the ground.'" Saul knew it was Samuel.
　　"Samuel said to Saul, 'Why do you bother me? Tomorrow, you
and your sons will be in the ground with me.'"

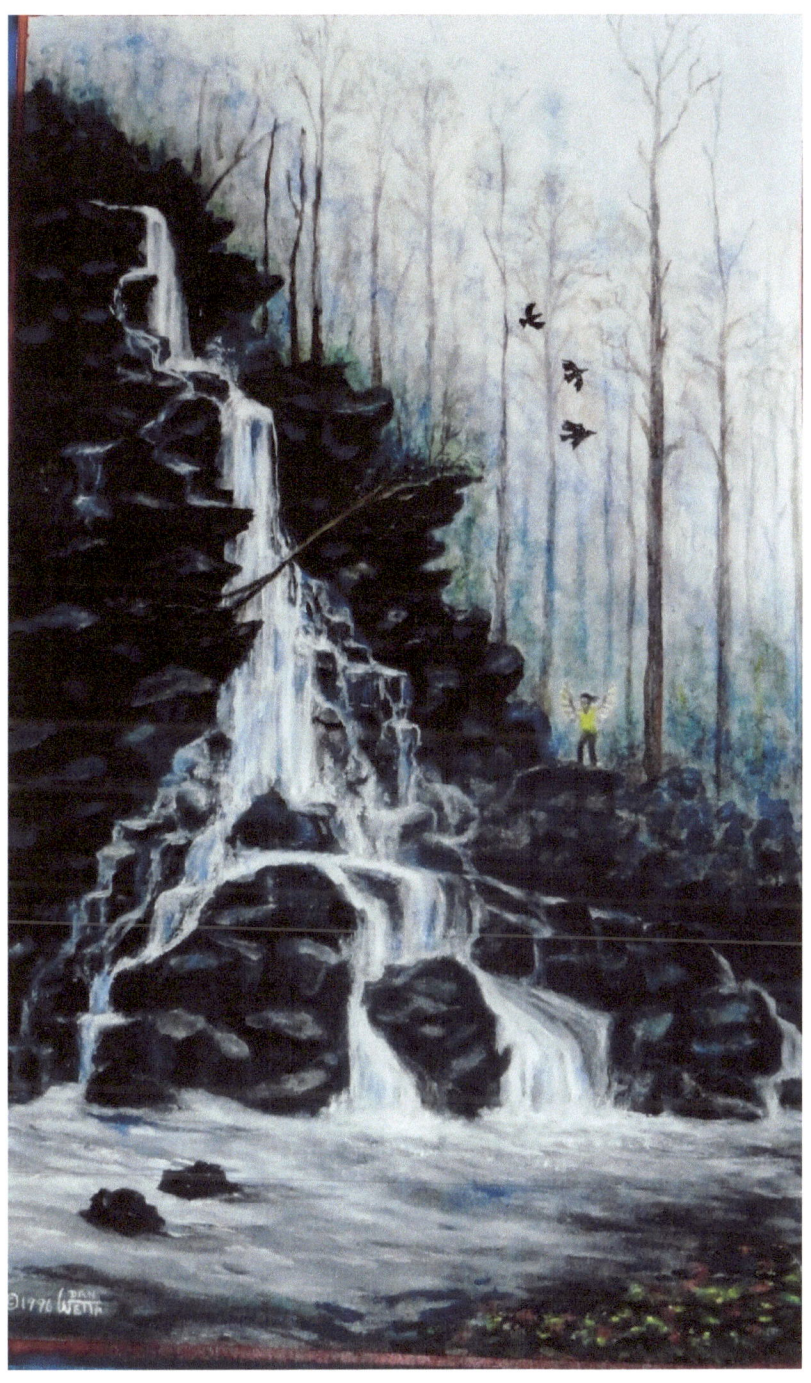

Title: Coal Mountain
Size: 22 x 30 inches
Medium: Acrylic on canvas
Copyright 1996 by Dan Wetta

Genesis 1:31 says, "God saw all that He had made and it was very good."

However, if God had put all the coal and oil above ground, the book of Genesis would probably have read, "God saw all that He had made and it was very bad."

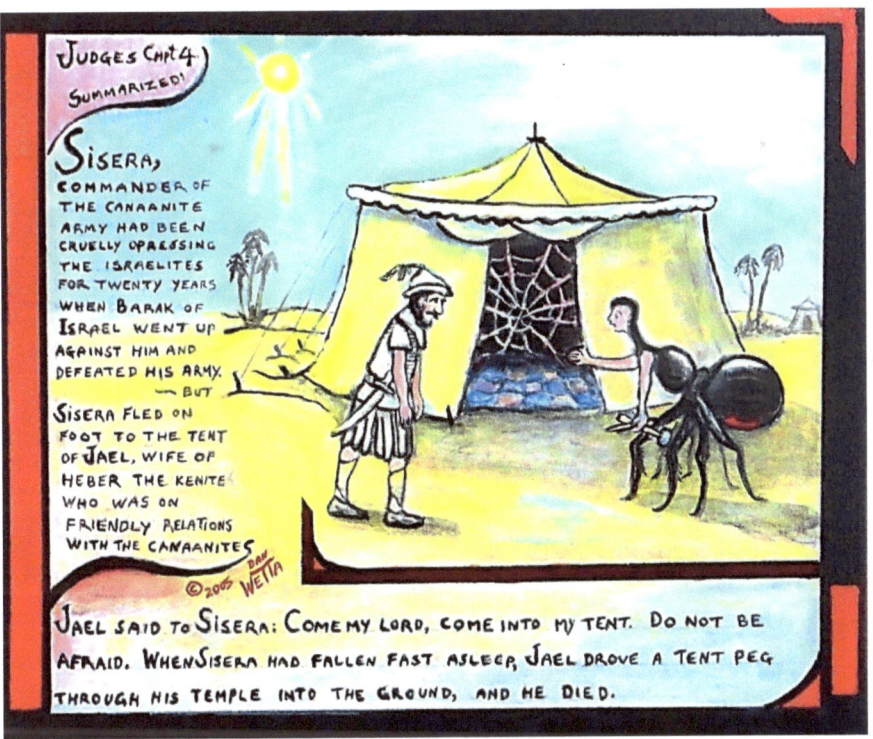

Title: Sisera and Jael
Size: 16 x 20 inches
Medium; Acrylic on canvas
Copyright by Dan Wetta 2005

This is my interpretation of Judges Chapter 4. It is a gory story.

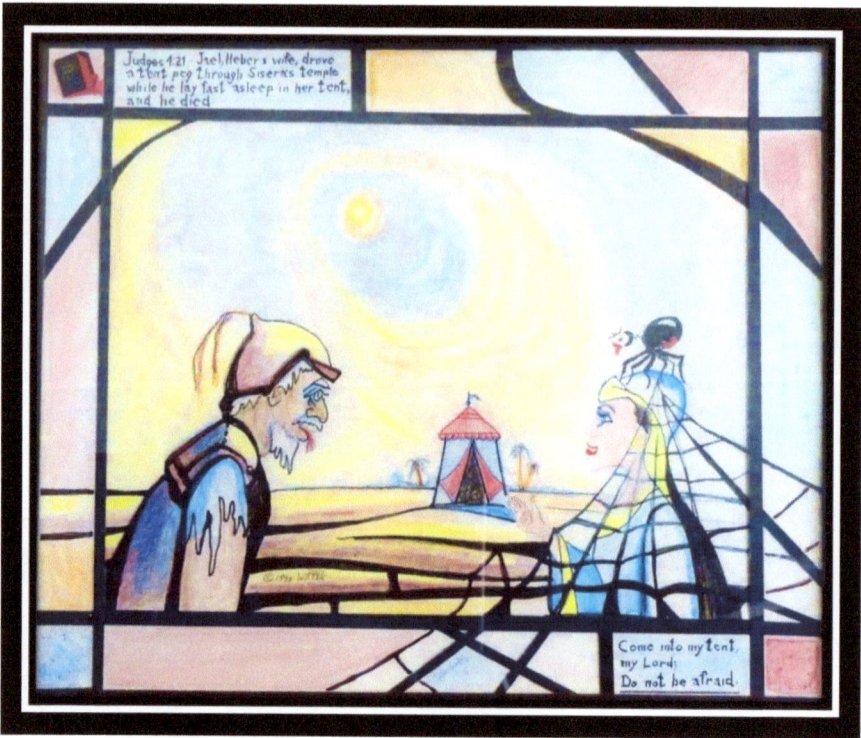

Title: Jael and Sisera stained glass design
Size: 16 x 20 inches
Medium: Mixed media on paper
Copyright by Dan Wetta 1995

I did two or three versions of this gory story at Judges 4:21.
Jael, Heber's wife, drove a tent peg through Sisera's temple while he lay fast asleep in her tent, and he died.

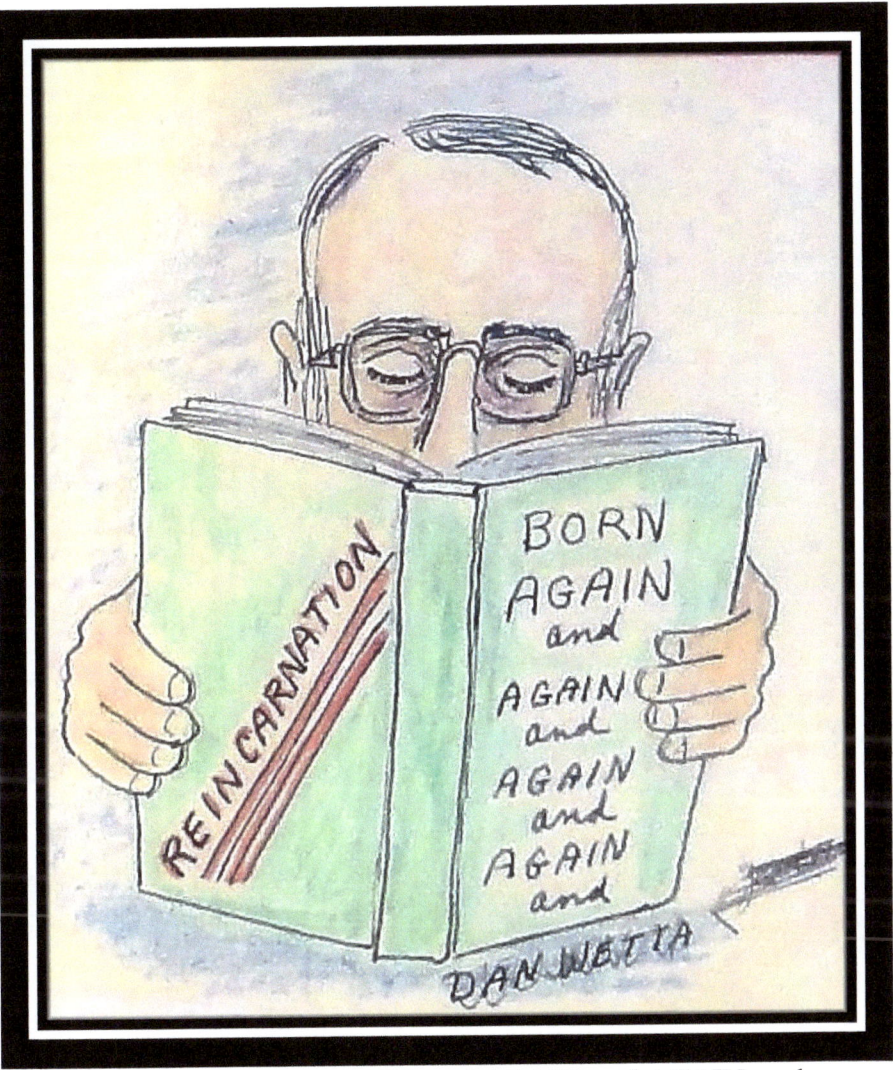

BORN AGAIN, and AGAIN, and AGAIN, and AGAIN, and AGAIN, and AGAIN, and

Title: Reincarnation
Copyright by Dan Wetta

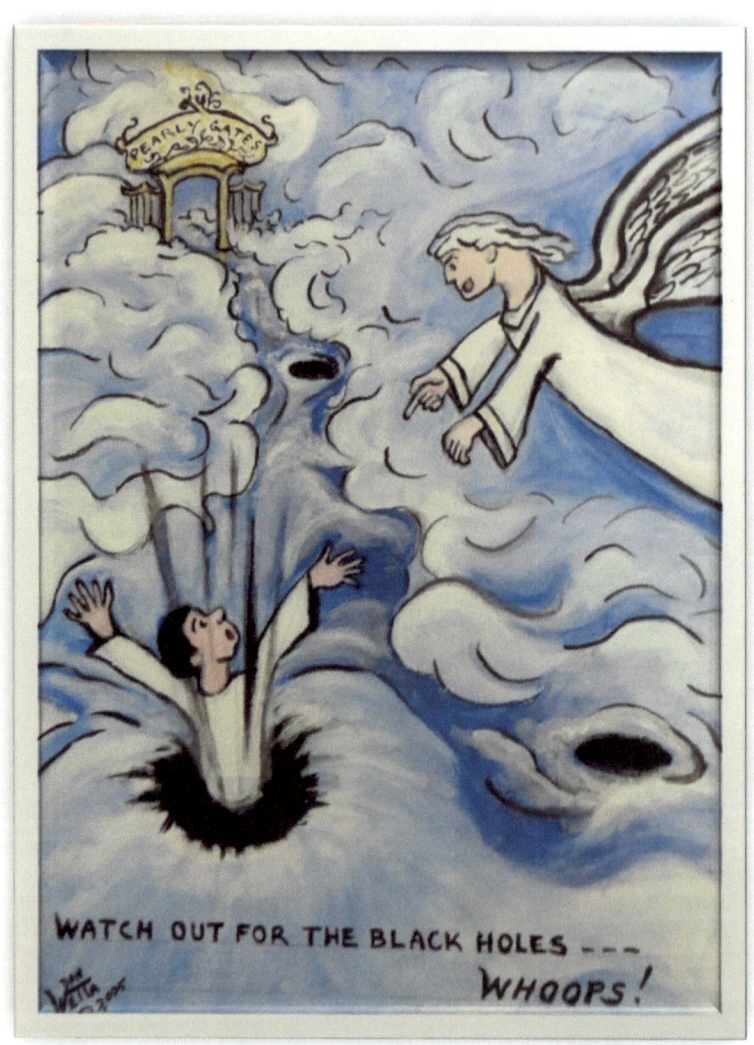

Title: Watch Out for Black Holes
Size: 18" x 24"
Medium: Acrylic on canvas
Copyright by Dan Wetta 2005

As they say: There are many pitfalls on the way to heaven

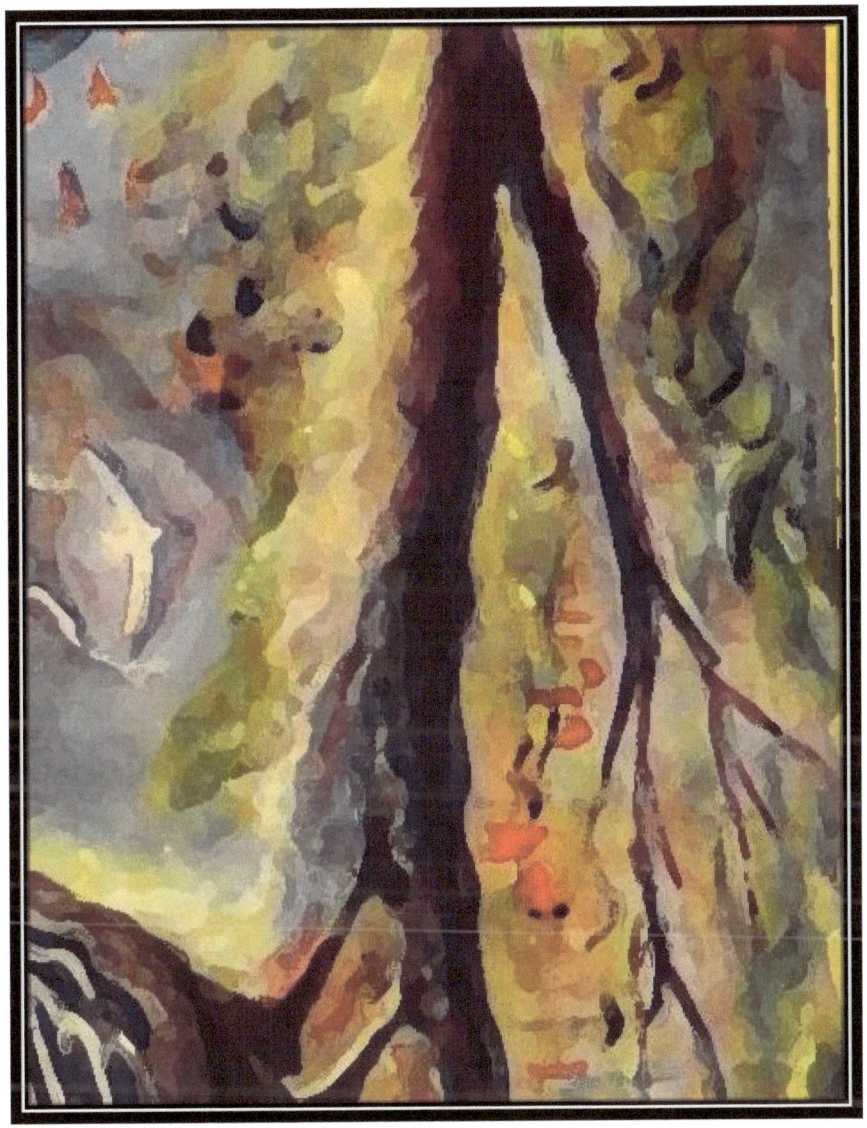

Title: Abstract Angel Gabriel One
Copyright by Dan Wetta 1995

This is a section cropped from my painting, "Angel Gabriel", with
artistic effects.

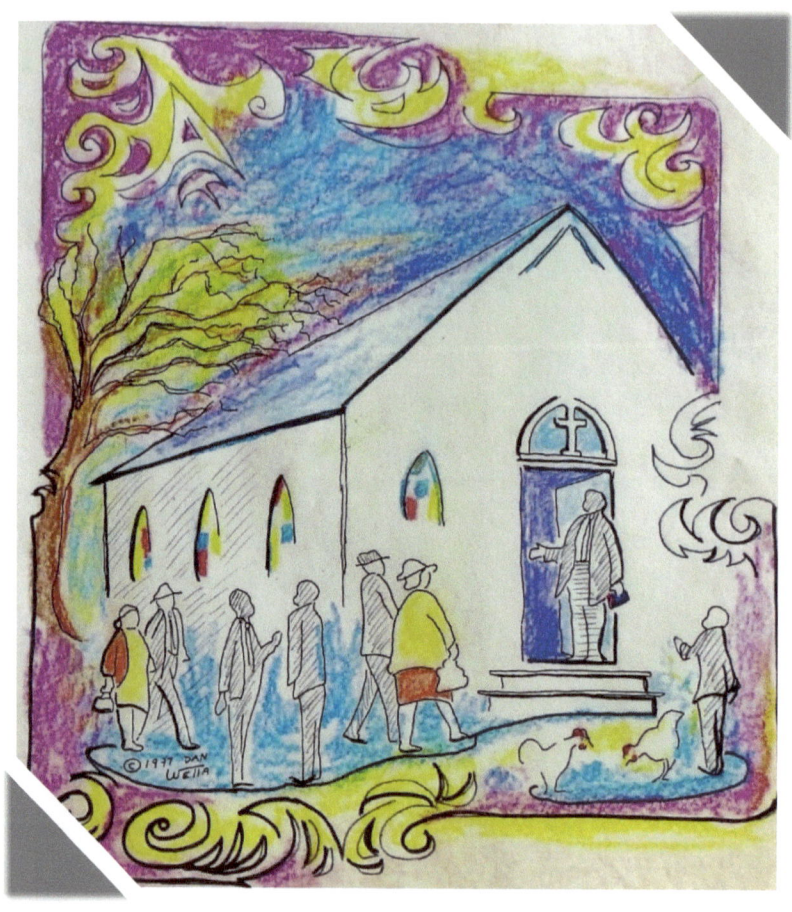

Title: Hurry, the Lord Has Something to Say
Copyright by Dan Wetta 1997

I was watching a TV show not long ago, and the leading actor said:
"God speaks to Jews, and Catholics speak to God."

On the other hand, I have heard many people proclaim:
"The Lord told me to do thus-and-so."

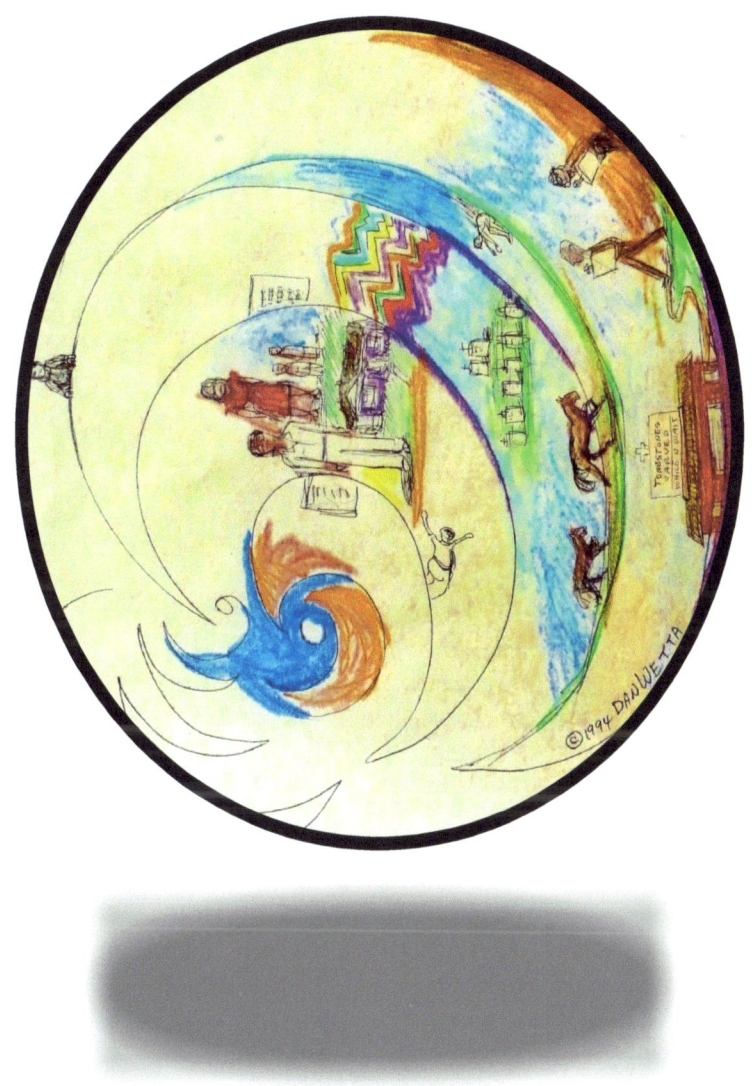

Title: Around and Around We Go.
Copyright by Dan Wetta 1994

Does this cartoon make you dizzy? Or maybe it's the title that causes the vertigo.

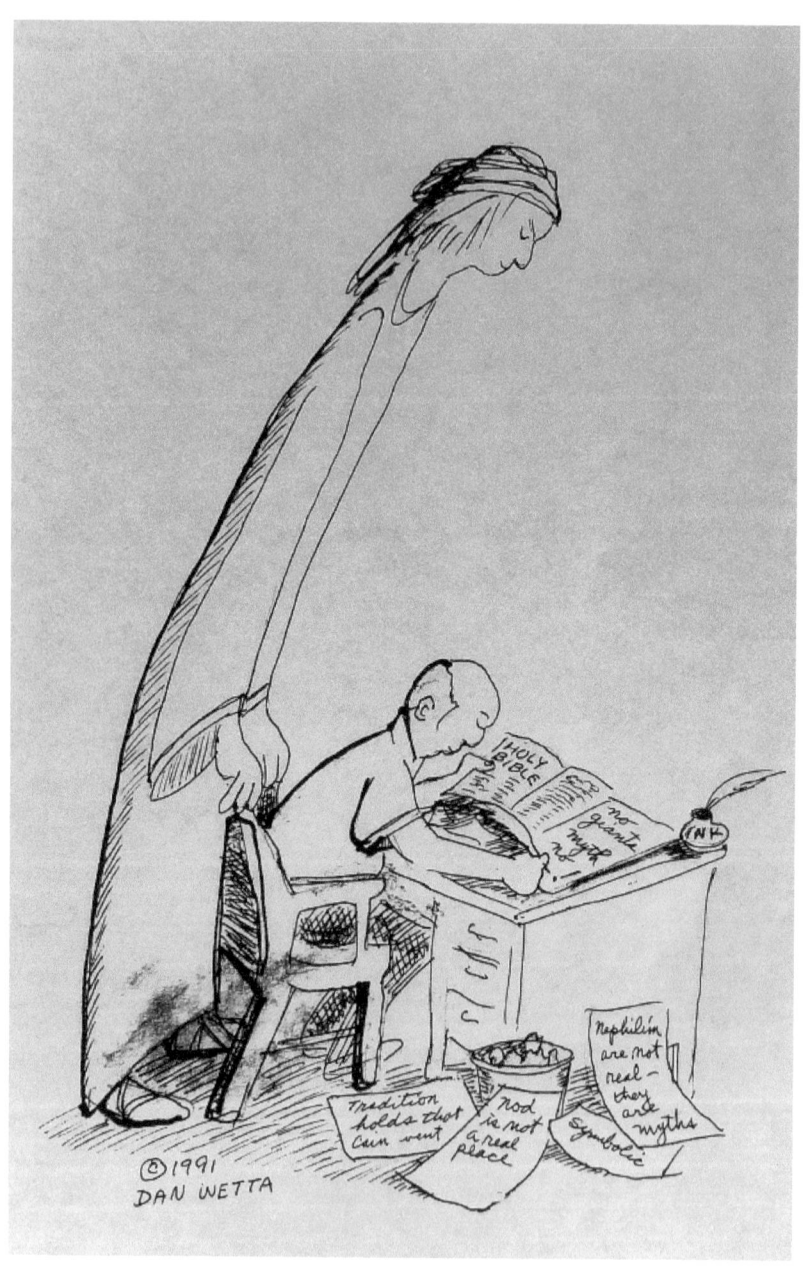

Title: Giants of the Bible
Copyright by Dan Wetta 1991

There are several references in the bible to giants who were upon the earth in ancient days.

In chapter 6 of Genesis, giants were called heroes of old, men of renown – but they fell out of favor with the Lord, and He drowned them in the flood, but after the flood, in chapter 11 of numbers, the men who went to spy out the land of Canaan came back and told Moses: "All the people we saw there are of great size. We saw the Nephilim there."

Deuteronomy 9:2-3 the people are tall and strong – Anakites.

Joshua 15:24: "From Hebron, Caleb the spy drove out Sheshai, Ahiman and Talmai, who were descendants of Anak the giant."

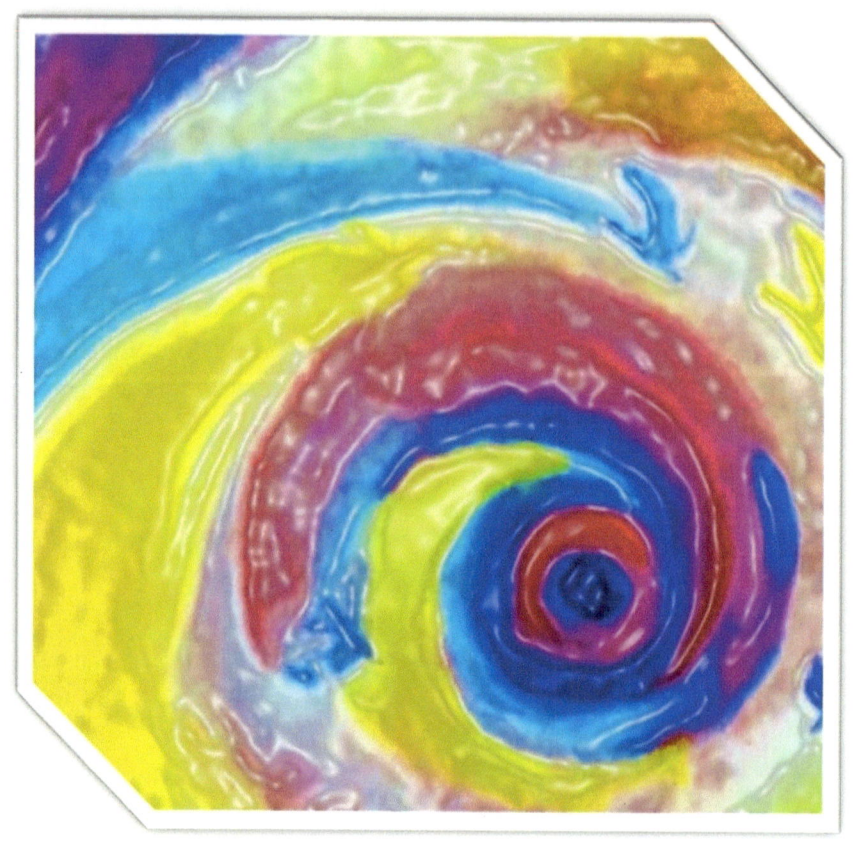

Title: Abstract Worm Hole in Sky
Copyright by Dan Wetta

This abstract detail was taken from my painting entitled "Worm Hole in Sky."

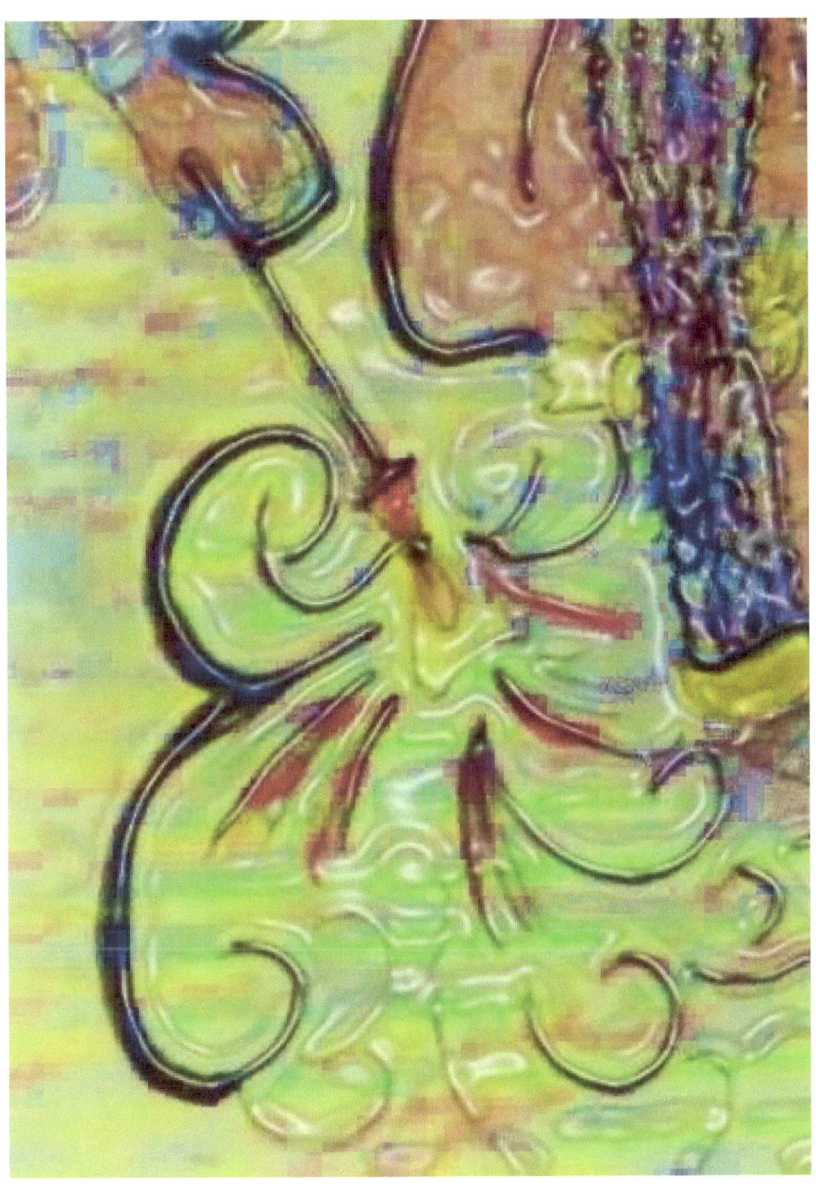

Title: Pharaoh's Daughter (abstract with artistic effects)
Copyright by Dan Wetta

This is from Pharaoh's Daughter and Baby Moses.

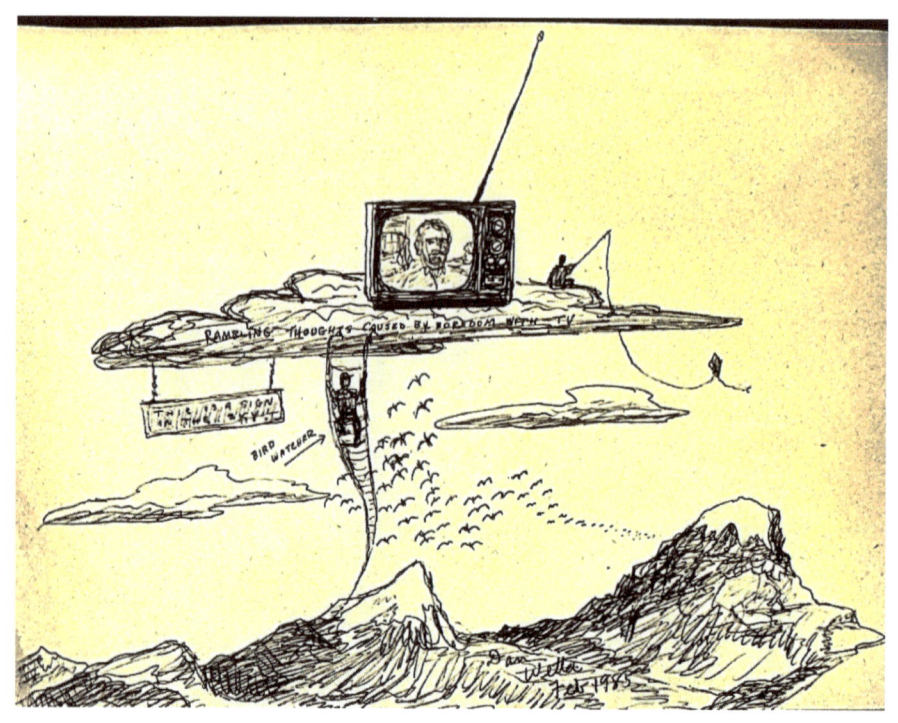

Title: Bored With TV
Copyright by Dan Wetta 1985

This is what happens to your brain when you watch too much boring TV.

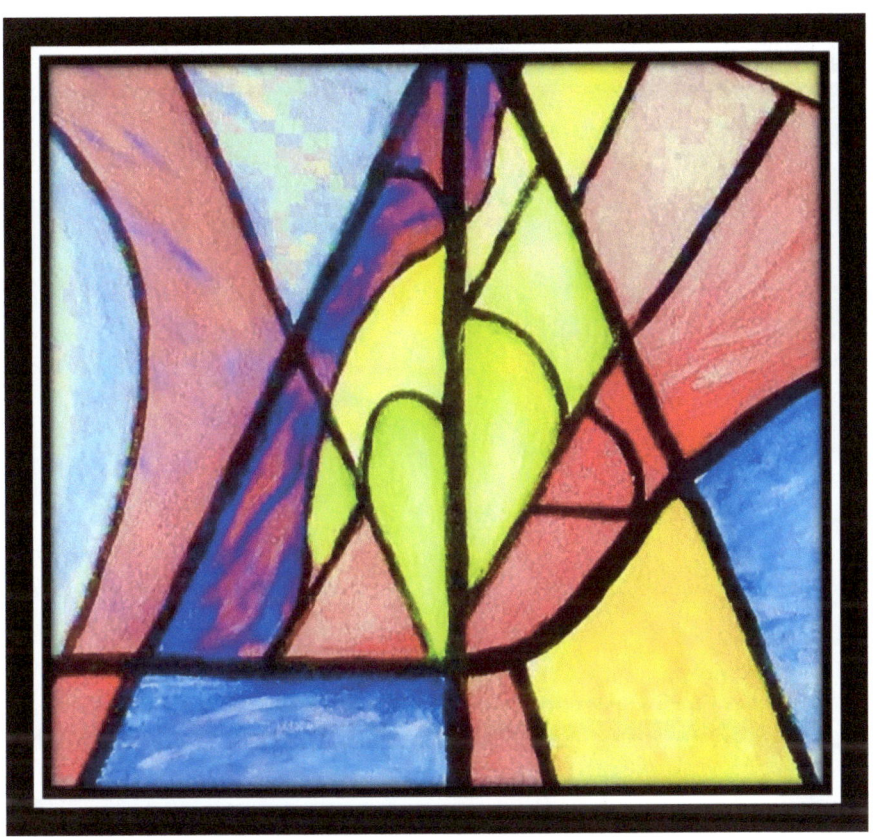

Title: Abstract Forty Six
Copyright by Dan Wetta 2006

This abstract was taken from my painting, "Caduceus."

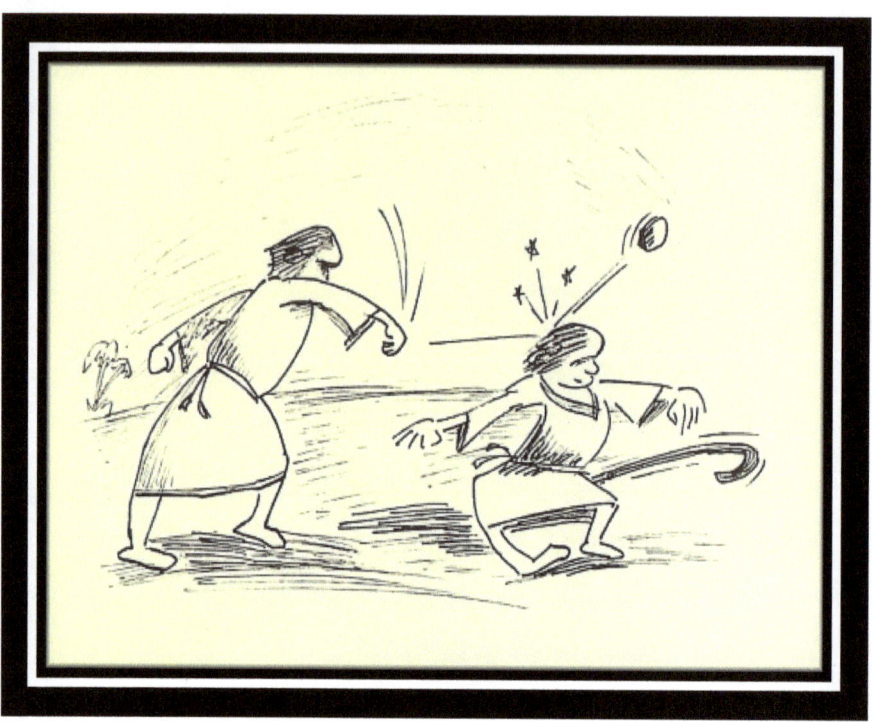

Title: Capital Punishment
Copyright by Dan Wetta

They didn't mess around with lawbreakers in the ole days!

Ex.21:14-29

1) If a man schemes and kills another man deliberately.

2) Anyone who kidnaps another and either sells him or still has him when caught.

3) Anyone who curses his father or mother.

4) A sorceress.

5) Anyone who has sexual relations with an animal.

6) Anyone who sacrifices to any god other than the Lord.

7) If a bull has had the habit of goring and the owner has been warned but has not kept it penned up and it kills a man or woman, the owner must be put to death, and the bull must be stoned too.

Title: Capital Punishment Text cartoon

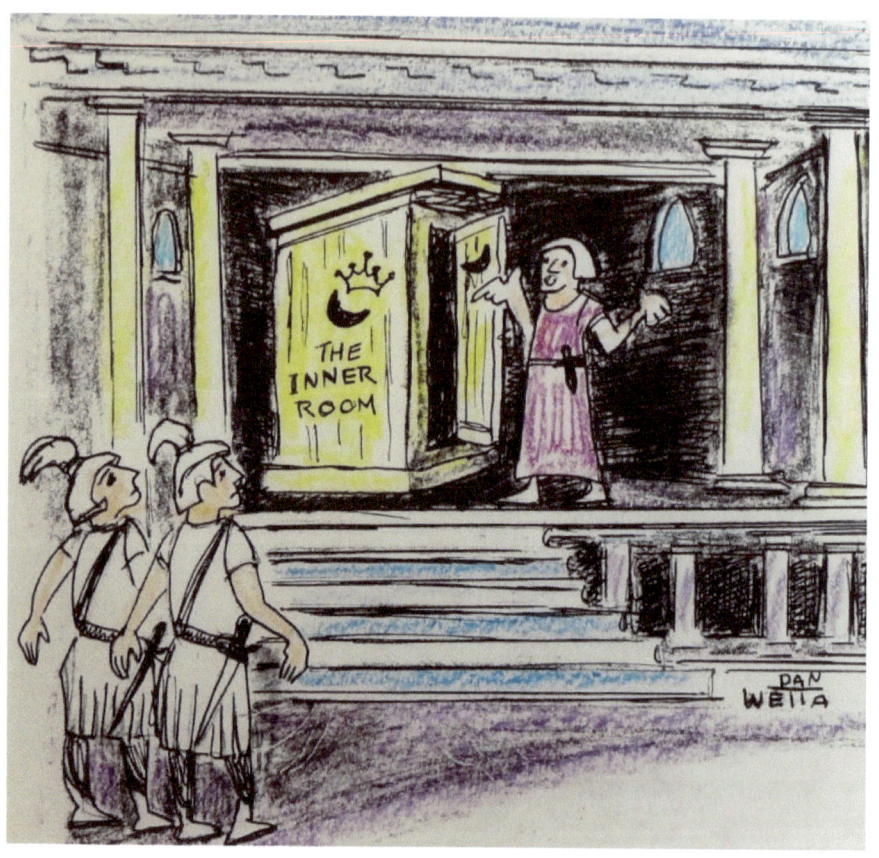

Title: The Inner Room
Copyright by Dan Wetta

Summary of Judges 3:15-26: The Moabite king had been oppressing the Israelites. There was a left-handed Israelite named Ehud who went to pay tribute to Eglon, king of Moab. Ehud had strapped a sword to his thigh under his clothing. Ehud said "I have a secret message from God for you, o king."

The king sent his attendants away. Ehud then drove his sword into the fat king's belly and left it there.

Ehud went out and closed the doors of the upper room behind him and locked them.

When the servants found the doors to the upper room locked, they said, "He must be relieving himself in the inner room."

When they finally unlocked the doors, they found the king lying dead on the floor.

Meanwhile, Ehud had escaped.

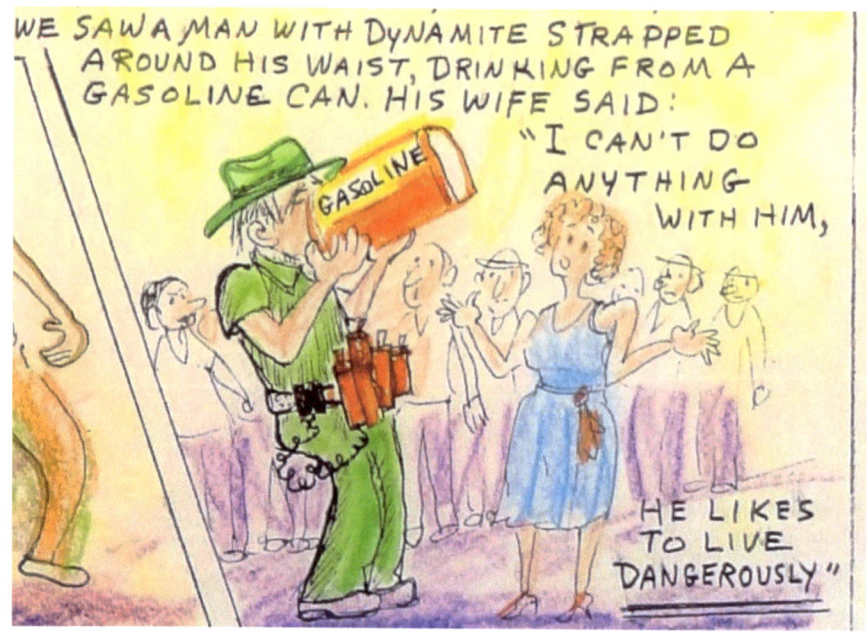

Title: Dangerous Gasoline
Copyright by Dan Wetta 1988

How times do change! This is an excerpt from a cartoon I did in 1988. That man was in a New Orleans neighborhood parade, which is mostly for families and their children.

Of course, that is not real dynamite strapped to the man's waist, and that is not gasoline in the can – but if he were to try to do that today, he would be arrested as a terrorist.

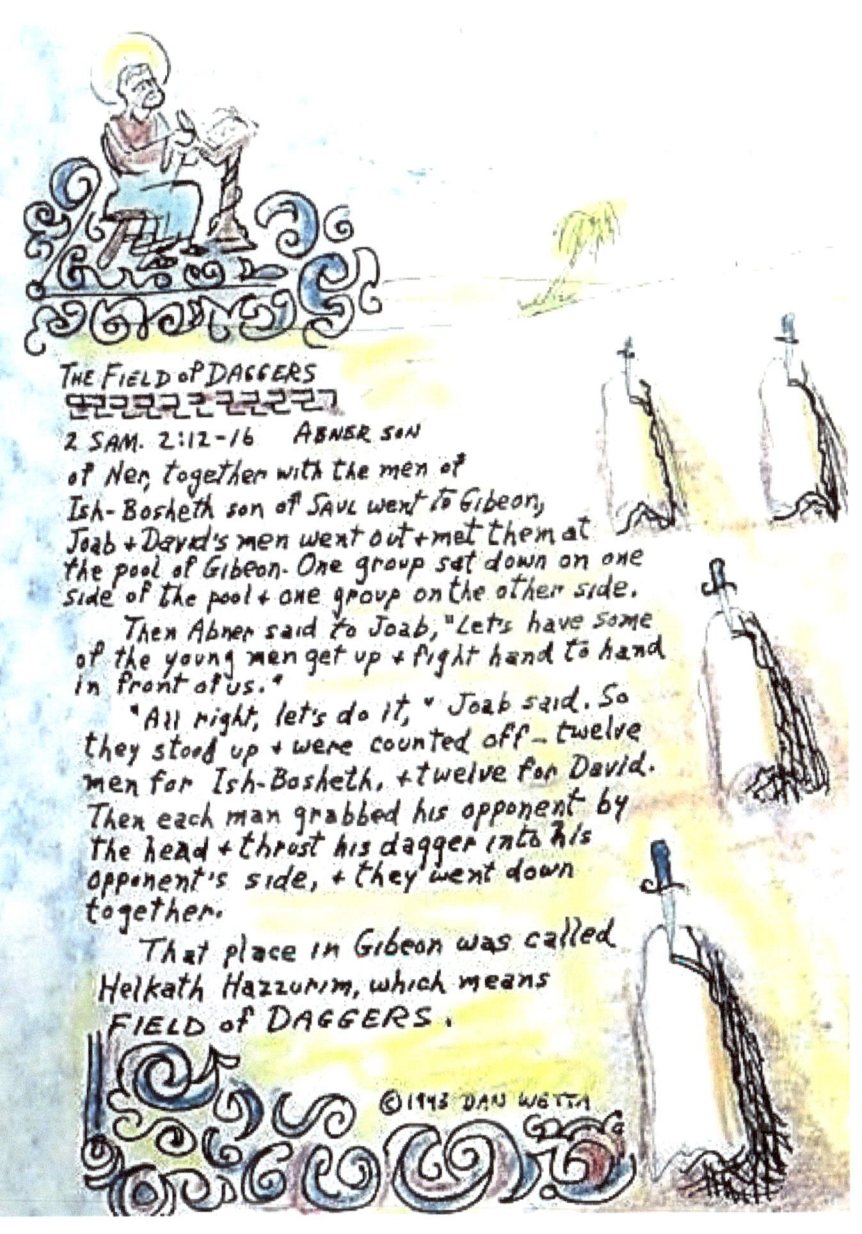

THE FIELD of DAGGERS
ㄷㄹㄱㄷㄱㄱ ㄹ ㄱㄱㄷㄹㄱ

2 SAM. 2:12-16   ABNER son
of Ner, together with the men of
Ish-Bosheth son of SAUL went to Gibeon,
Joab + David's men went out + met them at
the pool of Gibeon. One group sat down on one
side of the pool + one group on the other side.

   Then Abner said to Joab, "Let's have some
of the young men get up + fight hand to hand
in front of us."

   "All right, let's do it," Joab said. So
they stood up + were counted off — twelve
men for Ish-Bosheth, + twelve for David.
Then each man grabbed his opponent by
the head + thrust his dagger into his
opponent's side, + they went down
together.

   That place in Gibeon was called
Helkath Hazzurim, which means
FIELD of DAGGERS.

   ©1993 DAN WETTA

Title: Field of Daggers Text
Copyright by Dan Wetta 1993

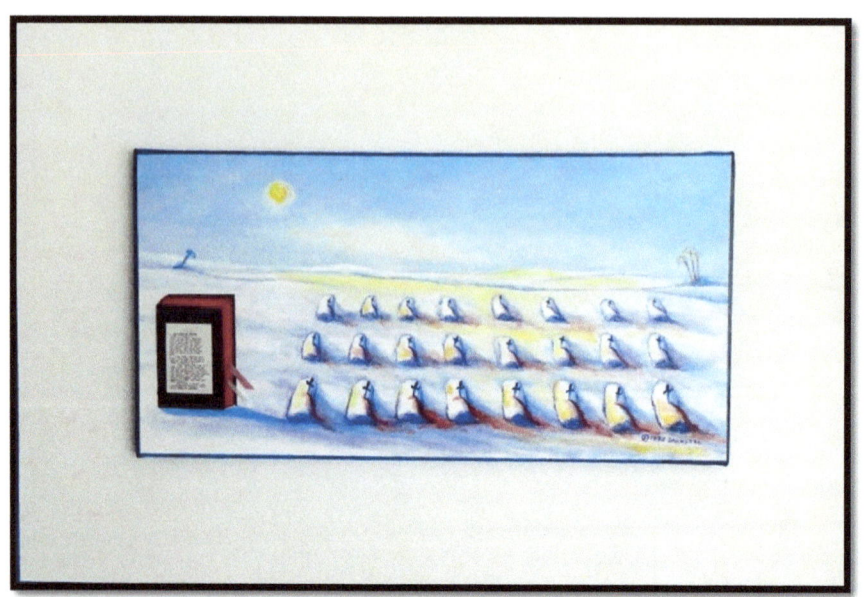

Title: Field of Daggers
Sub-title: Field of Jackasses
Size: 12x24 inch canvas on 24x36 canvas board
Medium: Acrylic on canvas

The text for this story is at 2 Samuel 2:16. Apparently one captain in Saul's army said to a captain in David's army, "Let's have twelve each of our men stab each other to death."

So they did, and twenty four men died and were buried in a place called the Field of Daggers. It was also called the Field of Flints, Field of Swords, and Field of Enemies.

I think those soldiers who stabbed each other were so dumb that they ought to call the place where they were buried – THE FIELD OF JACKASSES.

One time my daddy caught my little brother JJ smoking. When my daddy asked him why he was smoking, JJ said that our brother Raymond told him to do it. My daddy asked JJ, "If Raymond told you to jump off the Huey P Long Bridge, would you do it?" JJ answered, "No, I'm not that dumb."

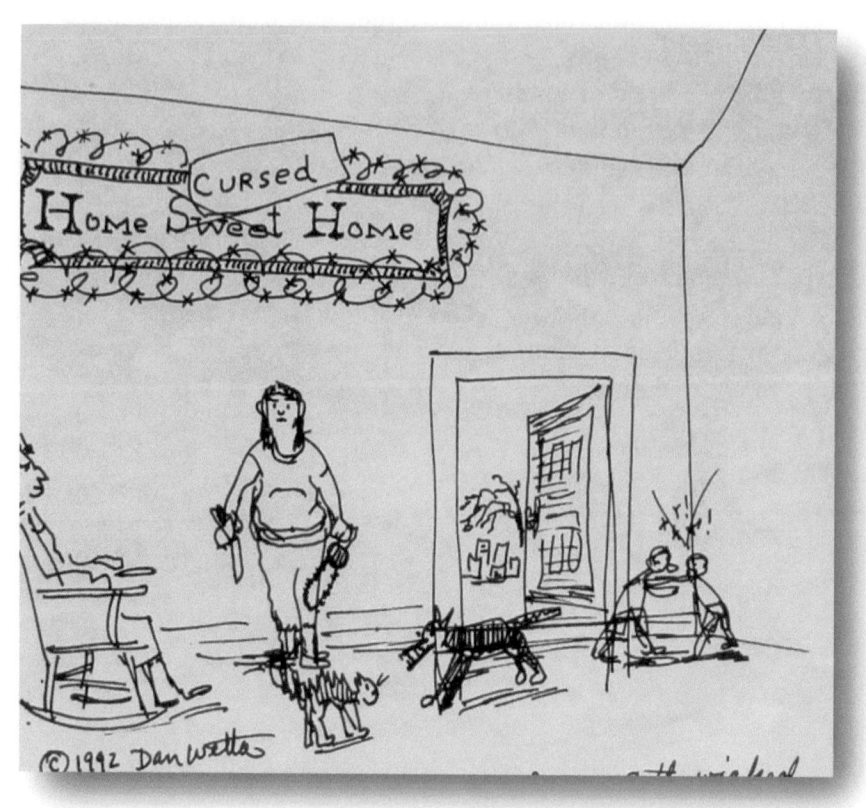

THE LORD'S CURSE IS ON THE HOUSE OF THE WICKED –
(Proverbs 4:33)

Title: Home Cursed Home
Copyright by Dan Wetta 1992

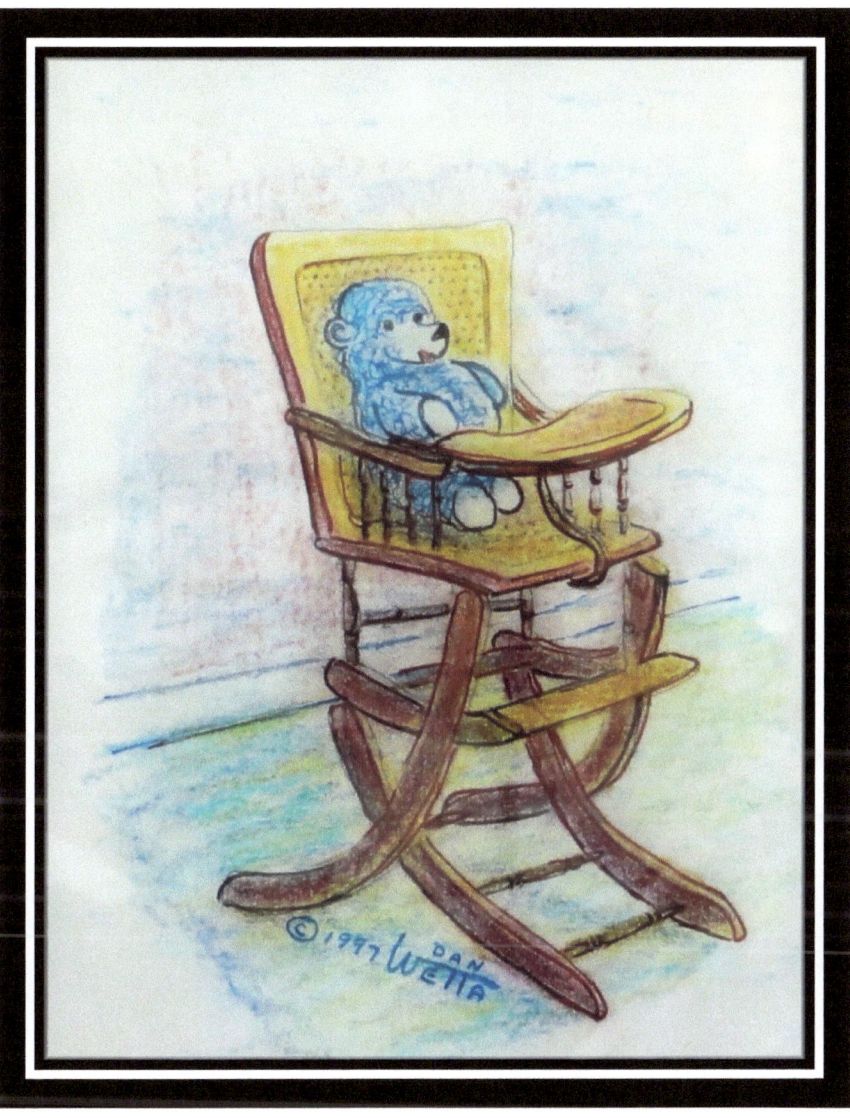

Title: Antique High Chair with Teddy Bear
Copyright by Dan Wetta 1997

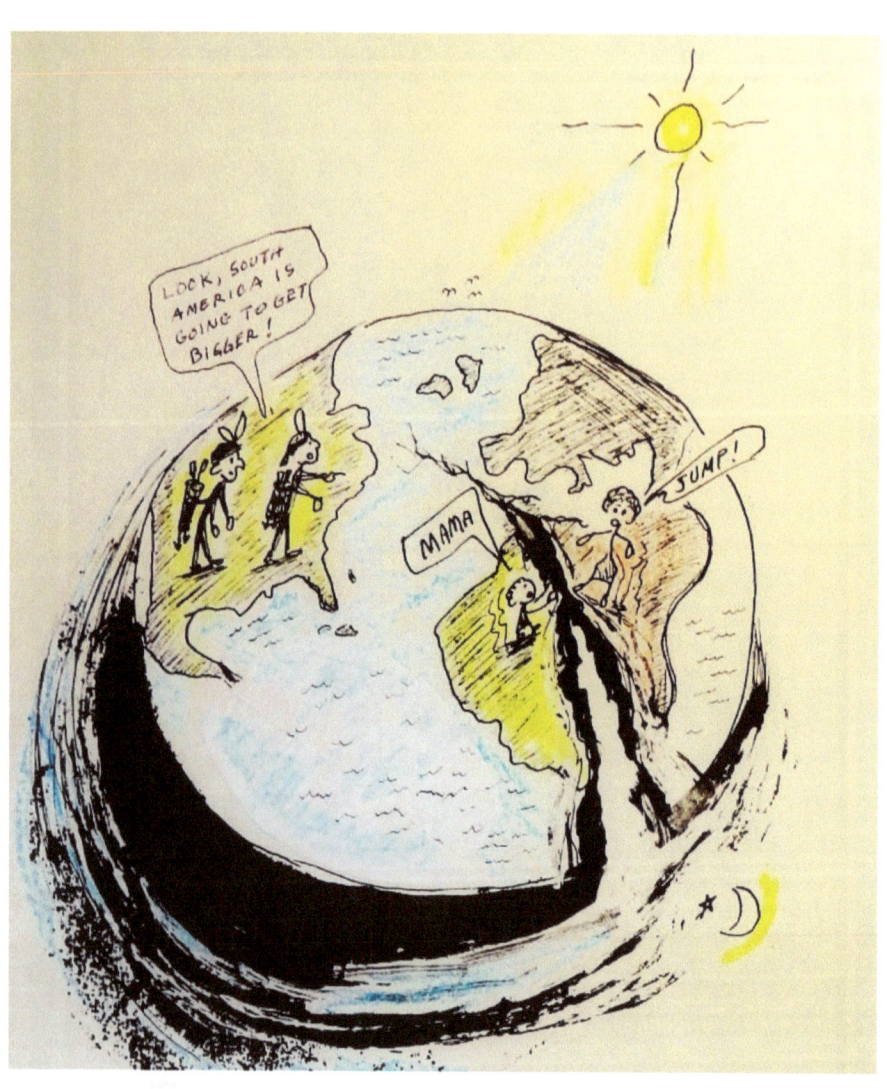

Title: The Earth Was Divided
Copyright by Dan Wetta

Genesis 10:25 says, "In the days of Peleg, the earth was divided."

This is a good example of interpretation differences:

Some scholars hold that Africa split off and floated over the ocean to become South America, while others say that it refers to the division of peoples at the time of the Tower of Babel.

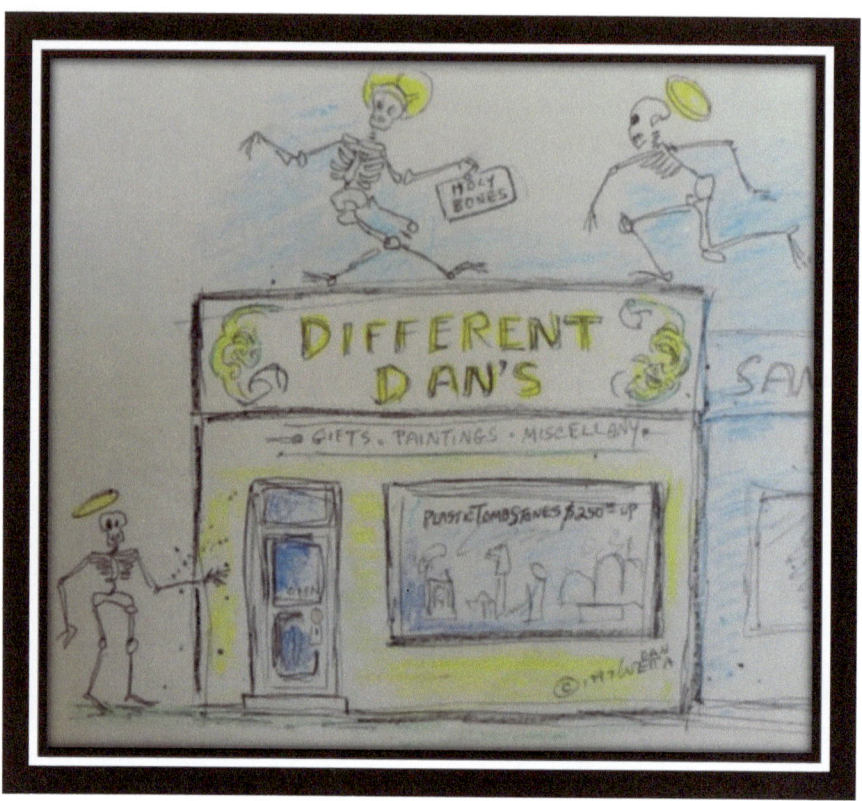

Title: Different Dan's
Copyright 1997

I think Michelangelo and his contemporaries used to swipe or buy cadavers and skin them to study the muscular structure of the human body. That is too gory for me.

But if you need some excitement, hide in a graveyard at midnight, and your imagination will take over. The dead will rise from their graves and do the dry-bones dance.

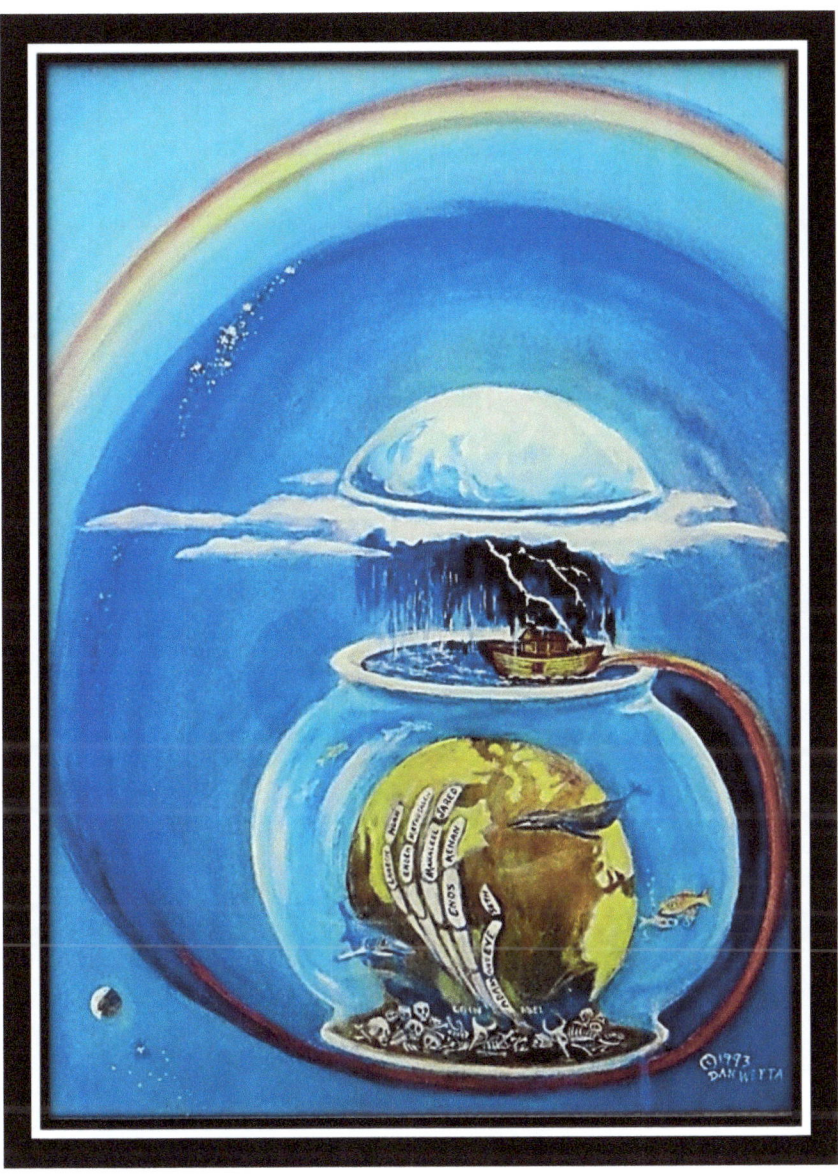

Title: Deluge
Size: 18 x 24 inches
Medium: Acrylic on canvas
Copyright by Dan Wetta 1993

The only way I knew how to depict the flood was to put the earth in a fishbowl with the ark floating on top.

When I finished the painting, it looked like the fish would have survived. However, bible scholars claim that fresh water from the rain killed the salt water fish and that salt water got into fresh water and killed the fresh water fish.

So if all the fish died in the flood, where did today's fish come from?

There is no mention of a fish tank in Noah's ark.

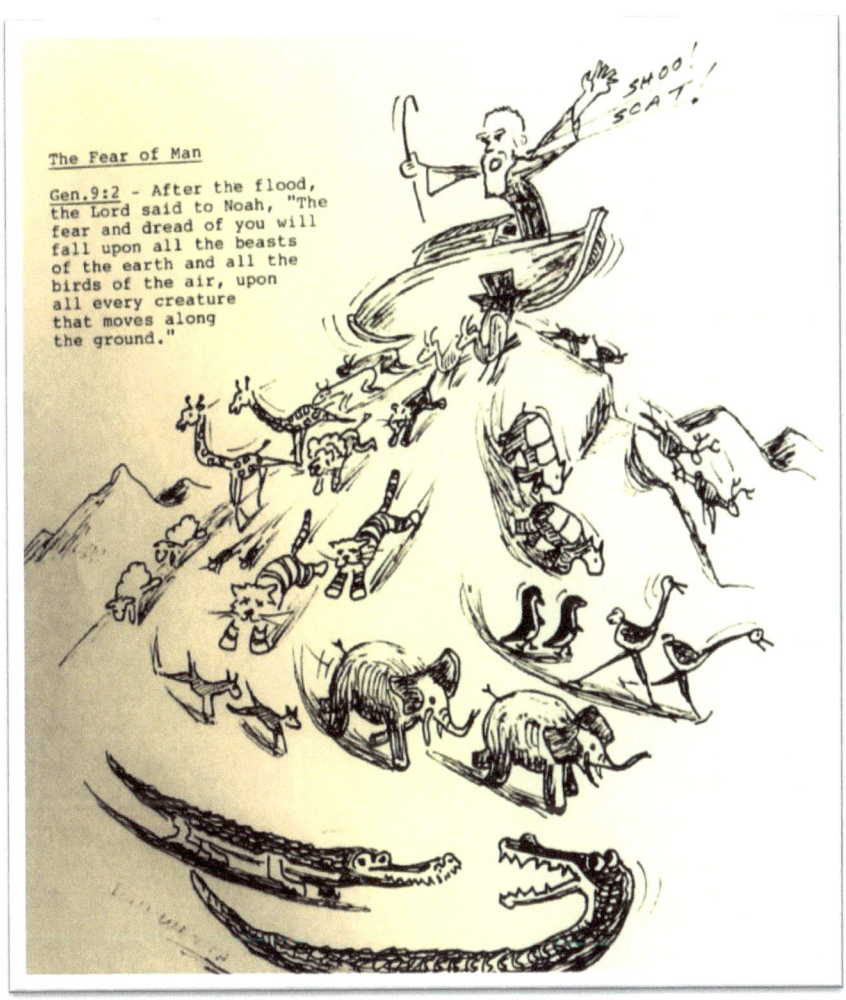

Title: The Fear of Man
Copyright by Dan Wetta

Genesis 9:2: "After the flood, the Lord said to Noah, 'The fear and dread of you will fall upon all the beasts of the earth and all the birds of the air, upon all and every creature that moves along the ground.'"

Maybe the animals were afraid of man way back then, but nowadays it seems like alligators, tigers, lions and grizzly bears never heard of Noah.

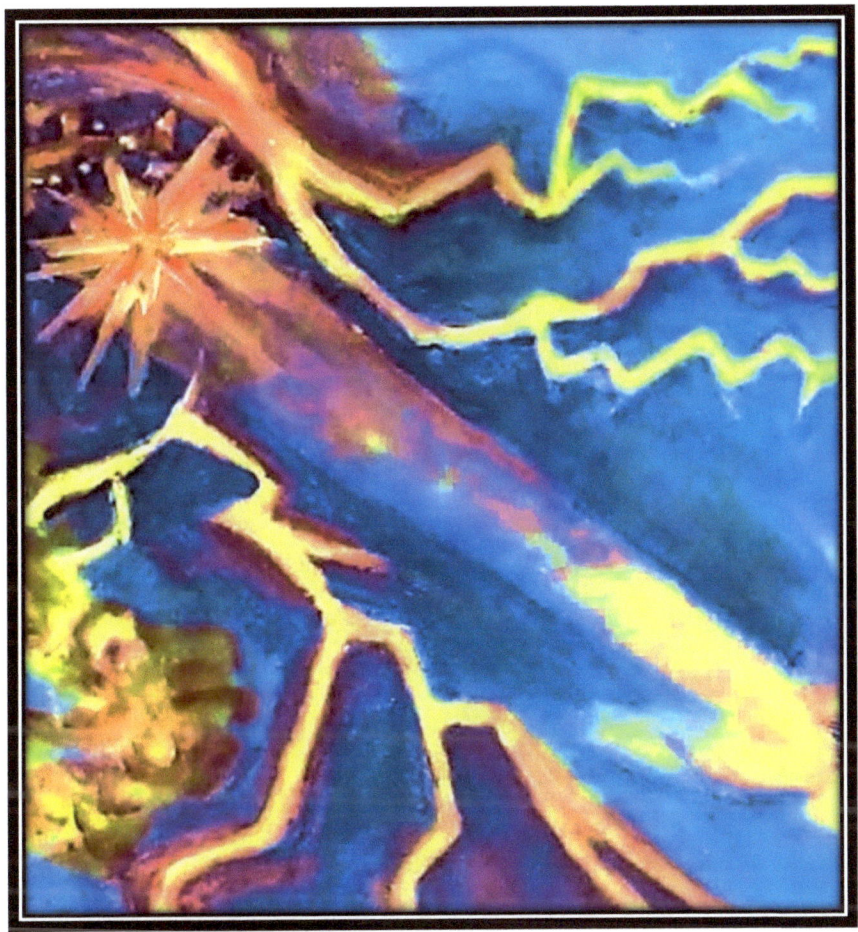

Title: Angel Gabriel Two abstract
Copyright by Dan Wetta 1995

This is from the painting, "Angel Gabriel."

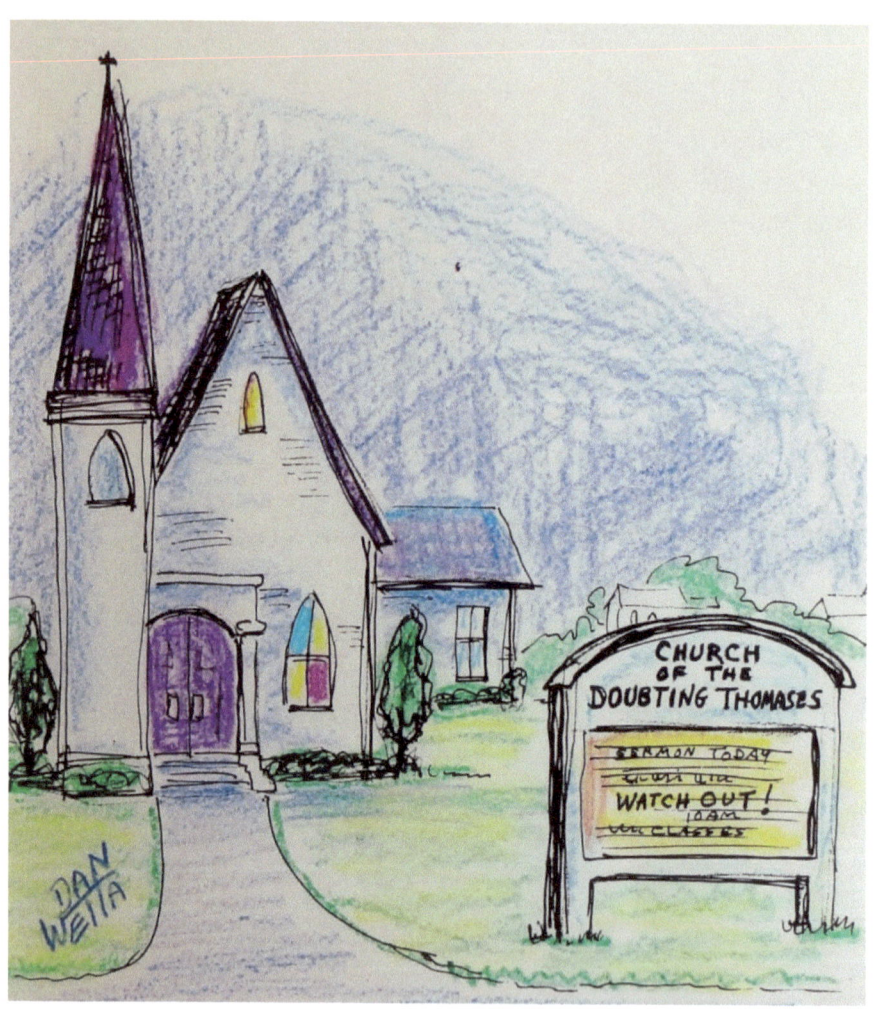

Title: Church of Doubting Thomases
Copyright by Dan Wetta

It all boils down to this: You either believe the bible or you don't.

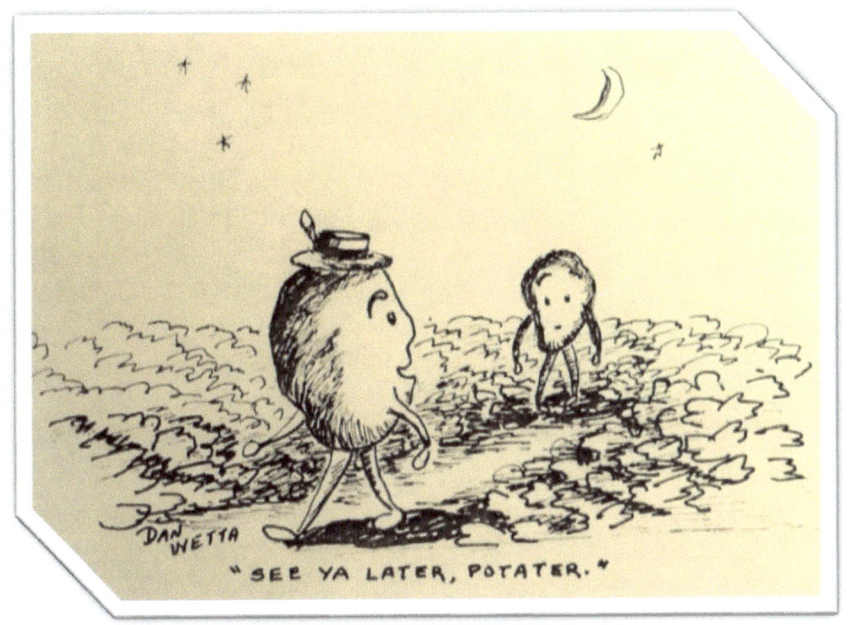

Title: OK! Enough about bible paintings for now!
Copyright by Dan Wetta

About Dan Wetta, Cartoonist and Artist

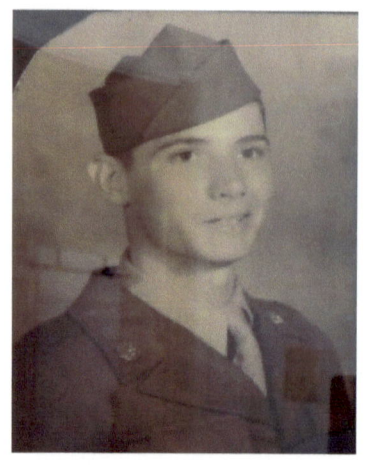

I was born on October 10, 1927, and I grew up during the Great Depression of the 1930's. I enlisted in the army in 1946 and was stationed at Camp Lee, Virginia, near Richmond, where I met my wife and settled down.

My father was a commercial artist, a steel and copper plate engraver for Dameron Pierson Stationery company in New Orleans. He was foreman ot their printing department. One of his tasks was to engrave printing plates to create paper money for Central and South American countries.

I began drawing and painting as a child, but did not want to become a commercial artist like my father because I wanted to paint things that interested me, so I made a living as an accountant-auditor.

I have exhibited at the Virginia Museum of Fine Arts and was a member of the Richmond Artists' Association for about fifteen years.

We used to have fun exhibiting at malls until one day a City of Richmond sales-tax agent came by with a note pad and began writing down the names of artists who did not have a sales-tax license.

When I got the city license, the IRS required me to file a quarterly FICA tax form, and the State said I had to have a business license, and then the malls got worried about liability, so they made us buy liability insurance.

Rules and regulations were taking up so much of my painting time that I said, "To heck with it!" and I quit exhibiting. As a result, I have acumulated quite a few paintings over the years.

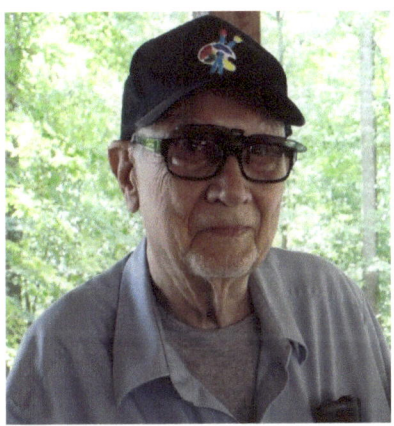

www.ingramcontent.com/pod-product-compliance
Lightning Source LLC
Chambersburg PA
CBHW040820180526
45159CB00001B/4